Nutshell Series
Hornbook Series
and
Black Letter Series
of
WEST PUBLISHING COMPANY
P.O. Box 64526
St. Paul, Minnesota 55164–0526

Accounting

FARIS' ACCOUNTING AND LAW IN A NUTSHELL, 377 pages, 1984. Softcover. (Text)

Administrative Law

AMAN AND MAYTON'S HORNBOOK ON ADMINISTRATIVE LAW, Approximately 750 pages, 1992. (Text)

GELLHORN AND LEVIN'S ADMINISTRATIVE LAW AND PROCESS IN A NUTSHELL, Third Edition, 479 pages, 1990. Softcover. (Text)

Admiralty

MARAIST'S ADMIRALTY IN A NUTSHELL, Second Edition, 379 pages, 1988. Softcover. (Text)

SCHOENBAUM'S HORNBOOK ON ADMIRALTY AND MARITIME LAW, Student Edition, 692 pages, 1987 with 1992 pocket part. (Text)

Agency—Partnership

REUSCHLEIN AND GREGORY'S HORNBOOK ON THE LAW OF AGENCY AND PARTNERSHIP, Second Edition, 683 pages, 1990. (Text)

STEFFEN'S AGENCY-PARTNERSHIP IN A NUTSHELL, 364 pages, 1977. Softcover. (Text)

NOLAN–HALEY'S ALTERNATIVE DISPUTE RESOLUTION IN A NUTSHELL, Approximately 300 pages, 1992. Softcover. (Text)

RISKIN'S DISPUTE RESOLUTION FOR LAWYERS VIDEO TAPES, 1992. (Available for purchase by schools and libraries.)

American Indian Law

CANBY'S AMERICAN INDIAN LAW IN A NUTSHELL, Second Edition, 336 pages, 1988. Softcover. (Text)

Antitrust—see also Regulated Industries, Trade Regulation

GELLHORN'S ANTITRUST LAW AND ECONOMICS IN A NUTSHELL, Third Edition, 472 pages, 1986. Softcover. (Text)

HOVENKAMP'S BLACK LETTER ON ANTITRUST, 323 pages, 1986. Softcover. (Review)

HOVENKAMP'S HORNBOOK ON ECONOMICS AND FEDERAL ANTITRUST LAW, Student Edition, 414 pages, 1985. (Text)

SULLIVAN'S HORNBOOK OF THE LAW OF ANTITRUST, 886 pages, 1977. (Text)

Appellate Advocacy—see Trial and Appellate Advocacy

Art Law

DUBOFF'S ART LAW IN A NUTSHELL, 335 pages, 1984. Softcover. (Text)

Banking Law

LOVETT'S BANKING AND FINANCIAL INSTITUTIONS LAW IN A NUTSHELL, Third Edition, approximately 500 pages, 1992. Softcover. (Text)

Civil Procedure—see also Federal Jurisdiction and Procedure

CLERMONT'S BLACK LETTER ON CIVIL PROCEDURE, Second Edition, 332 pages, 1988. Softcover. (Review)

FRIEDENTHAL, KANE AND MILLER'S HORNBOOK ON CIVIL PROCEDURE, 876 pages, 1985. (Text)

KANE'S CIVIL PROCEDURE IN A NUTSHELL, Third Edition, 303 pages, 1991. Softcover. (Text)

KOFFLER AND REPPY'S HORNBOOK ON COMMON LAW PLEADING, 663 pages, 1969. (Text)

SIEGEL'S HORNBOOK ON NEW YORK PRACTICE, Second Edition, Student Edition, 1068 pages, 1991. Softcover. (Text) 1992 Supplemental Pamphlet.

Commercial Law

BAILEY AND HAGEDORN'S SECURED TRANSACTIONS IN A NUTSHELL, Third Edition, 390 pages, 1988. Softcover. (Text)

HENSON'S HORNBOOK ON SECURED TRANSACTIONS UNDER THE U.C.C., Second Edition, 504 pages, 1979, with 1979 pocket part. (Text)

MEYER AND SPEIDEL'S BLACK LETTER ON SALES AND LEASES OF GOODS, Approximately 400 pages, October 1992 Pub.

Commercial Law—Continued

Softcover. (Review)

NICKLES' BLACK LETTER ON COMMERCIAL PAPER, 450 pages, 1988. Softcover. (Review)

STOCKTON AND MILLER'S SALES AND LEASES OF GOODS IN A NUTSHELL, Third Edition, approximately 425 pages, 1992. Softcover. (Text)

STONE'S UNIFORM COMMERCIAL CODE IN A NUTSHELL, Third Edition, 580 pages, 1989. Softcover. (Text)

WEBER AND SPEIDEL'S COMMERCIAL PAPER IN A NUTSHELL, Third Edition, 404 pages, 1982. Softcover. (Text)

WHITE AND SUMMERS' HORNBOOK ON THE UNIFORM COMMERCIAL CODE, Third Edition, Student Edition, 1386 pages, 1988. (Text)

Community Property

MENNELL AND BOYKOFF'S COMMUNITY PROPERTY IN A NUTSHELL, Second Edition, 432 pages, 1988. Softcover. (Text)

Comparative Law

FOLSOM, MINAN AND OTTO'S LAW AND POLITICS IN THE PEOPLE'S REPUBLIC OF CHINA IN A NUTSHELL, Approximately 450 pages, 1992. Softcover. (Text)

GLENDON, GORDON AND OSAKWE'S COMPARATIVE LEGAL TRADITIONS IN A NUTSHELL. 402 pages, 1982. Softcover. (Text)

Conflict of Laws

HAY'S BLACK LETTER ON CONFLICT OF LAWS, 330 pages, 1989. Softcover. (Review)

SCOLES AND HAY'S HORNBOOK ON CONFLICT OF LAWS, Student Edition, 1160 pages, 1992. (Text)

SIEGEL'S CONFLICTS IN A NUTSHELL, 470 pages, 1982. Softcover. (Text)

Constitutional Law—Civil Rights

BARRON AND DIENES' BLACK LETTER ON CONSTITUTIONAL LAW, Third Edition, 440 pages, 1991. Softcover. (Review)

BARRON AND DIENES' CONSTITUTIONAL LAW IN A NUTSHELL, Second Edition, 483 pages, 1991. Softcover. (Text)

ENGDAHL'S CONSTITUTIONAL FEDERALISM IN A NUTSHELL, Second Edition, 411 pages, 1987. Softcover. (Text)

MARKS AND COOPER'S STATE CONSTITUTIONAL LAW IN A NUTSHELL, 329 pages, 1988. Softcover. (Text)

NOWAK AND ROTUNDA'S HORNBOOK ON CONSTITUTIONAL LAW, Fourth Edition, 1357 pages,

Constitutional Law—Civil Rights—Continued

1991. (Text)

VIEIRA'S CONSTITUTIONAL CIVIL RIGHTS IN A NUTSHELL, Second Edition, 322 pages, 1990. Softcover. (Text)

WILLIAMS' CONSTITUTIONAL ANALYSIS IN A NUTSHELL, 388 pages, 1979. Softcover. (Text)

Consumer Law—see also Commercial Law

EPSTEIN AND NICKLES' CONSUMER LAW IN A NUTSHELL, Second Edition, 418 pages, 1981. Softcover. (Text)

Contracts

CALAMARI AND PERILLO'S BLACK LETTER ON CONTRACTS, Second Edition, 462 pages, 1990. Softcover. (Review)

CALAMARI AND PERILLO'S HORNBOOK ON CONTRACTS, Third Edition, 1049 pages, 1987. (Text)

CORBIN'S TEXT ON CONTRACTS, One Volume Student Edition, 1224 pages, 1952. (Text)

FRIEDMAN'S CONTRACT REMEDIES IN A NUTSHELL, 323 pages, 1981. Softcover. (Text)

KEYES' GOVERNMENT CONTRACTS IN A NUTSHELL, Second Edition, 557 pages, 1990. Softcover. (Text)

SCHABER AND ROHWER'S CONTRACTS IN A NUTSHELL, Third Edition, 457 pages, 1990. Softcover. (Text)

Copyright—see Patent and Copyright Law

Corporations

HAMILTON'S BLACK LETTER ON CORPORATIONS, Third Edition, approximately 550 pages, 1992. Softcover. (Review)

HAMILTON'S THE LAW OF CORPORATIONS IN A NUTSHELL, Third Edition, 518 pages, 1991. Softcover. (Text)

HENN AND ALEXANDER'S HORNBOOK ON LAWS OF CORPORATIONS, Third Edition, Student Edition, 1371 pages, 1983, with 1986 pocket part. (Text)

Corrections

KRANTZ' THE LAW OF CORRECTIONS AND PRISONERS' RIGHTS IN A NUTSHELL, Third Edition, 407 pages, 1988. Softcover. (Text)

Creditors' Rights

EPSTEIN'S DEBTOR-CREDITOR LAW IN A NUTSHELL, Fourth Edition, 401 pages, 1991. Softcover. (Text)

EPSTEIN, NICKLES AND WHITE'S HORNBOOK ON BANKRUPTCY, Approximately 1000 pages, November, 1992 Pub. (Text)

Creditors' Rights—Continued

NICKLES AND EPSTEIN'S BLACK LETTER ON CREDITORS' RIGHTS AND BANKRUPTCY, 576 pages, 1989. (Review)

Criminal Law and Criminal Procedure—see also Corrections, Juvenile Justice

ISRAEL AND LAFAVE'S CRIMINAL PROCEDURE—CONSTITUTIONAL LIMITATIONS IN A NUTSHELL, Fourth Edition, 461 pages, 1988. Softcover. (Text)

LAFAVE AND ISRAEL'S HORNBOOK ON CRIMINAL PROCEDURE, Second Edition, 1309 pages, 1992. (Text)

LAFAVE AND SCOTT'S HORNBOOK ON CRIMINAL LAW, Second Edition, 918 pages, 1986. (Text)

LOEWY'S CRIMINAL LAW IN A NUTSHELL, Second Edition, 321 pages, 1987. Softcover. (Text)

LOW'S BLACK LETTER ON CRIMINAL LAW, Revised First Edition, 443 pages, 1990. Softcover. (Review)

SUBIN, MIRSKY AND WEINSTEIN'S THE CRIMINAL PROCESS: PROSECUTION AND DEFENSE FUNCTIONS, Approximately 450 pages, October, 1992 Pub. Softcover. Teacher's Manual available.

(Text)

Domestic Relations

CLARK'S HORNBOOK ON DOMESTIC RELATIONS, Second Edition, Student Edition, 1050 pages, 1988. (Text)

KRAUSE'S BLACK LETTER ON FAMILY LAW, 314 pages, 1988. Softcover. (Review)

KRAUSE'S FAMILY LAW IN A NUTSHELL, Second Edition, 444 pages, 1986. Softcover. (Text)

MALLOY'S LAW AND ECONOMICS: A COMPARATIVE APPROACH TO THEORY AND PRACTICE, 166 pages, 1990. Softcover. (Text)

Education Law

ALEXANDER AND ALEXANDER'S THE LAW OF SCHOOLS, STUDENTS AND TEACHERS IN A NUTSHELL, 409 pages, 1984. Softcover. (Text)

Employment Discrimination—see also Gender Discrimination

PLAYER'S FEDERAL LAW OF EMPLOYMENT DISCRIMINATION IN A NUTSHELL, Third Edition, 338 pages, 1992. Softcover. (Text)

PLAYER'S HORNBOOK ON EMPLOYMENT DISCRIMINATION LAW, Student Edition, 708 pages, 1988. (Text)

[VI]

Gender Discrimination—see also Employment Discrimination

THOMAS' SEX DISCRIMINATION IN A NUTSHELL, Second Edition, 395 pages, 1991. Softcover. (Text)

Health Law—see Medicine, Law and

Human Rights—see International Law

Immigration Law

WEISSBRODT'S IMMIGRATION LAW AND PROCEDURE IN A NUTSHELL, Third Edition, approximately 350 pages, 1992. Softcover. (Text)

Indian Law—see American Indian Law

Insurance Law

DOBBYN'S INSURANCE LAW IN A NUTSHELL, Second Edition, 316 pages, 1989. Softcover. (Text)

KEETON AND WIDISS' INSURANCE LAW, Student Edition, 1359 pages, 1988. (Text)

International Law—see also Sea, Law of

BUERGENTHAL'S INTERNATIONAL HUMAN RIGHTS IN A NUTSHELL, 283 pages, 1988. Softcover. (Text)

BUERGENTHAL AND MAIER'S PUBLIC INTERNATIONAL LAW IN A

NUTSHELL, Second Edition, 275 pages, 1990. Softcover. (Text)

FOLSOM'S EUROPEAN COMMUNITY LAW IN A NUTSHELL, 423 pages, 1992. Softcover. (Text)

FOLSOM, GORDON AND SPANOGLE'S INTERNATIONAL BUSINESS TRANSACTIONS IN A NUTSHELL, Fourth Edition, approximately 540 pages, 1992. Softcover. (Text)

Interviewing and Counseling

SHAFFER AND ELKINS' LEGAL INTERVIEWING AND COUNSELING IN A NUTSHELL, Second Edition, 487 pages, 1987. Softcover. (Text)

Introduction to Law—see Legal Method and Legal System

Introduction to Law Study

HEGLAND'S INTRODUCTION TO THE STUDY AND PRACTICE OF LAW IN A NUTSHELL, 418 pages, 1983. Softcover. (Text)

KINYON'S INTRODUCTION TO LAW STUDY AND LAW EXAMINATIONS IN A NUTSHELL, 389 pages, 1971. Softcover. (Text)

Judicial Process—see Legal Method and Legal System

Juvenile Justice

FOX'S JUVENILE COURTS IN A NUTSHELL, Third Edition, 291

Products Liability—Continued pages, 1988. Softcover. (Text)

Professional Responsibility

ARONSON AND WECKSTEIN'S PROFESSIONAL RESPONSIBILITY IN A NUTSHELL, Second Edition, 514 pages, 1991. Softcover. (Text)

LESNICK'S BEING A LAWYER: INDIVIDUAL CHOICE AND RESPONSIBILITY IN THE PRACTICE OF LAW, Approximately 400 pages, 1992. Softcover. (Coursebook)

ROTUNDA'S BLACK LETTER ON PROFESSIONAL RESPONSIBILITY, Third Edition, 492 pages, 1992. Softcover. (Review)

WOLFRAM'S HORNBOOK ON MODERN LEGAL ETHICS, Student Edition, 1120 pages, 1986. (Text)

WYDICK AND PERSCHBACHER'S CALIFORNIA LEGAL ETHICS, Approximately 430 pages, 1992. Softcover. (Coursebook)

Property—see also Real Estate Transactions, Land Use, Trusts and Estates

BERNHARDT'S BLACK LETTER ON PROPERTY, Second Edition, 388 pages, 1991. Softcover. (Review)

BERNHARDT'S REAL PROPERTY IN A NUTSHELL, Second Edition, 448 pages, 1981. Softcover. (Text)

BOYER, HOVENKAMP AND KURTZ' THE LAW OF PROPERTY, AN INTRODUCTORY SURVEY, Fourth Edition, 696 pages, 1991. (Text)

BURKE'S PERSONAL PROPERTY IN A NUTSHELL, 322 pages, 1983. Softcover. (Text)

CUNNINGHAM, STOEBUCK AND WHITMAN'S HORNBOOK ON THE LAW OF PROPERTY, Student Edition, 916 pages, 1984, with 1987 pocket part. (Text)

HILL'S LANDLORD AND TENANT LAW IN A NUTSHELL, Second Edition, 311 pages, 1986. Softcover. (Text)

Real Estate Transactions

BRUCE'S REAL ESTATE FINANCE IN A NUTSHELL, Third Edition, 287 pages, 1991. Softcover. (Text)

NELSON AND WHITMAN'S BLACK LETTER ON LAND TRANSACTIONS AND FINANCE, Second Edition, 466 pages, 1988. Softcover. (Review)

NELSON AND WHITMAN'S HORNBOOK ON REAL ESTATE FINANCE LAW, Second Edition, 941 pages, 1985 with 1989 pocket part. (Text)

Regulated Industries—see also Mass Communication Law, Banking Law

GELLHORN AND PIERCE'S REGULATED INDUSTRIES IN A NUTSHELL, Second Edition, 389 pages, 1987. Softcover. (Text)

Remedies

DOBBS' HORNBOOK ON REMEDIES, Second Edition, December, 1992 Pub. (Text)

DOBBYN'S INJUNCTIONS IN A NUTSHELL, 264 pages, 1974. Softcover. (Text)

FRIEDMAN'S CONTRACT REMEDIES IN A NUTSHELL, 323 pages, 1981. Softcover. (Text)

O'CONNELL'S REMEDIES IN A NUTSHELL, Second Edition, 320 pages, 1985. Softcover. (Text)

Sea, Law of

SOHN AND GUSTAFSON'S THE LAW OF THE SEA IN A NUTSHELL, 264 pages, 1984. Softcover. (Text)

Securities Regulation

HAZEN'S HORNBOOK ON THE LAW OF SECURITIES REGULATION, Second Edition, Student Edition, 1082 pages, 1990. (Text)

RATNER'S SECURITIES REGULATION IN A NUTSHELL, Fourth Edition, approximately 320 pages, 1992. Softcover. (Text)

Sports Law

SCHUBERT, SMITH AND TRENTADUE'S SPORTS LAW, 395 pages, 1986. (Text)

Tax Practice and Procedure

MORGAN'S TAX PROCEDURE AND TAX FRAUD IN A NUTSHELL, 400 pages, 1990. Softcover. (Text)

Taxation—Corporate

SCHWARZ AND LATHROPE'S BLACK LETTER ON CORPORATE AND PARTNERSHIP TAXATION, 537 pages, 1991. Softcover. (Review)

WEIDENBRUCH AND BURKE'S FEDERAL INCOME TAXATION OF CORPORATIONS AND STOCKHOLDERS IN A NUTSHELL, Third Edition, 309 pages, 1989. Softcover. (Text)

Taxation—Estate & Gift—see also Estate Planning, Trusts and Estates

MCNULTY'S FEDERAL ESTATE AND GIFT TAXATION IN A NUTSHELL, Fourth Edition, 496 pages, 1989. Softcover. (Text)

PEAT AND WILLBANKS' FEDERAL ESTATE AND GIFT TAXATION: AN ANALYSIS AND CRITIQUE, 265 pages, 1991. Softcover. (Text)

Taxation—Individual

DODGE'S THE LOGIC OF TAX, 343 pages, 1989. Softcover. (Text)

HUDSON AND LIND'S BLACK LET-

Taxation—Individual—Continued

TER ON FEDERAL INCOME TAXATION, Fourth Edition, approximately 400 pages, 1992. Softcover. (Review)

MCNULTY'S FEDERAL INCOME TAXATION OF INDIVIDUALS IN A NUTSHELL, Fourth Edition, 503 pages, 1988. Softcover. (Text)

POSIN'S HORNBOOK ON FEDERAL INCOME TAXATION, Student Edition, 491 pages, 1983, with 1989 pocket part. (Text)

ROSE AND CHOMMIE'S HORNBOOK ON FEDERAL INCOME TAXATION, Third Edition, 923 pages, 1988, with 1991 pocket part. (Text)

Taxation—International

DOERNBERG'S INTERNATIONAL TAXATION IN A NUTSHELL, 325 pages, 1989. Softcover. (Text)

BISHOP AND BROOKS' FEDERAL PARTNERSHIP TAXATION: A GUIDE TO THE LEADING CASES, STATUTES, AND REGULATIONS, 545 pages, 1990. Softcover. (Text)

BURKE'S FEDERAL INCOME TAXATION OF PARTNERSHIPS IN A NUTSHELL, 356 pages, 1992. Softcover. (Text)

SCHWARZ AND LATHROPE'S BLACK LETTER ON CORPORATE AND PARTNERSHIP TAXATION, 537 pages, 1991. Softcover. (Review)

Taxation—State & Local

GELFAND AND SALSICH'S STATE AND LOCAL TAXATION AND FINANCE IN A NUTSHELL, 309 pages, 1986. Softcover. (Text)

Torts—see also Products Liability

KIONKA'S BLACK LETTER ON TORTS, 339 pages, 1988. Softcover. (Review)

KIONKA'S TORTS IN A NUTSHELL, Second Edition, 449 pages, 1992. Softcover. (Text)

PROSSER AND KEETON'S HORNBOOK ON TORTS, Fifth Edition, Student Edition, 1286 pages, 1984 with 1988 pocket part. (Text)

Trade Regulation—see also Antitrust, Regulated Industries

MCMANIS' UNFAIR TRADE PRACTICES IN A NUTSHELL, Third Edition, approximately 475 pages, December, 1992 Pub. Softcover. (Text)

SCHECHTER'S BLACK LETTER ON UNFAIR TRADE PRACTICES, 272 pages, 1986. Softcover. (Review)

Trial and Appellate Advocacy— see also Civil Procedure

BERGMAN'S TRIAL ADVOCACY IN A NUTSHELL, Second Edition, 354 pages, 1989. Softcover. (Text)

CLARY'S PRIMER ON THE ANALYSIS AND PRESENTATION OF LEGAL ARGUMENT, 106 pages, 1992. Softcover. (Text)

DESSEM'S PRETRIAL LITIGATION IN A NUTSHELL, Approximately 375 pages, 1992. Softcover. (Text)

GOLDBERG'S THE FIRST TRIAL (WHERE DO I SIT? WHAT DO I SAY?) IN A NUTSHELL, 396 pages, 1982. Softcover. (Text)

HEGLAND'S TRIAL AND PRACTICE SKILLS IN A NUTSHELL, 346 pages, 1978. Softcover. (Text)

HORNSTEIN'S APPELLATE ADVOCACY IN A NUTSHELL, 325 pages, 1984. Softcover. (Text)

JEANS' HANDBOOK ON TRIAL ADVOCACY, Student Edition, 473 pages, 1975. Softcover. (Text)

Trusts and Estates

ATKINSON'S HORNBOOK ON WILLS, Second Edition, 975 pages, 1953. (Text)

AVERILL'S UNIFORM PROBATE CODE IN A NUTSHELL, Second Edition, 454 pages, 1987. Softcover. (Text)

BOGERT'S HORNBOOK ON TRUSTS, Sixth Edition, Student Edition, 794 pages, 1987. (Text)

MCGOVERN, KURTZ AND REIN'S HORNBOOK ON WILLS, TRUSTS AND ESTATES–INCLUDING TAXATION AND FUTURE INTERESTS, 996 pages, 1988. (Text)

MENNELL'S WILLS AND TRUSTS IN A NUTSHELL, 392 pages, 1979. Softcover. (Text)

SIMES' HORNBOOK ON FUTURE INTERESTS, Second Edition, 355 pages, 1966. (Text)

TURANO AND RADIGAN'S HORNBOOK ON NEW YORK ESTATE ADMINISTRATION, 676 pages, 1986 with 1992 pocket part. (Text)

WAGGONER'S FUTURE INTERESTS IN A NUTSHELL, 361 pages, 1981. Softcover. (Text)

Water Law—see also Environmental Law

GETCHES' WATER LAW IN A NUTSHELL, Second Edition, 459 pages, 1990. Softcover. (Text)

Wills—see Trusts and Estates

Workers' Compensation

HOOD, HARDY AND LEWIS' WORKERS' COMPENSATION AND EMPLOYEE PROTECTION LAWS IN A NUTSHELL, Second Edition, 361 pages, 1990. Softcover. (Text)

Advisory Board

[XIV]

JURISPRUDENCE
LEGAL PHILOSOPHY
IN A NUTSHELL

by

SURYA PRAKASH SINHA
Professor of Law
Pace University School of Law

ST. PAUL, MINN.,
WEST PUBLISHING CO.
1993

COPYRIGHT © 1993 By WEST PUBLISHING CO.

610 Opperman Drive

P.O. Box 64526

St. Paul, MN 55164–0526

Library of Congress Cataloging-in-Publication Data

Sinha, S. Prakash.

Jurisprudence in a nutshell / by Surya Prakash Sinha.

p.   cm. — (Nutshell series)

Includes index.

ISBN 0–314–01379–2

1. Jurisprudence. 2. Law—Philosophy. I. Title. II. Series.

K231.S57   1993

340—dc20

92–33896

CIP

ISBN 0–314–01379–2

Sinha—Jurisprudence NS

To
Jessica and Sonya

In fond memory of
Wolfgang Friedmann and Ernest Nagel

*

OUTLINE

PART III. THEORIES OF LAW IN EMPIRICIST EPISTEMOLOGY

JURISPRUDENCE
LEGAL PHILOSOPHY

IN A NUTSHELL

*

CHAPTER 1

INTRODUCTION

Jurisprudence has two meanings. In the civil law tradition of Europe it means the collectivity of decisions of a particular court. In the common law tradition of England, United States, and other common law countries it means legal philosophy.

Philosophy consists in raising fundamental questions and seeking the truth. Thus, in philosophy of science we ask what are patterns of scientific explanation, what is accidental and nomic universality in the character of scientific laws, what are major components in theories, such as the logical skeleton of the explanatory system, its empirical content, and its conceptual or visualizable material, what is the cognitive status of theories, and so on. Or, in moral philosophy we ask such questions as what is it that people do when they engage into a moral discourse. In legal philosophy we raise such questions as what is law, what is justice, what is an offense, what is punishment, what are rights, and the like.

This book examines the central question about the nature of law. What is law? How is to be defined? What are its essential aspects? To that end, it examines various theories that have been

1

propounded in the course of human thought to explain the nature of law.

First the earth was created. Then civilization began. And then laws appeared.

As to the origin of earth, geology gives us theories about it. History gives us legends about it. There are mainly four such legends, namely, the Mesopotamian cosmology, the theology of Memphis, the Vedas of India, and the Book of Genesis of the Hebrews.

The epic Enuma Elish of the Mesopotamian cosmology was composed during 1894–1595 B.C. and is largely based on the Sumerian cosmology. Enlil, the god of air, separates earth from heaven from the primeval world matter. God Tiamet, the monsters borne by Tiamet, and the winds created by god Marduk participate in the creation. Apsu and Tiamet are the parents of the gods. From Apsu's carcass Ea forms the subterranean sea. Marduk creates heaven, earth, the heavenly bodies, and vegetation. Together with Ea, he creates humans.

The theology of Memphis was written in Egypt during 715–664 B.C. and it refers to events about 3,000 B.C. Much influenced by the speculations of the priests of Heliopolis of the preceding centuries, this theology of ancient Egypt presents a new chief God, Ptah, who creates the world from the power of his mind and from the speech that conveys his thoughts.

The Vedas of India were composed during 1500–500 B.C. They present two views of creation. According to Hymn X, 121 of the Rg Veda, the actions of god Hiranyagarbha brought on the creation. However, a highly abstract and logical concept is found in Hymn X, 129. According to this Hymn, there was neither non-existence in the beginning nor existence. The universe was developed from the single primordial substance so that He, the first origin of this creation, whether he formed it all or did not form it, whose eye controls this world in highest heaven, he verily knows it, or perhaps he knows not.

The Book of Genesis of the Hebrews was composed during the period from the tenth or ninth century B.C. to the fifth century B.C. It is composed from the "J", the "E", and the "P" sources. The "J" source begins in the tenth or ninth century B.C. God in it is called Jahweh (Yahweh). The "E" source is later in date and, in it, God is called Elohim. The "P" or the Priestly source dates to the fifth century B.C. and is set forth by Priest Ezra. The Genesis has it that the world was created by one eternal God as a purposeful event and evil is the punishment for disobedience to God.

Whether the world began in the theories of geology or in legends of history, humans and protohumans walked in it by 500,000 B.C. The fully modern human, or the *Homo Sapiens,* emerged by 30,000 B.C. With the development of food production, the population grew and civilization became possible. The Middle East exhibits one of the earliest instances of transition from hunting and

gathering to grain cultivation between 8500 and
7000 B.C. Cultivation spread to Europe, India,
China, and parts of Africa. Historians suggest
that it is likely, though not certain, that agriculture surfaced independently in the Americas, mon-
soon Asia, and west Africa.

The earliest civilized communities are seen in
the valleys of the Tigris–Euphrates and the Nile
around 3500–3000 B.C. Soon they appeared in the
Indus Valley, although lack of sufficient archaeological investigation has impeded the knowledge of
the origin of this civilization. A thousand years
later, civilization moved on from river valleys to
rain-watered land.

A distinctive social order became possible due to
agricultural surplus. The palace city of Knossos
on the Island of Crete, for one example, thrived on
trade by sea. Techniques of chariot warfare were
perfected shortly after 1700 B.C. along the northern fringes of Mesopotamia. Consequently, the
warrior tribes of central Asia and the Ukraine
spread out to dominate all of Europe, western Asia,
and India. Others, with the same technique, conquered the Yellow River valley of China. The
interaction between these conquerors and the in-
digenous peoples produced, by about 500 B.C.,
three distinctive civilizations in Greece, the Ganges
River valley, and the middle reaches of the Yellow
River. In the Middle East, the three empires of
Egypt, Asia Minor, and northern Mesopotamia
competed for supremacy and succeeded in achiev-

ing a somewhat unstable unification of the area under the Assyrians.

Civilized history began in these four centers.

Seven to twelve centuries thence, laws made their first appearance. We see them first in 2360 B.C. in the reign of Urukagina of Lagash. In 2300 B.C., they were promulgated in the reign of Sargon of Akkad. In 2100 B.C., they were adopted in the reign of Ur–Nammu of Ur. More extensive laws were promulgated in 1930 B.C. by Lipit–Ishtar, the King of Isin. The famous laws of Hammurabi appeared during the reign (1792–1750 B.C.) of this King of Babylon.

The laws of Hammurabi were expressions of what this King desired the law of the land to be. The written text was not an authoritative statute but a memorandum of decision based on Babylonian notions of justice. His laws were largely amendments and alterations reforming the existing laws and consisted of a heterogeneous series of decisions by judges in a number of separate cases. Their scope exhibited no attempt to cover all possible situations. Their methodology demonstrated very little of systemization.

The Middle Assyrian Laws probably go back to the fifteenth century B.C. but were inscribed on clay tablets during the reign of Tiglath–Pilesar I, from 1115 to 1077 B.C. These are even less comprehensive in scope than the laws of Hammurabi. They, too, are in the nature of amendments and modifications of the existing laws.

The Hittite laws probably date back to the seventeenth century B.C. but were inscribed on clay tablets in the thirteenth century B.C. They record judicial formulae and decisions of the royal court at Hattusas. Their scope is not comprehensive of all areas of law. They were subsequently enlarged by the decisions and ordinances of King Telepinus, who reigned from 1511 to 1486 B.C. The Hittite Laws were an attempt to unite the various classes and groups of the Hittite Empire.

The Hebrew Laws are neither decisions of judges nor ordinances of kings but are claimed to be laws dictated by God Himself. They are found in the first five books of the Old Testament, which are known as Torah (Law) to the Jews and Pentateuch (Five Rolls) to the Greeks. They were compiled from the "J", "E", and "P" sources as well as the "D" source, the Deuteronomic code.

Laws have continued to flourish subsequent to these beginnings. Also, much thought has been invested over the centuries in understanding the nature of law. It is the purpose of this book to study this thought.

CHAPTER 2

PREPARATION FOR THE
STUDY OF THEORIES
OF LAW

Human thought has given us a variety of theories about the nature of law. In order to understand them, it is important to apprise ourselves of the non-universality of law as a central principle of social organization, the irreconcilable epistemologies that underlie these theories, and the tendency to ideological incipience that is often found in these theories.

A. NON–UNIVERSALITY OF LAW

At any given period of history since its civilized beginnings, there have always existed, contemporaneously, three or four civilizations. Each is characterized by a coherent life-style stretching over a large geographical area and extending over a long period of time. The realization of this civilizational pluralism has enabled modern historians to conceive of a world history which views the history of humankind as a whole and not, say, in the manner of the national histories fashionable in the nineteenth century or the history of Western civilization invented in the twentieth century.

7

The appreciation of this fact of civilizational pluralism has important consequences for the jurist as well. It affects our task of apprehending the nature of law and defining it.

It is possible to discern the most fundamental principle of life for each civilization and, consequently, the most central principle of its social organization. Law can be said to be that principle for the Western civilization, but not for other civilizations. This fact explains that most, though not all, theories about law have issued from the Western culture, not from the Chinese, Indian, Japanese, or African cultures. This is not because of some higher spiritual or intellectual attainment denoted by law or some cultural superiority of the West, as claimed by such jurists as Sir Henry Sumner Maine (1822–1888) of England, but because law and its institutions have performed a central role in the particular historicity of the West whereas other principles have played that role in other societies. Since law has occupied such a central place in the Western life, it is only natural that Western thinkers would be more occupied with thinking about its nature than others in whose societies law has not played such a central role.

We shall see how law became so central to the Western life but not to the Chinese, Indian, Japanese, or African life.

1. The Western Civilization

Why did law become a central principle of life in Western civilization? The answer lies in the particular historicity of this civilization, as distinguished from that of the others.

In the principal stages of early Greek history, the territorial state was the most important political organization. It prevailed over all other bases of human association. And the world was explained through the laws of nature.

The earliest Greek invaders took to the sea. They conquered Knossos in Minoan Crete and established themselves among the Aegean Islands and on the mainland. For two hundred years following the destruction of Knossos in 1400 B.C. by the mainland Mycenaeans, the Mycenaeans carried both trade and raid into practically all coasts of the Mediterranean. One of the last such raids was against Troy in 1184 B.C. at the mouth of the Dardanelles, about which Homer wrote. Shortly after 1200 B.C., the Greek-speaking Dorians came from the north and invaded the Mycenaean centers of power. The displaced refugees went across the Aegean to settlements on the coast of Asia Minor. They had not brought with them any pre-existing pattern of governance. Therefore, they created a viable set of laws and governmental systems to assure cooperation in the new settlement. They thus originated the earliest Greek city-states, or the poleis. Again, it was law that came to be the means for governance and cooperation in these settlements.

On the mainland, the polis developed slowly, as the semi-migratory tribes began to settle permanently and join with neighbors to constitute a polis. Local chieftains began settling disputes by sitting in council under a high king. When the council was off session, individuals were appointed for a limited period with delegated authority that eventually acquired a legal definition. In this way, law and its institutions maintained their central role in the social life of the polis.

The compelling pull of the poleis influenced all areas of Greek cultural activity. The polis was small in size, from 50 to 500 square miles. It had a small population. Therefore, men participated in politics directly. Various forms of government evolved, namely, monarchy, oligarchy, tyranny (one-man rule), and democracy. The polis was generally successful in ordering the affairs of men. However, the inquiring mind of the Greeks sought learning. It first sought this from the East. When they failed to find an agreement among the priestly experts of the Middle East on fundamental questions, they, in Ionia, began thinking about these questions themselves. They began explaining the phenomena by imaginative reason. Using reason they dismissed gods as the ruling force of the universe. Instead, they used natural law to explain the phenomena.

There are four stages through which the Greek thought evolved, namely, the Heroic Mind, the Visionary Mind, the Theoretical Mind, and the Rational Mind. The Heroic Mind grounded thought in concrete experiences of the physical senses and gave it the flourishes of fantasy and myth, as in Homer's epics. The Visionary Mind was prompted by the firm establishment of the polis and it sought ordering through ideas interlaced with senses. The instruments of its expression were poetry and drama, as of Pindar, Aeschylus, and Sophocles. The Theoretical Mind was spurred by the emergence of Athens as a metropolis following the Persian wars. It called for analytical powers to look beneath the surface. The Rational Mind turned to concepts of rational order, as in Plato and Aristotle. It used concepts of *logos, arete,* and *metron* to express its world-view. *Logos,* which means word, conceptualized the Greek instrument for finding truth and justice by thinking and discussing issues. *Arete,* which means virtue, conceptualized man's special worth as a reasoning creature. *Metron,* which means measure, conceptualized measurement and proportion in order to avoid *hubris,* or excess.

Man was thus possessed of reason, freedom of choice, and the ability to make decisions. Therefore, he lived for his own sake rather than for the sake of some other exalted human being or supernatural power. This marks the emergence of individualism. The political consequence of this individualism was the independence of the polity whose citizens possessed political and legal rights held in common under the rule of law. Law provided the means for realizing these rights. Consequently, it became central to this mode of social organization.

The Athenian dominion was overpowered by the Spartan supremacy at the end of the Peloponnesian War in 404 B.C. The Macedonian conquest in 338 B.C. meant the loss of the sovereignty of the local polis. The Macedonian kings embraced Hellenism. Alexander directed it eastward. As a result, large numbers of Greeks emigrated, so much so that the Ptolemic and the Seleucid empires depended greatly upon these immigrants.

Soon Rome emerged as a power. In 509 B.C., at the end of the Etruscan rule, it established an aristocratic republic in the Latin cities of central Italy and, by 226 B.C., it expanded over all of Italy south of the Appenines. It drove the Carthaginians from Sicily by 241 B.C. It conquered Macedonia and Greece in 146 B.C., Seleucid Asia in 64 B.C., and Egypt in 30 B.C. The Republic broke down in favor of a military dictatorship as a result of involvement with wars of the east and civil wars between rival generals. A series of Emperors ruled the Roman Empire. In this long period of peace, the Hellenistic civilization spread to Italy, Gaul, and Spain. Latin remained the prevailing language, but intellectuals such as Lucretius (d. 55 B.C.), Cicero (d. 43 B.C.), and Vergil (d. 19 B.C.) used it to express Greek philosophy, rhetoric, and poetry. Philosophers such as Cicero argued that government originated in a voluntary agreement of citizens and that law must be the paramount principle of government. This idea resulted in the emergence of Roman Law, a point of significance from the viewpoint of our inquiry.

Christianity and other competing mystery religions remained largely obscure until about 200 A.D. Eventually, however, Christianity became an important historic force. During A.D. 235–84, the Romans suffered civil war and invasion from the Steppe barbarians. Emperor Constantine (ruled A.D. 306–337), established a new capital at Byzantium. He renamed it Constantinople and decreed Christianity as the state religion. Emperor Theodosius (d. A.D. 395) prohibited all rival faiths. However, there was a disagreement among the Christians as to the doctrine. Most German kingdoms embraced a version disliked by their Roman subjects. Consequently, Emperor Justinian (A.D. 527–65) launched campaigns into the western Mediterranean for the purpose of recovering the unity of the empire.

The primacy of politics over other bases of human association was reasserted in the disturbed events of the Dark Age during A.D. 600–1000. The Empire suffered three waves of barbarian invasion. The first occurred with the Hunnic invasion of central Europe that brought Goths, Burgundians, Vandals, Franks, Anglo–Saxons, and other Germanic peoples into the Roman territory between

A.D. 378 and 450. The second began with the invasion of the Avars from southern Russia at the death of Justinian. The last occurred when the Magyars crossed the Carpathian passes in A.D. 846. Then followed the massive and spontaneous conversion to Christianity. Russia converted in 989, Hungary in 1000, and Denmark, Sweden, and Norway between 831 and 1000.

In 1054, the Latin (Roman Catholic) Christendom formally separated from the Greek (Orthodox) Christendom and spread in Europe during the medieval times through conversion and conquest.

Christianity produced a significant shift in jurisprudential thought. It made a shift from natural law philosophy to revelation, although it still retained the concept of *logos* as reason and as a principle of cosmic ordering. The power of God came to sustain both spiritual and secular orders. Human existence became meaningful only insofar as it reconciled man with his Maker. A divinely-ordained unity sustained the European order in these medieval times. The theologian and the scientist alike proceeded to discover the inner coherence and harmony of this order. In law, Gratian (d. 1140) argued the pros and cons of discordance within the laws of the Church. Irnerius (d. 1130) inaugurated a systematic study of Roman Law as a means of sorting out confusions in the local law of Europe. The individual was subordinated to a collective world order. Obedience to authority became the main emphasis. Collective ends became the goal of the work ethic.

With the Renaissance, however, man returned to the center of things. During 1500–1648, Europe transformed itself through the rival movements of Renaissance and Reformation. Renaissance, dating from about 1350 in Italy, inspired the ideal of giving rebirth to the knowledge, skills, and elegance of the ancient past. Reformation reasserted religious concerns in the face of the rampant secularism of Renaissance. The primacy of God was no doubt preserved but secular measurements were increasingly used to judge events and acts, instead of the divine measurements of God and His commandments.

The classical concepts of *logos* were reasserted by the humanists and the Christian Platonists. *Logos* replaced the Age of Faith by a rational status of man. *Arete* was revived to give man a new intrinsic worth. *Metron* was reinstated to determine not only the limits of man but of macrocosm itself. A neoplatonic philosophy emerged that placed the fundamental relationship of man and his world at the center of cosmology. Its tenets, which achieved this result, were its belief in the correspondence of the microcosm and the macrocosm, its belief in the harmonic structure of the universe, and its belief in the approach to God through the mathematical symbols of center, circle, and sphere.

Individualism reasserted itself by four major means: by insisting, in the manner of the Protestants, on man being his own mediator with God, by challenging the centralized political authority, by legitimizing political needs of the individual rulers, and by instituting capitalism in the economic arena. A cultural pluralism came to flourish. In this individualistic, non-feudal, non-tribal, non-communal, and non-caste frame of society, it was law that provided the technique needed to organize the society.

In the period that followed, i.e., from 1648 to 1789, the Chinese inventions of gunpowder (invented about 756), printing (about 1100), and the compass (early twelfth century) came to the West and advanced it into the era of the national-industrial state. Church and state retreated from enforcing conformity to truth and the passions of Reformation and Counter–Reformation were replaced by the competence of trained professionals in various walks of life. No longer was in this pluralism a need to create and impose an overall synthesis of all truth and knowledge. Specialized professions flourished, including law. Professionalism increased among soldiers and diplomats. War was formalized, as at the battle of Fortenoy in 1745 when the French and the English officers offered each other the courtesy of firing the first shot. International law was promoted, providing the states the technique of reconciling their sovereignty with the calculations of the balance of power.

Intellect was relieved from its preoccupation with the religious debate. It was freed to make advances in agricultural and manufacturing technology. Theories no longer accepted that God intervened in man's everyday life. Consequently, innovations were made in mathematics, science, historiography, empirical philosophy, and political theories. This made Europe rich and advantaged. It planted seeds for Europe's eventual dominance of the world and the overthrow of the cultural autonomy of other great civilizations of the world.

Two revolutions transformed the Western civilization during the period 1789–1914: the industrial revolution, primarily centered in England until 1870; and the democratic revolution, primarily centered in France after 1789. Colonization and trade, which had begun about the year 1000, produced an enormous expansion of wealth and power for Western nations. The industrial revolution enhanced this wealth and accelerated the growth of population. The democratic revolution established the notion that governments were manmade. Therefore, they could be changed or manipulated. Skilled leadership in politics could win the support of the majority. With that support, the government commanded much greater power than hitherto. In these processes, law played its significant role in providing a central mechanism for social organization.

Social changes further intensified during the period 1914–1945. This was a result of the discovery through the two World Wars (1914–1918 and 1939–45) that, firstly, economies can concentrate effort on particular goals and, secondly, that human societies can be deliberately manipulated, both for war as well as for peace, as in Hitler's Germany, Stalin's Soviet Union, and Franklin D. Roosevelt's United States. Society and economy were no longer natural but, rather, quite amenable to conscious control.

Law played a central role in the control and management of these matters. It continues to do so in the period following 1945.

Therefore, as we look at the history of Western civilization, we can see how law has been a central principle of social organization due to the particular historicity of this civilization. The most fundamental principle of the Western way of life is *nomos*. This notion grew in the Greek cradle of Western civilization. It eventually developed to take on the meaning of law, whereby is meant a constituted order of society comprising individual rights and duties.

We first find the word *nomos* in Hesiod (c. 8th century B.C.), when it denoted law laid down for men. The word is not seen in Homer (c. 8th century B.C.), either in *Iliad* or *Odyssey*. However, we do find the comparable concept of *themis* both in Homer and in later compositions of Hesiod. *Themis* meant that which is laid down and established. The *themistes* (plural of *themis*) were ordinances of the divine Zeus which were granted to man for his benefit and the King was entrusted with them. As the self-consciousness of man grew, there occurred a corresponding shift of emphasis from *themis* to *dike* (meaning order, right, judgment, that which is right) to *nomos*.

There are three aspects to *nomos* in Hesiod: an entity ordained by Zeus to replace Homer's *themis;* an independently established practice or usage; and that which is in conformity with nature's regularities. There are, thus, two significant notions in it: one, the notion of natural phenomenon which pre-existed and whose regularity governed man's actions, and, two, the notion of the given way of life, which giving accrued either from divine directives or human usages. Virtue issued from concrete *arete* (excellence or goodness) and not from abstract truth. *Nomos* soon took on the meaning of *thesmos,* i.e., authoritatively laid down law for the benefit of the community.

As the rule of *logos* (word) grew and abstract meaning gained ascendancy, *nomos* began to be expunged of its divine aspect. The pre-Socratic thinking searched for the *arche,* or the first principle, that which is at its beginning in its basic sense. Thus, Anaximander (611?–547 B.C.) proposed that whatever existed did so in being exposed to the order of time, and Heraclitus (540–475 B.C.) separated human *nomoi (anthropeioi nomos)* from the divine *nomos (nomos theios).* The subject matter of *nomoi* became the cosmic totality, which included both man's usages and nature's phenomena. An organizational scheme underlay all occurrences. Consequently, *nomos theios* became the basic structure that sustained all the human *nomoi.*

Nomos was thus taken out of the domain of gods and made very much of this world. It thereby provided the dominant constitutional element of the *polis.* Pindar (522?–443 B.C.) regarded *nomos* the supreme ruling authority and poets Aeschylus (525–456 B.C.), Sophocles (596?–406 B.C.), and Euripides (5th century B.C.) extolled the ancient custom, which essentially referred to an unwritten *nomos,* or the *nomos agraphos.* The substantive meaning of *nomos agraphos* was a constitution of the *polis* that pleased the gods so that deviation from it resulted in the decay of good order (*eunomia*).

As the 6th and 5th centuries B.C. rolled along, unwritten customary rules (*nomoi agraphoi*) and rules of equity gave way to codified laws. However, according to the Sophists of the mid–5th century B.C., neither custom (*nomoi agraphoi*) nor codes (*nomos gregrammenoi*) provided a sufficient foundation for an order of justice. The abstract conception of righteousness or justice (*dikaiosyne*) replaced the concept of divine order (*dike*). *Nomos* came to be contrasted with *physis,* a concept which had already been introduced by such pre-Socratic thinkers as Xenophanes (6th century B.C.) and Heraclitus and which meant nature, or natural form of a person or thing. It denoted not a product of culture but an elementary phenomenon. *Physis,* for Democritus (460?–362? B.C.), was real in our everyday knowledge of the world and *nomos* was unreal. *Physis* was necessary and grown, not conventional. *Nomoi* were arbitrary and conventional. Since *physis* was the real order of things, it possessed the capability for revealing the true basis for justice, or for moral and legal conduct, or, in other words, for ethos (*nomos agraphos*) and statute law (*nomos gegrammenos*).

In this way, natural *nomos* came into being as a result of the *nomos-physis* controversy. Thus, Democritus thought that men must obey *nomoi* for their own well-being because of their natural propensity for causing hurt to each other. Plato (427–347 B.C.) regarded *nomos* as participating in the idea of good and justice. According to Plato, the divine intellect (*nous*) was the *physis* in which *nomoi* participated. Although Aristotle (384–322 B.C.) denied to *nous* the position granted by Plato as a participation in good and justice, he too believed, like Plato, that *nomoi* were inevitable for man if he were to exist differently from beasts. He thought that there was a general idea of just and unjust in accordance with nature. *Nomos,* thus, became natural law. Aristotle regarded man-made conventions just only if they did not violate the universal (*koinos*) unwritten *nomos.* This universal *nomos* represented the natural order of things present under the rule of god (*theos*) and reason (*nous*).

In its final development, *nomos* acquired the meaning of a constituted order of society compris-

ing individual rights and duties, which is a fundamental principle of life for the Western civilization.

2. The Chinese Civilizations

We have seen above how law came to be a
central principle of life in Western civilization due
to the particular historicity of that civilization.
However, the history of the Chinese civilization did
not proceed along the Western lines. Therefore, it
did not produce for itself the concept of law as its
central principle. Instead, it created its own.

Farming began in the Yellow River valley before
3000 B.C. The neolithic Black Pottery people were
probably ancestral to the historical Chinese, but
the archaeological evidence from the city of Anyang (about 1400–1100 B.C.) suggests significant
differences between Anyang and the Black Pottery
villages. The first rulers of China were probably
the Hsia. The second dynasty was that of the
Shang (1523–1028 B.C.), but information is almost
non-existent about that society and its government.
The Shang dynasty was displaced by the Chou in
1051 B.C. The rulers probably exerted an effective
control over a large area of northern China during
the early or the western Chou period (1051–771
B.C.). However, a barbarian attack in 771 B.C.
destroyed that authority. In the year following,
the later or the eastern Chou dynasty (770–256
B.C.) was inaugurated. The Chinese civilization

expanded rapidly during the period known as the age of the Warring States (402–221 B.C.).

Significant ideas emerged during this period which laid the foundation for the Chinese civilization. The Chou conquerors abolished human sacrifice and other rituals of the Shang religion and they explained their own supreme power in terms of a mandate from Heaven. Heaven was conceived as somewhat of an anthropomorphic deity which granted earthly rule to the specially selected Son of Heaven, the Emperor. The Son of Heaven could rule as long as he behaved piously and properly. He could lose Heaven's mandate by impiety or impropriety. A cosmology accompanied this idea whereunder the cosmic order involved a reciprocal interaction between heaven, earth, and men. Earthly affairs revolved around the emperor just as the heavens turned on the pole star. The emperor was responsible not only for war and politics but also for the terrestrial phenomena that affected human activity, such as weather. It was the duty of the emperor to behave in accordance with the prescribed rites in order to attain the harmony between earth and heaven that was necessary for human welfare.

The fact of wars challenged the belief that correct observance of traditional rites would bring order and prosperity. The Legalists repudiated the pieties of the past. Nevertheless, what prevailed in the end was the conservative, though modulated, piety of the sage Confucius (551–479 B.C.).

Confucius did not regard Heaven and spirits as proper objects of inquiry, although he did not doubt their reality or power. He directed attention to the human aspects of things. He looked back nostalgically to the days of the early Chou, the Shang, and the Hsia empires, and even to the divine emperors of the legendary age when, he felt, times had been good because a harmonious relationship existed between Heaven and earth. That harmony was lacking now. So, Confucius asked, what a wise man should do. He gave an answer to this question. His disciples recorded it in the Five Classics.

The study of the Classics became essential for a well-educated man. Consequently, they provided a common core from which grew fundamental attitudes and values for the subsequent generations. Confucianism emphasized decorum and self-control. Other schools of thought, most importantly Taoism, emphasized human passion and mysteries of nature. Together, they offered a balanced and stable pattern of thought which provided the cement of civilization down to modern times, albeit with changes and enrichment, but without fundamental interruption.

China's unification brought great disturbances among the peoples of the steppe. In 221 B.C., the ruler of the state of Ch'in waged wars against the steppe barbarians. He also subdued his rivals within China and declared himself the First Emperor (Shih Huang-ti) of the new Ch'in dynasty.

He prescribed a uniform script, completed the Great Wall, embraced the Legalist school, and repudiated anything that set limits to his power. Therefore, he repudiated Confucianism because it compelled the emperor to govern according to the traditional rites. He prohibited Confucian teaching and he burned Confucian books, except for a single copy of each work retained in the imperial archives.

Civil war broke out at his death in 210 B.C. The Han dynasty was founded in 202 B.C. that ruled until A.D. 220, except for a brief interruption in A.D. 9–22. The Han emperors reverted to Confucianism and repressed rival doctrines. Consequently, the educated class, in time, developed a remarkable uniformity of outlook.

After the reunification of China by the Sui dynasty in A.D. 589, the Sui emperors and their successors of the T'ang dynasty (A.D. 618–907) reestablished an effective frontier guard against the Turkish confederacy. The Sui organized an efficient and ruthless bureaucracy. They completed the Grand Canal that linked the Yangtse with the Yellow River, thereby providing a major route of economy. They succeeded in reconstituting an imperial China even stronger than it had been during the Han dynasty. Although strong central power prevailed only until 755, its disruption did not disrupt the economic development. More importantly, although foreign trade and interregional exchanges flourished, they failed to challenge the

traditional dominance of the landlord-official class.
The classically educated members of this class pursued arts and decorum worthy of gentlemen. The
gentlemanly ideal was considerably elaborated during the T'ang and early Sung (960–1279) period.

In the early T'ang period, Buddhism practically
achieved an official status. But it was system-
atically persecuted after 845 due to the Confucianist distrust of it. Nevertheless, it taught the Con-
fucians how to read new meanings into old texts by
analogy and symbolic interpretation. It also
helped them discover new meanings in the Classics
by bringing to their attention the metaphysical
and cosmological questions. The Taoists took from
it not only aspects of doctrine but monastic organization and schooling as well. Neo–Confucianism
was thus initiated even prior to 1000. The policy
of the Sung rulers to preserve things authentically
Chinese guaranteed its preeminence. Neo–Confucianism achieved great heights under the later
Sung, especially with philosopher Chu Hsi (1130–
1200) and his followers, whose attempt was to be
faithful to the ancients.

During the Mongol period, socio-economic
changes challenged and eroded the traditional values. Nevertheless, the old Confucianism reasserted itself in the end.

China took to maritime enterprise in the early
part of the Ming period (1368–1644). However,
after the expeditions of the court eunuch Cheng-ho
from 1405 to 1433, the Ming emperor forbade sea-

going. The Ming restoration of the Neo–Confucian orthodoxy hurt the mercantile class, but the trading community faded in importance due to the impressive productivity of Chinese agriculture. As a result, conservative Confucianism prevailed again. Printing (invented in 756) was used to disseminate Confucian literature. Gunpowder (invented about 1100) was used to subdue local warlords. The compass (invented in the early twelfth century) was used to stave off seaborne enterprise. In fact, Confucian institutions had achieved such perfection and inner strength that no upheaval made more than a transitory impression upon them. The jolt did not come until the social breakdown of China in the twentieth century.

A barbarian band from Manchuria came to Peking with a Ming general in order to suppress a domestic rebellion, but soon the Manchus founded their own Ching dynasty and consolidated their hold over China. The Manchu emperors distrusted the native Chinese. Yet, the civil administration employed both the Chinese and the Manchus. The recruitment examinations were based on the knowledge of the Confucian Classics.

The Manchus secured the Chinese frontier against the steppe nomads through a process that began with the Treaty of Nerchinsk of 1689 with Russia and ended with the smashing campaign of 1757 against the Kalmuk confederacy. Japan abandoned its sea adventures in 1636, which meant the elimination of the main source of raids

on the China coast. The local representatives of
the Chinese administration concluded agreements
with the Europeans which tamed the activities of
the European merchant ships. Restoration of
peace brought prosperity. The Europeans brought
such novelties as new geographical information,
improved astronomical skills, pendulum clocks,
and Jesuit priests, but conservatism continued to
prevail in the cultural life. The Chinese cultural
life, having perfected its own inner balance, took
no more than a casual notice of the European
novelties. Scholars invented critical methods to
establish true meanings of old Confucian texts.
Wayward interpretations, such as indulged in by
the earlier Neo–Confucianists, were discouraged by
the rigorous Han School of Learning.

Dynastic decay began about 1775. Peasant
grievances grew because of the pressure of population. Revolts began, culminating with the disastrous Taiping rebellion in 1850. The European
trade inflicted more problems. The British government tried to introduce European patterns of commerce at Canton after it abolished the East India
Company's monopoly of China trade in 1834.
When the Chinese officials banned the import of
opium, the British and European traders took to
extralegal forms of such trade. The Chinese attempted to stop these activities and dispatched a
special commissioner to Canton. A dispute over
the punishment of British sailors for a murder on
shore gave the British an excuse for war in which
British gunboats overwhelmed Chinese coastal de-

fenses. The war ended with the Treaty of Nanking (1842) whereby the British extracted from the Chinese all they wanted. Promptly enough, other Western powers followed suit. However, this affront to power did not result in interrupting the traditional patterns of Chinese life and culture.

After the opium war of 1839–41, Western adventurers flooded the treaty ports. They refused to remain in the humble position appropriate to foreign merchants in the Confucian tradition, especially since they had the guns and diplomacy of their governments behind them. To the Chinese this was immoral and unjust, but they could not come around to abandoning the Confucian ways in order to effectively meet the Western challenge.

In 1860, the French and the British seized Peking and burned the Imperial summer palace in retaliation for the imprisonment of some of their diplomats. China's enemies began chopping off its territory and its tributary dependencies. Thus, the land beyond the Amur River was ceded to Russia in 1860, Indochina (Vietnam, Cambodia, and Laos) to France in 1885, and Burma to England in 1886. Control of customs was ceded to the foreign powers in 1863, postal services in 1896, and railway construction in 1888. Since China had come to consider Korea its dependent kingdom, it intervened in it in 1894–95. It was defeated by Japan. Not only did it have to withdraw from Korea, it was made to transfer Formosa and other islands to Japan, as well, and concede a base to Japan on the mainland

Liaotung Peninsula. In addition, it had to pay an indemnity.

The continual concessions to the foreigners struck to many Chinese as a betrayal of the national interest by their government. Secret societies sprang up for the purpose of overthrowing the Manchus. But when the Boxers, so-called by the Westerners because of their calisthenic exercises, attacked the hated foreigners and missionaries, the Western powers occupied Peking (1900) and made China to agree to pay an indemnity.

In 1911, the revolutionary activity against the discredited Manchu rule became quite open. A republic was installed in 1912 without much bloodshed. New kinds of ideas began to attract the educated class. Legalism made its appearance. Western-style codes were adopted in order to attain freedom from Western domination. However, traditional concepts continued to persist. Thus, the new codes were applied when they coincided with the traditional ideas of equity and propriety. They were ignored when they conflicted with these ideas. The increased number of trials resulting from these codes was considered as a sign of decadence.

But the intellectual and political leaders of China turned their back upon Confucianism. Sun Yat–Sen (d. 1925) founded the Kuomintang Party, even though he suffered from intellectual confusions in his hurry to absorb Western culture with speed. The Kuomintang confronted local war lords, Japanese puppets, and rival Communists. Its military commander, Chiang Kai-shek, succeeded in recovering most of China from local warlords by 1928, but it failed to destroy the Communists. The consequent civil war continued sporadically throughout the period between the two World Wars. As the Japanese were defeated in 1945 and ended their occupation of China, Chiang Kai-shek and the Kuomintang clashed with Mao Tse-tung and the Communists. The conflict resulted in the Communist victory in 1949.

Socialist legality on the Soviet model was established in the years following 1949. Although attacks were made in 1952–53 on such concepts of legalism as separation of law from politics, equality before law, independence of the judiciary, limitation of actions, and non-retroactivity of legislation, the Soviet-style socialist legality was nevertheless adopted in the Constitution of 1954. However, the Soviet model was abandoned when relations with the Soviet Union broke off in 1960. China reverted to a path of its own. Priority was given to social transformation over economic growth. Soviet-style centralism was discarded. Persuasion was emphasized over force. The adversary was treated not beyond redemption. The practice of self-criticism was adopted. The masses were asked to be vigilant of their leaders. The Central Committee itself was invited to practice self-criticism.

To be sure, there have been significant departures from the traditional thought. The cosmology of natural phenomenon and human behavior has been abandoned. Former methods of mediation, such as appeal to the family, clan, neighbors, or local dignitaries have been replaced by mediation of those politically involved, such as the people's mediation committees, of which there are more than 200,000 in the country. The view that each party in a dispute must sacrifice something of his own in order to reestablish harmony has been supplanted by the need to assure success of some policy. But the principle of legality is repudiated in favor of education and persuasion. The honorable course to follow is conciliation, not recourse to law. Law is considered quite appropriate for dealing with counter-revolutionaries beyond reform, but it is not considered appropriate for resolving internal social contradictions. Conflict resolution largely proceeds upon an appeal to conscience, rather than pursuit of rights in the courts of law. Law is resorted to only when all else has failed. Recourse must first be had to human sentiment (*ch'ing*), next to reason (*li*), and only lastly to law (*fa*). Law is for the morally perverse, the incorrigible criminal, and the foreigner who is alien to Chinese values.

The essential principle of Chinese life is *li*, not law. The origins of *li* are found in a 350–year period that began with the early years of the Western Chou dynasty (1122 B.C.) and moved through the Book of History (Shu Ching), the Book of Poetry (Shih Ching, 1122–600 B.C.), and the Spring and Autumn Annals (Tsao Chuan, 770–464

B.C.). *Li* acquired its full meaning through the Analects (Lun Yu) of Confucius (551–479 B.C.). It was further developed in the works of his successors and followers during the period of Warring States (463–222 B.C.) and was compiled in the Book of *Li* (Li Chi) during the early part of the former Han dynasty (206 B.C.–A.D. 8).

In the Book of History, *li* had the meaning of ceremonies or religious rituals. It indicated sacrifices usually associated with ancestor worship and it partook of magical powers. This meaning changed in the Book of Poetry to correct and proper behavior. It pointed to man's proper way of life that was essential to man himself and to his relation with others. Man's way of life had to be harmonized with the totality of cosmic events represented in the concept of heaven (*t'ien*). The king's primary concern was to conform to the appointment of heaven (*t'ien-ming*). Cultivation of virtue or excellence of character (*te*) promoted harmony between heaven (*t'ien*) and earth (*ki*). What was crucial, therefore, was not the belief in the supernatural but the belief in interdependence of nature and human behavior. It was up to man to follow a conduct that would maintain harmony between him and nature. Filial piety (*hsiao*) was that virtue which maintained harmony in the family and, as its ultimate result, between man and nature's events. The imperative of *li* required aligning human order with nature's order. Therefore, while appointment of heaven (*t'ien-ming*) issued directives concerning various matters, there was no all-powerful personal lawgiver in control of man's destiny.

In the later documents of the Shu Ching and in the Spring and Autumn Annals, *li* expanded to cover all aspects of human existence. The ruler's (Son of Heaven's) responsibility was to govern in accordance with *li*. Failure to do so led to imbalance and confusion. The order of the society proceeded on the basis of five relationships, called *wu lan*, namely, the relationships between father and son, ruler and subject, husband and wife, elder and younger brother, and between friends. Correspondingly, there were five lessons of behavior, called *wu chiao*. This produced particularized *li*. Shu Ching narrates three *li* for observances in the worship of the spirits of heaven, the earth, and the men. It articulates five *li* for worship, calamity and mourning, state grants, war, and festivities. Infraction of one's duty disrupted the harmony between the human and non-human spheres and invited appropriate action for restoring that harmony. Consequently, there were five punishments (*wu hsing*) corresponding to the five lessons of behavior (*wu chiao*). *Fa* (laws, regulations, statutes) laid down the procedure for enforcing punishment. It was regarded with suspicion and antipathy. The practice of *li* in a spirit of benevolence and harmony was preferred to *fa* and *hsing*. Therefore, new enactments (*chih*) were seen as an omen that the state was about to perish. *Li* was preserved orally and transmitted through example and education.

Li, then, is something internal to human conduct, not something imposed from above by a human divine agency. Its practice is internally enforced as a demonstration of man's personal ability to contribute to the maintenance of universal harmony and the cultivation of his being and his society.

With Confucius, *li* became a principle of social organization and control. Filial piety (*hsiao*) was the moral essence of *li,* whose effectiveness derived from the moral impetus of virtue or excellence of character (*te*). *Te* was directed toward the expected cultivation of benevolence or humaneness (*jen*), righteousness in the sense of that which is right to do as one's duty (*i*), wisdom or practical knowledge (*chih*), and confidence (*hsin*). Law (*fa*) was considered hideous. Insistence was put upon a positive motivation of the people to avoid detrimental conduct, conform to *li,* and avoid litigation (*sung*).

The Book of *Li* (Li Chi) gave a fully developed expression of *li.* The Book contains 3,300 rules of behavior which are made concrete in customs, habits, and ceremonies. They are devised to maintain an all-embracing social harmony in accordance with valued ways of life.

One's failure to perform his duty in accordance with *li* invites a socially agreed sanction or moral education, including exhortation and punishment, in order to secure proper conduct in the future. Similar is the case with non-criminal matters as well, wherein the self-regulating procedures of *li* are relied upon and prevention of litigation is preferred over taking recourse to law.

3. The Indian Civilization

The Indian civilization, too, has its own particular historicity that has produced its own unique principle of life. This principle is not law, as in the Western civilization.

The origin of the Indus Valley civilization is not fully known due to insufficient archaeological investigation. According to the currently available data, it began shortly after the appearance of the earliest civilized communities in the valleys of Tigris–Euphrates and the Nile about 3500–3000 B.C. It spread to the south and the east as a result of transition from river-valley farming to rain-watered cultivation.

The Indus cities were destroyed in about 1500 B.C. by the Aryan invaders from the West. These wandering bands gradually settled down to agricultural life, but they continued to expand into southern and eastern India. The Sanskrit verses of Rg Veda and the epic Mahabharata descended from this Heroic age.

An aristocratic chariot culture prevailed in that age. However, the chariot and the aristocratic predominance were displaced by the coming of iron about 900 B.C. Great centralized monarchies emerged in the Ganges valley. By 800 B.C., the Ganges valley was well on its way to civilized complexity in which centralized monarchies supported courtly centers, artisan skills, and inter-regional trade. Sea trade with Mesopotamia was also resumed.

The core institution of social organization that emerged during this period and which, with subsequent modifications, continues to this day, was caste. A caste is an exclusive group of persons whose customs govern intimacies of dining and intermarriage with each other. It has a system of definite rules of behavior toward members of other castes. Strangers, intruders, wanderers, and displaced persons automatically become another caste. New occupations create new castes. A large caste is divided into subcastes. It is not clear how such a mode of social organization originated but it has been sustained by three main principles. First is the idea of ceremonial purity, along with its fear of contamination by a member of a lower class. Second is the pyramidical structure of castes in which each caste has another to look down upon and thus be satisfied psychologically. Consequently, there is no need to compel the newcomers to surrender their ways and be assimilated into the population as a whole. The third is the doctrine of *varna* and reincarnation. *Varna* divides all people in four large castes in the descending order of Brahmans, who pray and perform rituals, Kshatriyas, who fight wars and defend the society, Vaisyas, who carry on trade, and Sudras, who perform unclean tasks. Reincarnation explains a man's situation in a logical manner in terms of reward or punishment for acts in the former lives of his soul.

The foremost identification for everyone was with his caste. Therefore, political and territorial administration became of only secondary importance. Caste also made it easy for newcomers to come within the fold of the Indian civilization without radically displacing their own customs and habits. This went well with India's unique religious evolution wherein the doctrine was passed on by word of mouth from teacher to pupil and which, for that reason, allowed for an easy blending of different doctrines.

The Vedas constituted the handbooks of religious ritual. As their language became increasingly unintelligible, the priests shifted the emphasis from gods to the act of worship and put forth their own claims in texts which are known as Brahmanas. A rival type of piety arose in another body of oral literature known as Upanishads. It recommended a godless asceticism. The Brahman priests, in their clever turn, reconciled the Upanishads with their Brahmanas by arguing that Upanishads were quite suitable for the last stage of a man's life.

A more serious challenge to the Brahmans came from the emergence of Jainism and Buddhism about 500 B.C. Jainism remained a faith for an elite. However, Buddhism became more popular. It moderated and defined the Upanishadic style of religious life. Eventually, though, it gave way to a transformed Brahmanical religion, namely, Hin-

duism.   The period between the sixth and the
second centuries B.C. witnessed the composing of
the manuals of human conduct of the Hindus
known as the *Dharma Sutras*.

The kingdom of Magadha had already consolidated itself in the Ganges region by the time Alexander of Greece invaded the Indus Valley in 327 B.C.
That invasion disrupted Indus defenses and alli-
ances.   Chandragupta   Maurya   of   Magadha
(reigned 321–297 B.C.) annexed the Indus region to
his kingdom.   His grandson Ashoka (reigned 274–
36 B.C.) annexed central and southern India to the
Mauryan empire.

Ashoka patronized Buddhism.   He supplemented
it with such innovations as pilgrimages and alms-
giving.   The monks found in it a complete way of
life.   However, the ordinary folks continued to
resort to the Brahmans for the rites of their daily
lives.

The Gupta empire (A.D. 320–535) inaugurated a
golden age for India after a period of invasions
from 190 B.C. to A.D. 250.   It extended over all of
northern India from the Arabian Sea to the Bay of
Bengal.   Again, society and culture remained
strongly apolitical.   Even for the Gupta rulers politics were relatively superficial.   Thus, for example,
they allowed the defeated rulers to remain in control of their lands and were content with ceremonial deference on state occasions.

The Guptas accepted the Hindu notion of authority that put their own edicts last in authority.

Authority, in this notion, was arranged in the descending order of Vedas, the Brahmana commentaries on Vedas, examples of holy men, and, only lastly, personal inclination, such as edicts of a king or public official. The *Dharma Shastras,* or the instructions in the sacred law, were compiled during the Gupta era. These have been basic for Hindu life ever since, although interpreted subsequently to accommodate contemporary needs. They gave the caste theory its classical formulation. They laid down the duties of the members of different castes. They asserted that a faithful performance of these duties would lead one to the salvation of his soul, which lay in the soul freeing itself from the cycle of reincarnation and uniting with the Absolute Soul, or God.

By 715, the Muslim invaders conquered Sindh in the northwest. They seized control of the Indian Ocean and separated India from her cultural dependencies in southeast Asia. The caste organization of the Hindu society kept the Hindus politically and militarily weak. Therefore, they were not able to repel the Muslims. Instead, they recoiled peaceably to conserving their own heritage. Philosophers such as Shankara (788–850) showed why the Muslim criticism of Hindu idolatry had been mistaken for the reason that the practice helped people achieve a pure and transcendental monism propounded by Islam. They even argued for the validity of Muslim rites.

However, the popular culture rejected everything alien and defended everything its own. Hidden practices came out in the open. For example, Tantrism surfaced to seek supernatural powers by magic charms and incantations. Temples became prominent. Secular aspects of civilization suffered a setback. Hinduism remained firmly rooted. Although the Indian society expanded geographically, the Muslim threat forced the Hindus to concentrate upon what was Indian and reject whatever was alien.

The Muslim conquest of India brought significant changes. For the Hindus, their conquerors became just another caste and thus fitted into the Hindu social system. However, the universal and missionary faith of Islam resisted the caste system. The egalitarian teachings of Islam were preached by the itinerant Sufi holy men. These appealed to the low-caste urban Hindus and to the newcomers to Indian society along the frontiers, especially in eastern Bengal, who had been put in the lower caste. Hinduism itself underwent changes. Since the Muslim invaders destroyed the temples, it took to the streets. Ceremonies became more public. Consequently, Islam attracted only the fringes of society. Thinkers such as Kabir (d. 1518) and Nanak (probably a disciple of Kabir in his youth) attempted a synthesis of the common core of truth in both Hinduism and Islam. Nanak even founded the new Sikh faith. The popular Hindu piety replaced Sanskrit as the religious language with vernaculars such as Hindi. Of course, the official aspects of the courtly culture became Muslim.

The Muslim rulers conquered the last independent Hindu state of Vijayanagar in the south in
1565. During the reign of the Mughal Emperor
Aurangzeb (1658–1707) almost all of the Indian
peninsula was brought under the Muslim control.
Hinduism lost state support. However, it was revi-
vified in the streets by the saint Chaitanya (d.
1527) and poets Sur Das (d. 1563) and Tulsi Das (d.
1623). The public religious excitement of these
new movements swept away the arguments of both
the Muslim and the Christian missionaries. Thus,
although the form of Hinduism was altered by the
political submission of the society, the overwhelming majority of Indians remained true to the Hindu
faith, Hindu traditions, and Hindu ways of life,
including the caste system of social organization.
Muslim law applied to Muslims but not to non-
Muslims, except in criminal matters.

The Mughal power declined with the revolts of
the Marathas and the Sikhs. The Mughal emperor
survived in name until 1857. The European trading companies equipped their own armed forces,
recruiting Indian soldiers (sepoys) under European
officers. The European rivalry for India ended in
a decisive victory for the British over the French in
1763 after a struggle that had begun in 1756.
After the Afghan invasion of India and the defeat
of the Marathas at Panipat in 1767, the local
princes had to choose between the Afghans and the
British. Most chose the British. By 1818, almost
all Indian states went under British control. With
the British triumph in the last Maratha war, there

was no rival left. British control was exercised through a Resident at princely courts and through direct administration in other parts.

The social institutions and relationships were left alone by the British. They, for example, kept the Persian language of the Mughals as the language of administration until 1837. However, the interaction between the Western and the Hindu cultures increased as a result of initiatives from both the British and the Hindus. Missionary activity made the knowledge of the European civilization more accessible, although few Indians became Christians. Such activity stimulated efforts for understanding the British culture, as pioneered by Ram Mohan Roy (d. 1833). Indian leaders urged the British authorities to reform traditional customs and institutions. In fact, the demand for reform was so much that the administration failed to keep pace with it.

However, the great majority of the population remained only vaguely aware of these developments.

The British suppressed the revolt of 1857 and promptly installed an autocratic civil service recruited from British universities. The civil service began imposing a long series of reforms.

The Indian reaction to Western civilization was peaceful. New ventures of industry and commerce were largely left to the outsiders, such as the Parsis and the Englishmen. Indian industries were strengthened as a result of disruption of supply lines from England during the two World Wars. This activity took place in enterprises in which the private sector and the government merged.

The Indian National Congress was organized in 1885 for the purpose of achieving self-government. After World War I, its leadership passed to Mohandas Gandhi. In 1905, the Muslim League was organized. In 1940, the League proclaimed its goal of establishing a separate Muslim state. Independence from the British came in 1947. India was divided into a Muslim Pakistan and a secular India.

During the British rule, the Hindu principles of *Dharma* were applied to such matters as marriage, inheritance, the caste system, and religious usages and institutions. A territorial law was newly created to govern other aspects of the newly reshaped society. This law applied to all subjects, regardless of their religion. The concept of a territorial law, in which the law existed as an autonomous body independent of religions, was an alien concept to Indian traditions.

Territorially, a distinction was drawn between the Presidency Towns of Bombay, Calcutta, and Madras and the rest of the colony, known as *Mofussil*. In the Presidency towns, English courts applied English law as it existed in 1726, suitably modified by the local authorities for Indian conditions. The jurisdiction of these courts originally existed in disputes involving an Englishman or in disputes in which the parties formally accepted that jurisdiction. In 1781, their jurisdiction was extended to all disputes. They applied Hindu law to Hindus and Muslim law to Muslims. In the rest of the colony, the *Mofussil* courts dispensed law. These had been established by the East India Company which, in 1765, had secured the privilege of collecting taxes in return for an annual payment to the Mughal Emperor. After the suppression of the revolt of 1857, these courts passed to the direct authority of the British government. The Regulation for the Administration of Civil Justice of 1772, issued by Governor–General Warren Hastings, defined their authority. They applied Hindu or Muslim law in matters of inheritance, marriage, caste, and religious usages and institutions. They applied general principles of justice, equity, and good conscience in other matters. The Regulation of 1781 created two superior courts for the provinces of Bengal, Bihar, and Orissa: one, the *Sadar Diwani Adalat,* for private law matters, the other, the *Sadar Nizami Adalat,* for criminal matters.

The court system was reorganized throughout the colony by the Indian High Courts Act of 1861. Although the Cornwallis Code of 1793 and the Elphinstone Code of 1827 had already been adopted for India in criminal matters, the task of organized codification began with the Charter Act of 1833. The first Law Commission submitted its famous *lex loci* report that proposed three codes, one for Muslim law, one for Hindu law, and one in the nature of territorial law (*lex loci*) for matters in which Hindu or Muslim law did not apply. Due to some serious objections made to these proposals, a second Law Commission was established in 1853 and it made its own proposals. However, it was only after the revolt of 1857 that an intensive legislative activity for India took place. The Indian Code of Civil Procedure was adopted in 1859, which was replaced by a Civil Code (1908), a Criminal Code (1860), and a Code of Criminal Procedure (1861). Other statutes were enacted, such as the Limitations Act (1859), the Succession Act (1865), the Contract Act (1872), the Evidence Act (1872), the Specific Relief Act (1872), the Negotiable Instruments Act (1881), the Transfer of Property Act (1882), the Trusts Act (1882), and the like.

As mentioned above, India achieved independence in 1947. The Constitution of 1950 provided for the continuity of the former law (Section 372). New legal activity followed. The modern tendency is to replace religious laws with secular laws.

However, nearly eighty percent of the population living in Indian villages continues to conduct its life through the traditional institutions. The influence of these traditions remains significant in the urban areas as well.

The essential principle of individual and communal life of most Indians is *dharma,* a term which experts agree is untranslatable, but whose concept is certainly not of law in the Western sense. *Dharma* originated in the Aryan tribal community at the very beginning of the present Indian civilization, i.e., about 2000 B.C. The community allocated the governmental leadership to the king (*raja*) and the spiritual leadership to the priest (*brahman*). By the end of the Rg Vedic period (1500–900 B.C.), a fourfold division of society came to prevail along the lines of the four *varnas*, which formed four classes of society, namely, the priest (*brahman*), the warrior (*kshatriya*), the peasant (*vaishya*), and the serf (*shudra*). The concept of *rta*, or the universal cosmic order, presented an order that was immanent, pre-existent, and independent of any other force. *Dharma* was that which upheld or sustained. *Rta* apprehended man's phenomenal surroundings and structured irregular phenomena into a form of regularity. Gods gave examples of *dharma* to uphold that which existed in order (*rta*). The purpose was to make man conscious of his own active, though ordered, way of life.

The sacred literature of Vedas (1500–900 B.C.) gave an expression to *dharma* as a complex of action, conduct, ordinance, and principle of regularity in various existential situations. Thus, *dharma* exhibited three aspects: one, expression of nature's most active parts; two, expression of natural and human phenomena; and, three, expression of both abstract and concrete relations of pure knowledge and human affairs.

The subsequent literature of Upanishads (900–500 B.C.) accepted *dharma* as the supreme force of the world but it related *dharma* intimately to practical necessities of everyday life in all its aspects. It was within the all-embracing function of *dharma* that the principle of *karma* (act or deed) operated. *Karma* is the principle that establishes a causal connection between the performance of one's deed and the reaping or suffering of its consequence in this or another life. The ultimate aim of soul is *moksha,* or its release from the cycle of life, death, and rebirth. *Karma,* sustained by *dharma,* leads to *moksha.* Good *karma* lies in the performance of one's duty.

The later literature of *dharma sutras* were in the nature of manuals of the precepts of *dharma* stated in the form of aphorisms. The subsequent *dharma shastras* presented more compositions in verse form.

All these various teachings of *dharma* are concerned with the issue of how a man can follow a way of life in conformity with *dharma.* *Dharma* is of three kinds: *svadharma, sadharana dharma.* and *purushartha.* *Svadharma* calls for performance of one's duty as determined by his class (*varna*) and by his stage of life (*ashram*). Its breach is a social offense, since its performance serves social solidarity for the present generation as well as for the future generations. *Sadharana dharma* guides one's conduct for the benefit of the community as a whole. This, in turn, benefits his own being as a part of the whole. *Purushartha* assists man in achieving his ends, which are *dharma, artha* (wealth or material possession), *kama* (pleasure), and *moksha* (salvation).

Dharma gained further elaboration and interpretation under the rubric of Hindu Law and it continues to govern personal relations of the Hindus in today's India, who constitute about 80 percent of the population of the country. The Islamic law does the same for the Muslims of the country. The secular law governs the rest of the population, with some overlapping applications. The fact that there exists a Western-style structure of legal administration must not delude us into thinking that that has replaced *dharma* with *nomos* as the essential principle of life for most Indians.

4. The Japanese Civilization

The historical emergence of social concepts in the Japanese civilization, too, demonstrates the non-universality of law.

At the outset of civilized history, the Japanese steadily raised their farming to the levels of the Chinese who flourished in the northeastern flank of the Chinese center. They adopted various aspects of the Chinese culture, such as Buddhism and Confucianism. The emperors of the Nara period (A.D. 645–784) emulated the T'ang court of China, although the baronial patrons practiced a rougher life-style in the provincial castles. A system of periodic distribution of rice plantations was introduced in the Taika era (beginning in A.D. 646).

Under this system, the distribution was made in proportion to the number of people to be fed. The social organization proceeded along the division of the society in ranks. Each rank performed a particular task for the regime. Their duties were collected in a compilation known as *ritsu-ryo,* which contained a series of prohibitions (*ritsu*) and the rules of administration (*ryo*) for each class. The *ritsu-ryo* provided the source of enlightenment for the people, as contrasted with the storehouse of legal rights and duties in the Western sense.

The sharing of public land was replaced in the ninth and tenth centuries by a feudal system. In this system, the seigniorial unit of *sho* became a sovereign domain which enjoyed fiscal privileges and whose master owned all the land within it.

The courtly culture did not disappear with this decline of imperial power. However, its character changed. The warrior barons, or the *samurai,* with their military expansiveness, did not much care for the antimilitaristic cultural idea of the T'ang China that had been imposed upon them. Instead, they developed their own warrior ideal that emphasized courage in battle, loyalty to the leader, and the personal dignity of the fighting man. Territory taken in wars became hereditary, but continued vigilance and prowess in battle were needed to keep it. The sword settled the disputes both between different bands and within a single band. The Emperor and the courtier class (*kuge*) lost much power. The Emperor was still revered

because of his sacred rights, but the warrior class
(*buke, bushi, samurai*) developed its own code of
conduct (*buke-ho*). Again, the basis of this code of
conduct was not anything like the Western concept
of law. Instead, it was based upon the duty of
faithfulness to the overlord.

Buke-ho applied to the warrior class and *ritsu-ryo* applied to others. This dualism persisted until
the warrior succeeded in establishing his dom-
inance over the peasant. Consequently, during the
period of the Ashikaga Shoguns (1333–1573), *buke-ho* came to be dominant and *ritsu-ryo* fell into
disuse.

The townsmen and the sailors began to achieve
prominence after about A.D. 1300 as the poor *sa-murai*, without much land, took to piracy and
searoving and as Japan achieved naval supremacy
in the southeast Pacific after China withdrew from
the seas in 1430's. With their riches brought
home, the town life assumed a new importance. It
gave rise to a warlike, self-reliant middle class that
developed an elaborate high culture. The drama
was based on the wars of the *samurai*. Painting
acquired a distinctive Japanese style. *Samurai*
manners achieved refinement, as in the elegant tea
ceremony and the use of silk clothes. Zen Buddhism had been originally imported from China
and was now, beginning in about 1200, mixed with
the samurai ideal. It developed into the Pure
Land Buddhism. Its monasteries defended themselves like a *samurai* clan, since they often were

important land-holders. Peasant uprisings sprouted after 1400 but did not amount to much. Prior to 1400, the cult of the Sun Goddess, from whom the imperial order descended, was confined to the imperial court and was patterned after Chinese-style ancestor worship. After 1400, it was reinterpreted and was invested with its own metaphysical theology under the new name of Shinto.

Civil wars were waged at the beginning of the period 1500–1700. The Portuguese arrived in the 1540's. European dress styles, Christian baptism, and European guns spread rapidly. The increased cost of armaments meant that it was necessary to have large territorial sovereigns. Consequently, there occurred a political consolidation of Japan under Hideyoshi (d. 1598). After his death, one of his companions, Ieyasu of the Tokugawa family, emerged successful at the end of a civil war and he proceeded to protect himself from his rival. He controlled the searovers. Eventually, he forbade it altogether.

The Dutch came in 1609. A new supplier of arms thus materialized for the Japanese. Therefore, the Shogun could now proceed safely against the Christian community. There was a Christian revolt in 1637 at Kyushu. In its wake, almost all Christians, whether European or Japanese, were executed.

The Tokugawa Shoguns ruled from 1603 to 1868. The end of warfare deprived the *samurai* of a meaningful occupation. Therefore, they spent their time in the ceremonies of their class or in amusing themselves in the sensuous life of the towns. They thereby bankrupted themselves but gave rise to a bustling market economy. The merchants were only too glad to accept the assignment of right to collect rice from villages, a right that had belonged to the bankrupt *samurai*s. In this way, the vulgar culture of the towns and the decorous culture of the officialdom existed contemporaneously and complementarily. At the basis of the social order was a strict separation of the social classes of the warriors, the peasants, and the merchants.

The Tokugawa Shoguns had made Neo Confucianism official and they had even prohibited the study of other philosophies. However, a few disaffected Japanese began studying Western as well as Chinese thoughts. Others employed Neo–Confucianism and its teaching of obedience to superiors as a justification for opposing the Shoguns' usurpation of authority from the Emperor. Yet others took to Shintoism in place of Neo–Confucianism. Consequently, when the Shoguns were forced to abandon the policy of isolation in 1854, men with alternative policies were just waiting in the wings.

However, the idea of law was quite absent in this period. Order was based on a series of *giri*, or proper rules of behavior, such as the *giri* of father and son, of husband and wife, of landowner and farmer, of lender and borrower, of merchant and customer, of employee and employer, and so on.

These *giri* were observed because violation brought
on social reprobation.

The policy of rigorous seclusion that had been in
effect since 1638 could no longer be enforced
against the Western navies. In 1853, the United
States sent Commodore Perry to Japan with four
warships and demanded that Japan let the United
States use its ports for trade and as coaling sta-
tions for the U.S. ships. The Japanese hesitated at
first, but the Tokugawa Shogun eventually accepted the American terms in 1854. This caused offense to the Japanese sensibility and the Japanese
overthrew the Tokugawa government in 1868.
The Emperor was restored, inaugurating the Meiji
era.

Soon the Japanese realized that adoption of
Western technology and political organization was
the only way to protect themselves from the West
and to end the national disgrace of unequal trea-
ties which had been extracted from them in 1858.
Consequently, feudalism was replaced by a democratic state. Western-style legislation was adopted
in order to link Japanese law with the laws of the
West. European-style codes of law were adopted.
Public institutions were modified extensively.
Thus, freedom of agriculture was established in
1871. Sale of land was instituted in 1872. A
Constitution was adopted in 1889. Departments
(*kin*) and municipalities were created in the administrative structure of the country. An industri-

al revolution was launched for achieving military strength.

The Europeans started World War I in 1914. Japan made its own Twenty-one Demands upon China in 1915. Chinese protests and American efforts to restrain Japan resulted in a general settlement in the Pacific area at the Washington Conference of 1922 which kept Japan away from China.

Western-style industrialization and democratic politics were adopted during this period. However, the traditional ways of Japanese life continued. Thus, in the industrial field, what governed the conduct was the attitudes that derived directly from the spirit of the *samurai* clans. Factory managers took it as their duty to be of service to the nation, to obey the superiors, and to discipline and protect the inferiors, rather than seeking profit as an end in itself. Honor and prestige were the goal of the firms. The old warrior values of courage, endurance, and loyalty were practiced by private ventures. Within the firm, human relations were patterned along the traditional mode that had existed between the *samurai* and the peasant. Managers commanded, the workers obeyed, and the workers were looked after throughout their life. In the political field, although the Constitution of 1889 introduced universal male suffrage to the Diet, behind-the-scene authority was exercised until the 1930's by an inner circle of elders who descended from the clique of clan leaders.

In the 1930's, the semisecret patriotic societies set up ambitious young army officers as a rival power to the civil government. Meanwhile, Japan set out on a course of military conquest, taking Manchuria in 1931 and most of China in 1937–41. However, trade embargoes were imposed upon Japan by the United States on such crucial supplies as oil and scrap iron with a view to restraining Japanese moves in the Pacific and securing U.S. interests there. In order to seize the oil fields in Borneo and create a "co-prosperity sphere" in Southeast Asia and the Southwest Pacific, Japan attacked the American fleet in Pearl Harbor in 1941. At the end of World War II, Japan surrendered to the United States in August, 1945. Subsequently, the Americans ended their occupation of the country. A modern era followed for Japan.

In this era, the law made in imitation of the West governs a very small segment of Japanese social life. Only the middle class individuals fashion their relations on the basis of freedom and liberty and other constituent concepts of that law. The majority of the people live their lives according to the Confucian idea of hierarchy based on natural order. There is a general dislike for involving oneself in public affairs. There is a general preference for leaving matters of government to a powerful minority. Recourse of law is considered shameful. Personal relations are pursued through *giri-ninjo*. The notion of legal rights is contrary to the Confucian hierarchy and is deemed to depersonalize human relations by putting all persons on

an equal basis. Law is deemed appropriate only
for depersonalized matters relating to business and
industry. The preferred procedures for settlement
of disputes are *jidan, wakai,* and *chotei.* In *jidan*
the parties settle the dispute amicably through
mediators; in *wakai* the judge brings the parties to
a settlement; in *chotei* the parties request the
court to appoint a panel of conciliators who are
charged with proposing an equitable settlement.
Resort to *chusai* (arbitration) is avoided in domestic contracts.

Thus, law has not been a central principle of
social organization in Japan due to the particular
historic being of this civilization.

5. The African Civilizations

Civilizations in Africa have grown in their own
particular historicity in which law has not been a
central factor. Look, for example, at the cultures
of the Tallensi, the Ashanti, the Hausa–Fulani, the
Yoruba, the Ibo, the Tiv, the Ganda, the Lugbara,
the Kikuyu, the Nandi, the Arusha, the Nyakyusa,
and the Nuer.

The **Tallensi** (occupying the basin of the Volta
rivers) respond to the cues of life, solve their common problems, and resolve their inter-group conflicts not through a central authority, or a temporal chief, or a council of elders. These problems
are handled by the kinship heads. The problems
are sorted out between those appropriate for the

clan head, those appropriate for the diviner, and
those appropriate for the family head.   People
know what is to be handled in their world and
what is to be settled in the world of spirits.   They
live in the world of tangible substance as well as in
the world of ancestors and spirits.   The spiritual
world has real effect in the material world.   It has
to be propitiated with solemn ritual and display.
Festivals and rituals emphasize the harmony of the
whole society.   Inter-clan wars exist, as between
the Namoos and non-Namoos, but they are regarded part of the social process that releases tensions
and precedes ritual affirmation of inter-clan solidarity.   Their society is stable, unchanging, fixed
in their locality and in their ways.   Measures of
self-help by the injured party resolve conflicts arising from violation of norms within the clan.   Members of the lineage group put their own pressure
upon the disputants of the lesser groups.

The **Ashanti** (Ghana and environs) believe in
the supremacy of the spiritual world.   A certain
form of social order is adopted because it is the
appropriate mode of linkage with the spiritual
world.   Family or lineage is the means for organizing action in the tribe and the nation.   Particular
spheres of competence belong to the lineage, the
tribe, and the nation, respectively.   The concept of
ntoro provides the bond with the spiritual world,
just as the concept of *mogya* provides the bond with
the material world.   The *mogya* makes the child a
member of its lineage, which is a group descending
from a common original female ancestor.   The

lineage group forms a part of the clan. The clan is made up of matrilineal descendants of a common female ancestor. The lineage head or elder is elected by the senior members of the lineage. His functions include deciding disputes among lineage members. The chief, or the *Asantehene*, has the task of performing rituals for propitiating the spirits and leading his tribe in war.

The relationship between these various groups is not that the *Asantehene* is supreme over the chief and the chief over the elder but that their specific competence, as laid down by tradition, is called into action when needed. The individual exists both in the world of his ancestors and in the world of his family and clan. Life is a matter of performance of obligations. Thus, land is held with the obligation to use it. Property is held with the obligation to employ it for the benefit of those sharing one's blood. The male has obligations to till the land, render services to those who have links with the spiritual world, serve the *Asantehene* in war, assist in the performance of rituals, pay levies duly imposed, raise the offspring, and so on. The norms for protecting the social order and avoiding injury to gods are laid down by tradition. Violation invites inquiry into the family, the tribe, and the nation. Severe sanctions are imposed for tribal offenses because of the great risk of injury to the tribe through gods.

The **Hausa–Fulani** (north central Nigeria, east of Niger and west of Lake Chad) states and the

Nupe state have developed from a people who have had their unique culture and conquered peoples of differing cultures. They ruled them by keeping their social distance from the mass and by preserving their monopoly of political and economic advantage. The ruling Fulani are more Islamized than their conquered peoples. In spite of inter-marriage with the conquered peoples, the Fulani keep to their image of superior separateness.

Life centers in villages and towns behind walls due to risks of armed attack and slave raiding in the open savanna or orchard bush land. Cultivation is carried out in outlying farms. Families live in compounds of related households. Their members are organized into work units called *gandu*. The king represents the most powerful person in the state. He manipulates rewards and deprivations. There is a system of control of succession to the kingship. Thus, the Habe state of Zazzau controls succession from four eligible dynasties, the Habe state of Abuja has a single royal lineage, and the Nupe state uses a system of rotation among three royal houses.

There is social mobility among the members of the society. The less advantaged can move to positions of greater power, prestige, and wealth. Each occupation has its own standard of *arziki*. *Arziki* denotes high achievement of admired values and is a composite of birth, prestige, political protection, large family, good farming, wealth, greater than average consumption, and so on. There exists an institution of clientage. Those seeking advantage seek the protection of a patron. Slaves are used in political office, in armies, in work as fiefs in slave villages, and in household tasks.

The ruling Fulani brought the Islam. It has tended to replace the clan and the extended family by the nuclear family and the individual. However, it has not succeeded in destroying the unity of the family, kin, and tribe, nor has it destroyed their world of spirits. Muslim law is no doubt applied in criminal matters, but in disputes among pagans it is traditional custom, not Muslim law, that is applied. Disputes are decided by the chief of the village, the *hakimi* or the overlord of fiefs, the *Alkali* court, and the *Salenke* court.

The **Yoruba** (southwestern Nigeria and western Benin) carry on their life in three types of settlement patterns: one, where there is a central town, surrounded by farm lands and hamlets, and there are subordinate towns at the periphery of the kingdom; two, where, due to plentiful land, numerous independent villages exist beyond the central town and its short belt of farm lands; and, three, where there are central towns that are populated largely by refugees and are surrounded by farm land, with no subordinate towns.

The king, called the *oba,* lives in a metropolitan town. Traditional bodies manage the affairs of the town and the state. The domestic family of the man is the smallest group and constitutes part of a larger group of descendants from a common male ancestor. In turn, this group forms part of the *idile* or the *ebi,* which is the largest lineage group of all, descending from a founding male ancestor.

Isoko are intermediate patrilineal segments in the *idile.* Members of the *isoko* cultivate their allotted part of the lineage land. They pursue a lineage craft. Jointly, they worship ancestors and gods.

Harmful effects of the supernatural can be lessened through Ifa, the god of divination, and by respecting social norms. Eshu, the messenger of gods, reports upon the infractions. Punishment results from these reports, which can be avoided by proper behavior. Decisions about the allocation and use of land are made by the *oba* for the kingdoms, by the chief for the community, and by the head of the lineage for the members of the family. Social organization remains kin-structured, in spite of urbanization.

The **Ibo's** (southeastern Nigeria) largest social unit is the tribe or the village group in a single territory. Its members descend from a common male ancestor. The members of a village have their own male ancestor, who descends from the tribal ancestor. The basic social unit is *ummuna,* which is a patrilineal group living together. The lineage groups are divided into halves of a larger whole for social and exogamous purposes. There exists a wide variety of social groupings of both the associational and the kinship kind. There are gods and spirits, oracles and diviners.

The council of elders governs the lineage groups. It also governs the members of a village, since they, too, are descendants of a common male ancestor. This council and the oracles supervise obedience to norms and settle disputes. There are two kinds of offensive behavior, one that disrupts the harmony of the relationship of a community to the earth goddess and the other which does not. The offender is punished with immediate physical deprivations and future spiritual deprivations.

The **Tiv** (northern Nigeria), having been crowded in their land, migrated to other lands. They are torn by conflict within and between groups, with no adequate authority to organize action. Witchcraft and mystical powers are part of life. Leadership flows from possessing the witchcraft power of *tsav,* as well as personal qualities. Spiritual forces manifest themselves in *tsav* and *akombo* (fetishes). The *mbatsav,* or the possessor of an exceptional degree of *tsav,* is able to use it for good or ill. All this is supplemented by *swem,* which is an impersonal sacred power.

Ancestors identify lineage groups, but they lack power of bringing fortune or misfortune. There are two concepts of lineage, *ityo* and *tar.* The *ityo* determines a person's status for the purposes of marriage, performance of rituals, and armed support. The *tar* determines the relationship of a lineage group to the land it occupies and the ways in which the harmony of that relationship is expressed. When that harmony is disturbed by an

offender, a group of elders called *jir* make sure it is
repaired.

The **Ganda** (Uganda and a plateau between
Lake Victoria and Lake Kyoga) have a number of
patrilineal clans descending from a male ancestor
and possessing common totems. The clans are
part of the kingdom. Each clan has a special duty
to perform for the king. It, for example, might
supply the chief herder, or a certain official for the
coronation ceremony, or a certain gatekeeper, or
the keeper of a certain shrine, or the keeper of the
bark clothes, and so on. Clientage is established
by the act of *kusenga,* whereby an inferior attaches
himself to a superior.

Kinship matters, such as inheritance, succession,
and dowry, are settled by the head of the clan.
Offenses such as murder, adultery, and theft are
redressed by a system of self-help as well as by a
system of decision-making bodies. Cases are decided by the village headmen or subchiefs. They are
appealed to the chief of the *ssaza,* a territorial
district. From *ssaza* they are appealed to the
katikiro, or the chief minister of the king, and
ultimately to the *kababa,* or the king himself.

The **Lugbara** (north Uganda, central Africa, the
Nile–Congo divide) organize their social action
through a structure of lineage grouping. Their
homesteads are scattered across the country and
are organized into family clusters based on a minimal lineage. The head of the lineage acts as the
cluster's head. Clans are divided in subclans. The

subclans are in turn divided into major, minor, and minimal lineages, each lineage being the agnatic core for a territorial group. Life is organized through the family cluster. The family head, or the elder, is the eldest son of the senior wife of his predecessor and he possesses complete authority in the cluster. The ancestors respond to invocations. These are performed by those with legitimate authority for it.

There is an interesting scheme for dealing with conduct offensive to the harmony within a lineage group or with its related lineage groups. First, an elder makes the determination whether the conduct is offensive. He invokes ghosts against the offender. Next, punishment follows in the form of sickness inflicted by an ancestor. After the offender recovers, a diviner validates whether the sickness occurred from the visitation of it by the ancestor. Finally, the offender is purified and harmony restored by a rite of sacrifice.

The **Kikuyu** (inhabiting a high plateau beside the slopes of Mount Kenya) have nine clans. Each clan is divided into exogamous subclans. The clans are identified not by territory but by common ceremonies. The *mbari* is the local kinship group based on common descent from a male ancestor, headed by its senior elder. It is the governing structure of the *itoro,* which is a group of people living on a piece of land who have accepted a particular *mbari* for associational purposes.

The society is organized into age-sets, which perform the military and governing functions. The age-sets cut across the society regardless of clan or district. Elders in the age-sect settle the disputes. The elders are selected for settling a dispute on the basis of family relationships between the disputants. The living interact with their ancestral spirits. However, the supernatural does not play any significant role in controlling deviant behavior.

The **Nandi** (Kenya, east Africa) live in scattered homesteads that are organized into groupings called *korotinwek* (singular, *koret*). The *koret* members are identified by territory, not lineage. The relationship system of *tiliet* provides the means for identifying the interrelationships of persons united by blood and marriage.

Karuret, or custom, provides a general standard of approved behavior. The *koret* is governed by a council of elders called the *kokwet* (plural, *kokwotinek*), and is headed by the *poiyot ap kokwet,* or the elder of the council. Its decisions are obeyed because of the force of public disapproval for noncompliance, fear of the power of the spirits, and private acknowledgment of guilt by the offender.

The *pororiet* constitutes a larger territorial grouping of warriors. There are sixteen such groupings, each with its own council, whose principal concern is war. The largest territorial grouping is the *emet,* of which there were originally six and eventually five. However, this grouping is no

more than a means of referring to a defined region.
It is not an integrated unit of social organization.
Moral standards are reinforced by the living, the
ancestral spirits, and the supreme god Asis.

The **Arusha** (Tanzania, on the southwestern
slopes of Mt. Meru) are a pluralistic people. Their
concern is more the preservation of peace among
themselves than the prosecution of norms of conduct. They are organized into pairs of units. The
polygynous family is divided into two units called
ilwasheta (singular, *olwashe*). The whole people
are divided into two clans, each clan into a pair of
clan sections, each section into a pair of subclans,
and each subclan into two *ilwasheta*. These *ilwasheta* are composed of various maximal lineages.
Each maximal lineage consists of several inner
lineages, each of which is divided into *ilwasheta*.
However, the *ilwasheta* are not divided into further two parts. Instead, they consist of a number
of families. Each family, though, is divided into
two *ilwasheta*.

Lineage relationships are determined by descent
from a common male ancestor. The maximal lineage is based on descent from the earliest known
male ancestor. The inner lineage consists of heads
of families who are sons of the same dead father.

The Arusha are divided into two territorial sub-
tribes. Each subtribe is divided into territorial
local groupings of family homesteads. Their male
heads are organized into age-groups or age-sets for
the purposes of war and governance. The assem-

bly of the territorial local grouping manages public affairs and settles disputes among its members. The objective of dispute settlement is the elimination of the dispute by an agreement between disputants and the performance of that agreement. Compromise and reparation are valued not for achieving harmony but for reducing violence.

The **Nyakyusa** (Tanzania, at the north end of Lake Nyasa in the Great Rift Valley) are organized in age-villages. Men of closely contemporaneous ages live in these villages from boyhood until death. Their headmen are selected at the coming-out ceremony, held every thirty-three or thirty-five years. New chiefs are elected at that ceremony and new age-villages are created. The old chief is replaced by two new chiefs and their respective chiefdoms, each of which consists of four age-villages. These, in turn, are divided into two age-villages.

Witches bring sickness and misfortune and protect persons from the evil use of witchcraft.

Wrongdoing is handled through the institution of "breath-of-men". Under it, the men of the village murmur about the violation of the norm and invoke supernatural punishment. The offender is punished by illness or misfortune. This leads to his reformation. Thereupon, a commensal feast is given at which he and his neighbors openly acknowledge guilt and punishment. The medicine man administers a medicine designed to prevent a repetition of the violation. Disputes are settled by a senior relative or a respected neighbor. Men use force to protect themselves from violation by others.

For the **Nuer** (savanna and swamps of southern Sudan), the smallest unit of social organization is the hut of a wife and her children, where sometimes the husband also lives. The homestead of huts and a cattle byre form the polygynous family. During rainy season, the family lives in the village. During the dry season, it lives in the cattle camp. Membership in the village community is determined by relationship to the dominant clan in the village. The community is not made up exclusively of a single lineage. Attached elements mix with lineage. A district of the tribe is formed by a group of villages or camps engaging in regular social relations. There are fifteen tribes. A tribe has distinctive sections. The tribal segments are divided into primary, secondary, and tertiary segments.

The social status seniority is defined by the age-set system, which also indicates the appropriate behavior patterns. However, age-set is not a significant means of social organization. Conduct is right (*cuong*) or wrong (*duer*). Compensation is provided for injuries resulting from wrongs. Self-help and duels are justified measures against them. The aggrieved person is assisted by his kinsmen in these measures. No use is made of spiritual punishment. The wronged person can seize the cattle of the offender. The owner will take no further action if he considers the seizure right. If not, he either negotiates or resorts to force. Disputes involving killing are settled with the intervention of the leopard-skin priest.

Thus, law is not the central principle of social organization in the thirteen African societies surveyed above.

Africa underwent powerful changes in the middle of the nineteenth century when an extremely vigorous state-building began. This occurred as a result of three factors. One, a substantial increase in food production that supported larger populations due to the success of the American crops of maize, peanuts, and sweet potatoes, although it is not known when these were first introduced in Africa. Two, the suppression of slave trade by the British by 1833 in west Africa and by 1897 in central Africa. Three, the increase in demand for African products, such as ivory and palm oil, which were traded in exchange for European machine-made cloth and other products. Guns and more efficient firearms overwhelmed the older military systems of, say, the spear-wielding Zulu war bands and the armored horsemen of Bornu in west Africa.

Muslim influences exerted upon Africa from the north and east, European from the west and south. Muslim ideas of law helped the rulers in east and west Africa in extending their power, as, for example, the Ashanti kingdom. However, these ideas did not displace the native traditions and customs in the villages. When Muslim movements came in conflict with the European Christians, they took on extremely zealous forms, such as the dervish brotherhood of the Sanusi founded in 1837 near Mecca by a native of Algiers, or the declaration in 1881 by Mohammed Ahmed of Sudan that he was the Mahdi, the restorer of Islam. The British forces crushed his rebellion in 1896–98.

The Christian missionaries brought school, hospitals, and knowledge of Western civilization. Africans began to be educated in the Western ways. However, the Europeanization of the sub-Saharan Africa remained insignificant, except in Algeria in the north and the Boer Republic in the south. The interior remained either under the control of ancient kingdoms like Bornu near Lake Chad or new regimes like the Zulu founded in 1817 by Shaka (1787–1828).

By 1914, native rulers throughout Africa except Ethiopia came under foreign imperial administration. The Europeans replaced slave labor with wage labor for their projects in Africa, although the fine distinction was lost upon the natives. France and England were the major contestants for the African soil. Late arrivals included Germany, which took over Tanganyika, south west Africa, and Cameroon in 1884; Italy, which had some successes in the Red Sea region but was defeated in Ethiopia in 1896; Belgium, which organized an international association in 1876 to explore and civilize the Congo basin; and Portugal, which revived its claims in Angola and Mozambique.

European colonial administrations grew rapidly between 1875 and 1914. However, they remained superficial in most of Africa. The natives resented the European activities. Thus, the Berbers of the Atlas mountain region rebelled against the French for decades, the Ashanti kingdom of west Africa fought against the British four times and was not annexed to the Gold Coast (modern Ghana) until 1902, and the Zulus of South Africa did not submit to British rule until the battle of 1879. Only Emperor Menelik II defeated Italy in 1896. In any case, the social structures of African societies persisted in their traditional modes.

Not much disruption was occasioned in Africa by World War I (1914–1918). The German colonies were easily taken over by the British and the French. Rebellions were minimal during the inter-war period. The Union of South Africa was set up in 1908 as a self-governing dominion under the British crown, giving full political autonomy to the white Boers and the British. Liberia was established in 1847 as a homeland for former slaves of America. Ethiopia remained independent until 1934, when it was attacked by Italy and made part of its imperial domains in northeast Africa. Egypt attained independence from the British in 1922.

As a consequence of the exposure of the Africans to the European experience, hundreds of thousands of persons moved to an environment in which old customs did not fit. When people of different tribes began living together in mission schools, mines, and town, they had to find some other basis for mutual accommodation than old kinships and tribal patterns. The two models that competed in this search were the Islamic and the Western. The Islamic model prevailed in those parts where it had been established for many centuries. However, in most sub-Saharan regions the Western model competed strongly with the Islamic model.

World War II ended in 1945. In its wake, independence came. The new nations have demonstrated a tendency for modernization along European principles. New legislation has been adopted to change the traditional ways. However, eighty to ninety per cent of the population continues to live by traditions and customs. It is generally unaffected by the reform legislation and is largely unaware of the laws and institutions of the cities. Law is not central to the social organization of the African societies.

Law, thus, is not universal. Different civilizations have created their own principles of life as a result of their own particular historicity.

The contrasts among these principles are fundamental. They contain concepts that do not have counterparts in others. For example, the Indian principle of *karma* or the Chinese connection between *li* and *jen* (humaneness) have no counterparts in the Western principle of life, whereas the

Western *nomos,* that contains the potential for man-made law, is non-existent in *dharma* or *li.*

Or, again, the *rta* conception of order in India is totally incompatible with the *nomos* idea of divine agencies creating the universe and gods issuing commands for governance, which task later came to be performed by human law-givers. *Dharma* produces in man a conviction of duty for compliance with the pre-existing order of *rta.* *Li* gives an idea of order in which ways of conduct regulate man's worldly existence in harmony with nature. Thus, order is granted from outside in *nomos,* it is granted from within in *li,* and it is pre-ordained in *dharma.*

Consequently, while *nomos* laid the groundwork for an idea of law from outside, *li* became the social obligation directed toward the harmonious state of the world, and *dharma* produced authoritative texts to teach man his duty to support the *dharmic* state of the world.

Accordingly, while *dharma* and *li* produced a general and all-pervasive way of life as an organizational principle of existence, *nomos,* especially written *nomos* (*nomos gegrammenos*), proceeded along the basis of specific commands. Thus, while the validity of the precepts of *nomos* depended upon the authoritative statement thereof made publicly available, the validity of the precepts of *li* never depended upon such a mode. While *nomos* was attributed to a law-giver, such an attribution is non-existent in either *li* or *dharma.* While *li* is concretized in the five *wu lan* relationships, *nomos* moved on to an abstract way of thinking, producing speculations about laws of nature. Discovery and speculation about the ways of the non-human nature did not interest the Hindu *dharma shastras,* either. The task of the authors and teachers of these *dharma shastras* was to show man his duty and to guide him in close adherence to *dharma,* not articulation and distribution of individual rights typical of the Western legal ethos. *Li,* too, does not dispense individual rights, since the rights approach, with its antagonistic behavior of claiming those rights, is excluded by the conception of seeking an all-embracing harmony within all human relations.

Where the source of obligation is from outside, as in the Western legal order, a need arises to justify rights and duties, but where the source of obligation is from inside, as in *dharma* and *li,* the important task becomes not the justification of laws and individual rights and duties under those laws but the discovery of that obligation and apprehending its hidden sources. The internal coherence of duty-bound ways of life, whether it be pre-ordained as in *dharma* or socially created as in *li,* is incompatible with institutionalization of rights which characterizes the Western legal order.

An appreciation of the non-universality of law is an important preparation for examining the theories about law and the claims made by them.

B. IRRECONCILABLE EPISTEM-
OLOGIES IN THE THEORIES
ABOUT LAW

It is also important to see the various epistemologies underlying these theories and appreciate their irreconcilability.

Epistemology is that branch of philosophy that studies knowledge and explores such matters as the nature of knowledge, its scope, its presuppositions, its laws, and the general reality of claims to knowledge. It is concerned not with psychological reasons which make people hold beliefs but with the question whether the beliefs are based on good grounds or whether they are sound. Its concern is not whether or how we can be said to know some particular truth delivered by some branch of knowledge, but whether we are justified in claiming knowledge of a whole class of truths, or even whether knowledge is possible at all.

The theories about laws exhibit three types of theories of knowledge, namely, the metaphysical-rational, the idealist, and the empiricist.

The metaphysical-rational epistemology claims that all knowledge is contained in nature and it is discovered by reason. This epistemology is at work in the classical theories of natural law.

The idealist epistemology maintains that the mind and the spiritual values are fundamental in the world as a whole. Philosophical idealism can be classified into immaterialism (Leibnitz, Berke-

ley, Collier), transcendental idealism (Kant), absolute idealism (Fichte, Schelling, Hegel), and neo-
Hegelianism (T.H. Green, F.H. Bradley, B. Bosan-
quet, J. Royce, J.M.E. McTaggart, M. Oakeshott, B.
Blanshard, etc.). It is Kant's transcendental idealism that concerns us here.

According to it, it is not possible to gain knowledge of the world either by rational thought alone
or by mere sense experience. Our perceptions
have to be organized within the pure *a priori*
intuitions of space and time in terms of rational
principles. These principles require that our perceptions refer to things in causal relation with one
another. The *a priori* intuitions of space and time,
when put in the categories of understanding, such
as substance and causality, quality and quantity,
and so on, make knowledge possible. Without this
procedure, there would only be a manifold fluctuat-
ing of sensations. We do not know if there are
things-in-themselves, but we cannot have knowledge of an objective world unless we place everything in spatio-temporal contexts and synthesize
our sensations according to the categories of understanding.

This process, according to Kant, is carried out
not by our empirical self but by our transcendental
self. Nothing can be known of the transcendental
self, since it is a condition of knowledge and not an
object of it.

Thus, the idealist theories of law proceed from
some fundamental ideas discovered through an inquiry into the human mind.

The empiricist epistemology claims that the source of knowledge lies in experience, rather than in reason. Experience is the as yet unorganized product of sense perception and memory, memory being the device to retain in mind that which is perceived. An awareness of that which is discovered in this way is experience. There is another sense of the term experience which indicates sensations, feelings, etc. However, what is crucial to empiricism is the view that knowledge depends upon the use of senses and upon what is discovered through them.

The empiricist epistemology is held in three main ways. One, it is claimed that all knowledge comes from experience, in the sense that it is directly concerned with sense experience or derived from it by experiential means of learning, association, or inductive inference. Two, it is claimed that all knowledge is dependent upon experience. That is to say, although not all knowledge is derived immediately from experience, all the materials for knowledge are ultimately derived from experience. Consequently, all concepts are *a posteriori*. Three, it is claimed that while there are ideas that are *a priori* and not derived from experience, we have knowledge of them only upon the general precondition of having experience.

These three epistemologies are irreconcilable. One cannot maintain, at the same time, that knowledge is contained in nature discoverable by reason *and* that it is gained from an inquiry into the human mind *and* that it lies in experience. Consequently, the theories about law based upon these epistemologies are respectively irreconcilable at the most fundamental level.

C. IDEOLOGICAL INCIPIENCE IN THEORIES OF LAW

There is an important difference between philosophy and ideology. Philosophy is a description of objective truth. Ideology is a statement of value preference. Both are legitimate activities. However, it is important to maintain the distinction between the two in order to distinguish what is being perceived as truth from what is promoted as preferred value. The distinction is often abandoned in many theories of law. For example, as shown in the subsequent chapters, the very methodology of natural law lends itself to the incipience of value preference in the philosophy of law. Or, in Kant we proceed from an inquiry into the human mind to learning his philosophy of law and find in our laps his ideology about maximization of man's freedom and his maxims of moral law. Or, in Hegel, we proceed along the unfolding of the Idea through his dialectics and end up with glorification of the state. Or, in Stammler, we are led through an analysis of just law but are simply given his principles of just law dogmatically asserted. Or, in Bentham we find the assertion of the ideology of his greatest-happiness principle. Or, in Savigny we follow the empirical method of his historical approach but discover preference for values of conservation rather than change. Or, in Marx and Engels, we find a condemnation of ideology but in turn an advocacy of their own materialist ideology. Or, in Duguit we proceed with a scientific positivism and end up facing his postulate of social solidarity that substitutes the dogmas of individualism, subjectivism, and moralism with the dogmas of collectivism, objectivism, and realism, leaving open further use of social solidarity for whatever content one wishes of it. Or, American realism gives a framework in which any ideology can be promoted. Even at that, the range of ideologues permitted is limited to those who become judges and comparable officials. Or, phenomenological theory of the surfacing of the immanent values provides a convenient disguise for any ideology.

When ideology is disguised as philosophy, philosophy is discredited and ideology is made suspect. We must be alert to this incipience as we examine these theories.

Since epistemology is the most fundamental level of discourse for us, we have organized the theories about law in the subsequent chapters according to their epistemological classification.

PART I

THEORIES OF LAW IN ME-
TAPHYSICAL–RATIONAL
EPISTEMOLOGY

CHAPTER 3

DIVINE AND PROPHETIC
THEORIES OF LAW

THEORIES

The essential aspects of the divine and the prophetic theories are that law is created by God for
governance of man and that it is transmitted to
humans through the agency of a prophet or a
ruler.

Such a perception of the nature of law is found
in some of the ancient legal systems, such as the
Babylonian laws, the Hebrew laws, and the Laws
of Manu, as well as in the Islamic law. Thus, the
Laws of Hammurabi explain that Hammurabi, the
king of Babylon, set forth truth and justice
throughout the land when the god Marduk commanded him to give justice and good governance to

the people of the land. Or, the Hebrew Laws claim in the Book of Exodus of the Bible (24, 31, 32, 34) that the Lord summoned Moses to Mount Sinai and gave him two tablets of stone that contained the law written by the finger of God. Or, the Laws of Manu of ancient India profess to be of divine origin in that the Supreme Being revealed his Sacred Law to Manu, the father of humankind, at the time of the creation of the world. Or, the *sharia* (the way to follow) of the Islamic law professes the prophetic theory in that the first source of this law is Koran, which is the scripture composed of the inspired utterances of the Prophet Muhammad (570–632 A.D.). It was written a few years after the Prophet's death. The second, third, fourth, and fifth sources, hierarchically, are *sunna, hadith, qiyas,* and *ijma. Sunna* consists of the way of life and conduct of the Prophet, his practices, and his behavior. *Hadith* is the story of an eyewitness concerning the Prophet and his tradition. *Qiyas* is deduction by analogy from the principles laid down in the Koran. *Ijma* is the unanimous consensus of the legal scholars of Islam (*fukaha*) whose task it is to discover and reveal the law.

CRITICISMS

There are four major difficulties with this way of looking at law.

Firstly, it requires faith in a divine being, such as God. It thereby confines rational inquiry within the limits of faith.

Secondly, there is no universally acceptable concept of God. For example, the Semitic religions of Judaism, Islam, and Christianity consider God as a personal being, anthropomorphically masculine. The Hindus consider God as the absolute soul, the individual soul being a part of that soul. Due to the human inability to comprehend the absolute, its contemplation is made possible through deities or objects of nature. The Chinese have some idea of the supernatural, but it is not that of a personal god.

Thirdly, these theories require acceptance of an agency as the spokesman for God, whether it be a prophet, as in the Hebrew or the Islamic theory, or a ruler, as in the Babylonian theory.

Fourthly, it enables the person interpreting, specifying, and applying the law to escape from the responsibility for making law through these acts since, arguably, the resultant law is the law of God and not a product of his own act.

CHAPTER 4

NATURAL LAW THEORIES

Essentially, the natural law theories do not accept the law posited by man as the true law. They point to something other than the positive law as the true law and ascribe to it a superior status over the positive law.

A. EARLY THEORIES OF NATURAL LAW

THEORIES

The early theories include theories that view natural law as law of virtue, as justice by nature, as law of right reason, and as law of God.

1. Natural Law as Law of Virtue

In this formulation, the proponents point to a law of virtue to be followed by the rulers and other members of society. We find three such formulations in *dharma* (India), Lao–Tsze (China), and Confucius (China).

a. Dharma (India, Vedic Period: 1500 B.C.–500 B.C.)

Dharma is the divinely ordained norm of good conduct. It prescribes duties of man as a member of his caste as well as his duties in a particular stage of life. In its first aspect, it prescribes duties for brahman (priest and teacher), kshatriya (warrior), vaishya (artisan and businessman), and shudra (servant or performer of unclean tasks). In its second aspect, it prescribed duties of brahmcharyin (student), grahastha (householder), vanprastha (forest dweller), and sanyasi (wandering ascetic).

The sources of these duties lie not in the edicts of rulers but in the holy scriptures (the Vedas), the tradition and practice of those who know the Vedas (smritis), and the customs of virtuous men.

b. Lao–Tsze (China, b. 604 B.C.)

Lao–Tsze maintains that the system of law most conducive to welfare is one that gives a full play to the inarticulate dictates of nature. It is within the bounds of natural justice that the ruler must enforce his laws. Justice and reason are the only legitimate judges and executioners. When the ruler replaces justice and reason by his caprice, he usurps the function of the law of nature. Thereby, he condemns himself.

c.   *Confucius (China, 550 or 551 B.C.–478 B.C.)*

Confucius holds that if a ruler directs people to the practice of virtue and regulates them to that practice through the medium of moral discipline, they will naturally have a strong sense of personal honor and will be orderly in their conduct. However, if the ruler emphasizes laws and resorts to punishment for their violation, the people will try only to live to the minimum requirements of law and will be destitute of a sense of personal honor. Therefore, the most important function of a judge is to see that under his jurisdiction there are no occasions for going to law. In order to qualify for a public office, a man should know how to avoid the four vices of tyranny, violence, oppression, and mechanical administration of law. Tyranny consists in punishing people without educating them. Violence consists in requiring people to conform to laws without first bringing these to their notice. Oppression consists in punishing the breaches of those ordinances and laws that people believe to be in disuse due to the ruler's laxness in their execution. Mechanical administration of the law consists in dealing with people in bargain-making so as to stick to the exact letter of the laws without looking for justice and mercy.

2.   Natural Law as Justice by Nature

Aristotle of Greece (385 or 384 B.C.–322 B.C.) ascribes to man a dual character in his relation to nature. Man is subject to nature inasmuch as he is a part of the universe and, therefore, subject to the laws of matter and creation. He is also the master of nature inasmuch as he dominates it by his spirit. His spirit enables him to will freely and, therefore, to distinguish between good and evil. What we are looking for, Aristotle maintains, is not only what is just without qualification but political justice. Political justice exists among free and equal men who share their lives with a view to self-sufficiency and whose mutual relations are governed by law.

Political justice is of two kinds, natural and legal. Natural justice exists everywhere with the same force and is not dependent on the people's thinking in any particular way. Legal justice is originally indifferent but it does not remain so when laid down, for example, as in laying down that a prisoner's ransom shall be a mina.

Laws are passed for particular situations. The things that are just by convention, expediency, or human enactment are not everywhere the same, whereas there is but one that is everywhere by nature the best.

He distinguishes the legally just from the equitable. The equitable, for him, is superior to the legal. The equitable is the correction of legal justice. Such correction is needed where law is defective. The defect results from the fact that while law must of necessity speak universally, it is not possible to do so without error.

Law binds both magistrates and the people, for, he argues, the rule of law is preferable to the rule of an individual. There must be magistrates in order to determine those matters that are left undetermined by law, but law is reason unaffected by desire and passions that pervert the mind.

According to Aristotle, laws are of two kinds, particular and universal. The particular law is laid down by each community and is applied to its members. It is partly written, partly unwritten. The universal law is the law of nature, since the law of nature is binding on all men, even those who have no association or covenant with each other. Written laws often change. The universal law does not change, since it is the law of nature.

3. Natural Law as Law of Right Reason

Marcus Tulius Cicero of Rome (106 B.C.–43 B.C.) maintains that true law is right reason in agreement with nature. It is universal in application, unchanging, and everlasting. To alter it is a sin. To repeal it is not permissible. To abolish it is impossible. No senate or people can free us from its obligations.

There is one eternal and unchangeable law valid for all nations and all times. There is one ruler, God, who is this law's author, its promulgator, and its enforcing judge.

Cicero argues that we need not look outside of ourselves for an expounder or interpreter of it. It is the highest reason, implanted in nature, which commands what ought to be done and forbids what ought not to be done. This reason, when firmly fixed and fully developed in mind, is law.

Law is intelligence whose function is to command right conduct and forbid wrongdoing. Consequently, the origin of justice is to be found in law, i.e., the supreme law, which existed before any written law existed. It is foolish to believe, he claims, that everything is just that is found in the customs or laws of nations. Justice is one, binding all humanity, and is based on law, which is right reason applied to command and prohibition. The standard of nature determines the difference between good and bad laws.

Thus, law is not a product of human thought or enactment of peoples. It is something eternal that rules the whole universe. It is, therefore, the primal and ultimate mind of God.

Although commands and prohibitions of nations have the power to summon people to righteousness and keep them away from wrongdoing, that power is coeval with God. Since divine mind cannot exist without reason and since divine reason has the power to establish right and wrong, this reason did not first become law when it was written down but when it came into existence with the divine mind.

Just as divine mind is the supreme law, so is reason perfected in man also the law. This perfected reason, in Cicero's view, exists in the mind of the wise man. Law is, thus, the distinction between things just and unjust made in agreement with nature.

4. Natural Law as Law of God

St. Thomas Aquinas (1224–1274) gives us the most developed statement of the Christian theological natural law.

In order to understand his effort, we must appreciate its historical context. During the dark period in Europe between the demise of the ancient civilization and the birth of the medieval order, the idea of natural law continued to prevail but the Fathers of the Church, most notably Ambrose, Augustine, and Gregory, linked it with the Christian doctrine of original sin. Political society and the state became institutions of sin. A break from this thought began in the twelfth century. Political society and the state now came to be regarded as the embodiment of moral purpose and as instruments for justice and virtue, not as institutions of sin. The new European civilization, which had already begun to form in the ninth century, rose upon the twin foundations of feudalism and the Christian Church. The Christian religion was organized in an international institution called the Church. It followed the hierarchical pattern of a political society in which Pope in Rome became its acknowledged head. The religion was adopted both by the spiritual and the worldly orders. Therefore, the new theory of law had to proceed along the lines of accepting Christianity as the supreme legal value. Consequently, the Fathers of the Church began to replace reason of the earlier natural law with Christian faith as the supreme law of the universe.

This new hierarchical society needed a hierarchy of laws. Thus, with the *Decretum Gratianum* of the twelfth century, the law of nature no longer remained content with being identified with reason. It became part of the law of God. The Church became its authentic interpreter, since the state had already been condemned by Augustine as an institution of sin.

The conflict between the spiritual lawgiving authority and the secular lawgiving authority was to occupy Europe for centuries. During this conflict, both sides invoked natural law. The result was the scholastic system of law most thoroughly formulated by St. Thomas Aquinas.

He explores the essence of law through four questions: whether law is something pertaining to reason; whether law is always directed to the common good; whether the reason of any man is competent to make laws; and whether promulgation is essential to a law.

As to the first question, he maintains that law is a rule and measure of acts whereby man is induced to act or is restrained from acting. Since it belongs to reason to direct to the end, it follows that law is something pertaining to reason.

As to the second question, he sets forth four premises. First, law belongs to reason by virtue of reason being a principle of human acts. Second, practical matters are the object of the practical reason. Third, the first principle in practical matters is the last end. Fourth, the last end of human life is bliss or happiness. These four premises lead him to the conclusion that law must in the end regard the relationship of itself to happiness. Since every part is ordained to the whole, the law must regard the relationship of itself to universal happiness. Thus, every law is ordained to the common good.

As to the third question, he argues that a law's foremost regard is to the common good. Since ordering for the common good belongs either to the whole people or to a public personage who has care of things, it follows that the making of a law belongs either to the whole people or to such a public personage.

As to the fourth question, he maintains that for a law to have the binding force appropriate to it, it must be applied to those who are ruled by it and that such application is made by the law being notified to them by promulgation.

With these propositions, he defines law as an ordinance of reason for the common good, which is made by one who has the care of the community, and which is promulgated.

He presents a hierarchical scheme of law in which divine law is supreme. This is so because the whole community of the universe is governed by divine reason. Not all of divine law is intelligible to man. The intelligible part reveals itself through eternal law, which is the incorporation of divine wisdom, and the *lex divina,* which is the enactment of God as found in the Scripture. Principles of eternal law are revealed in natural law. From natural law are derived all human laws.

The hierarchy appears as follows:

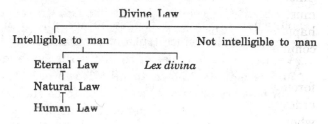

[302A]

Aquinas claims six propositions from his above-mentioned premises.

One, natural law is not a habit, since natural law is something appointed by reason whereas habit is that by which we act. If the term habit is used to mean that which we hold by a habit, then, he explains, natural law may be called a habit inasmuch as sometimes the precepts of natural law are in the reason only habitually, as distinguished from being considered by reason actually.

Two, the precepts of natural law are many, but they are based on one common foundation. That common foundation is that good is to be done and evil is to be avoided. This is so because the first principle in the practical reason is the one founded on the notion of good.

Three, natural law prescribes acts of virtue, since each one's reason naturally dictates to him that he act virtuously. Of course, not all acts of virtue are prescribed by the natural law, since there are things done virtuously to which nature does not incline at first but which have been found conducive to well-being through the inquiry of reason.

Four, natural law is the same for all in its general principles, since truth or rectitude regarding the general principles of reason is the same for all and is equally known to all. However, as to certain matters of details, which are to be likened to conclusions from those general principles, it is the same for all in the majority of cases. In some few cases it may fail both as to rectitude due to certain obstacles and as to knowledge due to the reason being perverted by passion, evil habit, or an evil disposition of nature.

Five, while natural law can be changed by addition, since both the divine law and the human laws have added many things over and above the natural law for the benefit of human life, it cannot be changed by subtraction, since it is not changeable in its first principles.

Six, there is a distinction between the most general precepts, or the first principles, of natural law and its secondary and more detailed precepts, which are conclusions derived from the first principles. While conclusions derived from first principles can be blotted out from the human heart by evil persuasions, the first principles can never be blotted out.

CRITICISMS

1. Dubious Ontology

The natural law theory suffers from a misleading ontological dualism. In it there is the existence of the empirical world, but there is also in it the reality of the transcendental that operates as an existential world and not merely its epistemological antecedent. The transcendental is claimed to have real existence because of its universality and pure rationality. An instrument of the cognitive process is thus converted into an object itself of human understanding. The epistemological device becomes reality itself. The postulates of reason become ontological facts that exist independently of understanding.

This engenders a thorough confusion of deontology and ontology, of value and reality, of the ideal and the factual. This artificial duality imposed upon a single object of understanding produces paradoxes that cannot be solved without recourse to the factual unity of the original problem, but— and here lies the failure of the theory to help us with the solution—a truer reality is assigned to the transcendental. The transcendental is not merely a cognitive focus but it is the reality itself, the very substance from which norms are to be derived. Since the variety of the experiential world obviously cannot be denied, the desired unity and coherence in the world is thus achieved by turning the cognitive schemata into facts themselves. We are left wondering how a legitimate theory of understanding can be anchored on such an ontology. This is so because natural law is claimed to be not merely a quest for ideal laws but the right law itself.

2. Inability of Abstract Reason to Schematize Historical Experience

Under natural law, abstract reason is the true reality. But however detailed a scheme one might attempt to build of the content of that reason and of natural law, it seems that the complexity of the historically developed needs, interests, conflicts, and institutions is too vast to be comprised under that scheme. If one still persists in that attempt, all one would accomplish are precepts that are too general and too vague to be of assistance in solving problems.

3. Logically Defective Procedure for Deriving Ought From Is

The procedure of the natural law theory is to derive norms from the ontologically ascribed facts of natural law. This raises a central problem in the relationship of *is* and *ought,* namely, whether *ought* can be derived from *is.*

The logic of norms is much more complex than the question of logical relation raised here by the method of natural law. Moreover, it is possible to use it for a descriptive statement of values (*ought*). Values themselves may be teleological (relative to purpose) or absolute (as in natural law). Furthermore, it may well be argued that, ontologically, values belong to the human world and, being part of that human world, are facts. Therefore, it is important to clarify that our question is whether natural law's absolute values or norms (*oughts*) derive from nature that exists (*is*), as claimed by it. Denial of that claim does not mean a denial of other relationships between norms and facts which do, in fact, exist. For example, in a judicial decision both *is* (facts of the case) and *ought* (norms of law) are combined in a logical scheme to produce a normative conclusion (judgment).

So, focusing upon the claim of the natural law theory, it is basic to deductive logic that one cannot derive a conclusion from that which is not contained in the premises either explicitly or enthymematically. Similarly, in inductive logic, which is a process of generalization of the nature of a whole class from the characteristics of a number of instances belonging to that class, it is basic that there can be no induction from the property of a thing to that which is other than it. Consequently, values cannot be derived from facts. When the natural law theory pretends to derive norms from its ontologically ascribed facts of nature, abstract reason, or God, it merely offers us an illusion. Values result not from facts but from the infusion of values made in those facts.

4. Failure to Recognize the Distinction Between Natural Laws and Normative Laws

It is a failure of the natural law theory not to recognize the fundamental nature of the distinction between natural laws and normative laws. Nature exists. Regularities exist in it. One may even admit that laws in nature exist independently of man's perceptive act, although there are epistemological theories in the philosophy of science that maintain that laws of nature or scientific laws are only logically necessary and not physically necessary, which necessity arises from the definitions and axioms from which we start and not in the sequence of sense impressions, and that it is illogical to transfer necessity from the world of conceptions to the world of perceptions. In any case, norms of behavior are not like such natural laws. Normative laws, whether moral or legal, are outside the competence of laws of nature, since they are produced by human decisions and not by regularities of nature. They are man-made and, unlike the laws of nature, they can be altered by human act. Moreover, when a law does not obtain in nature it ceases to exist, but when a norm is violated it does not cease to be a norm. Admittedly, existing norms are subject to the application of standards for their goodness or badness, but these standards are made by man, not nature outside man.

Sometimes the distinction between the natural laws and the normative laws is challenged by arguing that the laws of nature are rationalizations of the physical world and could be nullified when fresh facts compel, so that, the argument goes, it is not true that laws of nature cannot be broken or altered by human acts. The fallacy of this argument lies in the confusion it makes between a regularity in nature and the man-made statements made thereof. We make a hypothesis about a supposed regularity and we accept the hypothesis as long as it has not been falsified. When fresh facts contradict it, the result is that what we supposed to be the law is not law and is replaced by a more adequate statement of it. The case is not that the law of nature has been broken or altered but that the supposed statement did not correctly formulate it. By creating the hypothesis about a regularity in nature we do not create the regularity itself.

Sometimes the distinction between natural and normative law is denied by claiming that as natural law cannot be broken so the normative law cannot be broken, either. Let us concede for the sake of argument that a normative law, say, a criminal law, cannot be broken since the consequence is punishment. However, punishment is not the necessary consequence since the authorities may decide not to prosecute the offender. That decision is fundamentally different from formulation of a hypothesis for natural law.

It may well be that norms may have to be limited by the constraints of nature (e.g., limited resources) or they may have to be compatible with nature in order to be effective, but that does not mean that they are made by nature. On the contrary, it is we who impose our standards, our norms, our ideals upon nature and thereby introduce morals into the natural world, despite the fact that we are part of it. Nature has its facts, its existence, its regularities, but not morals for the use of humans. Man's moral world is fashioned by his own ideals. The facts of nature are neither moral nor immoral.

5. Removal From Man of His Responsibility for Moral Decision–Making

This is probably the most serious danger of natural law. By claiming to provide certainty and guidance to moral conduct, natural law responds sympathetically to man's yearning for such certainty. But that is an illusion. No such certainty exists in moral decisions. Moral decision is the painful task of choosing among alternative values. Pure obedience to nature was given up by mankind the moment man began to improve his condition in the wild, whether it was by means of husbandry and plow or steam engine, surgery, and space shuttle. Much less can nature provide answers to moral dilemmas faced by man. The danger of natural law lies in the disguise that it provides to the need to make a decision between alternative values. There exist deep and abiding conflicts of values. A choice has to be made among them.

That choice is made by man, who must consequently take the responsibility for that moral decision rather than hiding behind nature. Natural law, by providing that disguise, removes the burden of that decision from man who indeed makes that decision.

6. Insensitivity to the Historicity of Man

The argument of the natural law theory is that a certain value is innate in nature. Its realization becomes a process of unfolding of that innate essence. The formal structure of that process is provided by the historical time. Necessity in history provides the law of its manifestation.

Such an account of value lends itself to a deterministic view of history that ignores its contingent aspects. If that value is a matter of unfolding as above, all efforts on our part become irrelevant for its realization. All we need to do is to await its unfolding.

Furthermore, this account of a value generates an assumption that the process of development of that value is autonomous. That is to say, that process is determined only by its internal law. However, the truth appears to be to the contrary. Values have resulted from social relations and the institutional forms of these relations. Both of these factors have existed in the context of historical times, governed by the dominant value at the time, the public choice process, and the ideological commitment. These conditions are not merely incidentals to the unfolding of an autonomous system of values. Rather, these are the very conditions that generate the values and provide them their specific character. The advent of man in the world is historical. He is not a passive incident in the unfolding in history of his trans-historic impersonal essence. Instead, his active dynamism makes history.

7. Non-universality of Its Universals

The natural law theory takes as self-evident the beliefs in the facts of natural law, such as a belief in an innermost being of man, or God, or abstract reason. However, such beliefs are not shared as universally, or even as generally, as the natural law adherents would like to think. Consequently, such beliefs hold no promise for serving as the basis for an universal approach to certain problems or value programs, such as that of human rights in the world.

8. Inadequate Consideration of Cultural Pluralism

The claim of the natural law theory is that its values, which are absolute and universal, exist in nature *a priori*. The claim of universality is made *a priori*, not sociologically. It should be noted that the origins of the idea of a universal moral unity among men lie in a very laudable desire to dismantle the particularist barriers among nations and peoples. Thus, the Stoics assimilated natural law with the general cosmic law that governed the universe so that all subjects of natural law were, by submitting to the universal cosmic law, held together in one harmonious society. However, the *a priori* claim of the theory fails to take an adequate account of cultural pluralism and it denies the relativity of ethics.

Human history suggests that in any particular period since the growth of civilized communities about 3500–2000 B.C., there have contemporaneously existed four civilizations in the old world and three in the new world. Moreover, various cultures have created their own particular ideas about the social order as a result of their particular historical circumstances. Each culture produces its own values. Sociologists call them the inner order of human beings. Anthropologists call them the pattern of a culture. Behavioral psychologists call them high-frequency, spatio-temporal behavior of the people in question. Man is engaged in a continuous task of generalizing his own view of his environment and in imposing his constructions and meanings. These characterize one culture in distinction from any other. These norms can be ascertained in a homogeneous culture as well as in a heterogenous culture. In any case, the normative content of the societies in the world is pluralistic and it is particular to its respective culture.

The response of natural law to the empirical diversity of values is that this diversity reflects the multiplicity of error against the singleness of truth: *error multiplex, veritas una.* But when we face the task of deciding which is truth and which is error, this theory deserts us, since it does not provide an adequate criterion for making that decision. More dangerously, and for the same reason, it lends itself to providing the disguise of universality to any particular ideology that wishes dogmatically to so generalize.

Our point about ethical relativity must not be misunderstood as precluding moral criticism of other people because no definite answers are achievable, or endorsing the thesis that contradictory ethical views may be asserted without either of them being mistaken, or merely saying that mankind has carved for itself coexisting and equally valid patterns of life. Recent anthropology, psychology, and sociology have shown that while there are differences among people, there are similarities as well. These similarities help us construct universal ethical yardsticks, without having to relapse into the *a priori* dogmatism of natural law.

The extreme relativity of ethics that argues anything-goes is untenable in light of learning gained from psychology, sociology, and anthropology.

Thus, psychologists have pointed out that it is possible to speak about good and bad, right and wrong, desirable and undesirable when granted that there is reliable knowledge of what man can be under certain conditions that we call good and granted that he is at peace with himself when he is engaged in becoming what he can be, that individuals and cultures do not differ widely with respect to what they consider the ultimate ethical goals, that cultural differences are compatible with identity in values inasmuch as judgment of the value of an act takes into account the particular circumstances under which it occurs, with the consequence that the same act may be right if it fits one set of conditions and wrong if it violates another set of conditions. Sociologists have suggested that society, culture, symbolic interaction, and the potentialities of biological organism interacting in the basic process of socialization have been the basic field conditions for the emergence of the human psyche and that it is probable that there may be certain identical basic structures and functions in the psychic systems of the world. They have pointed out that the pluralistic value-universe is not limitless and that all patterns of moral standards are interdependent with all the other factors operative in the determination of action. Some have suggested the limitation of possibilities due to the facts that human infants are invariably dependent, that they confront the emotional problems of sibling competition, and that they are possessed of similar neurological defense mechanisms. Anthropologists have debated whether the variety in ethical codes is basic or superficial, whether the variations relate to means or ends, whether there are universals or near-universals that cut across cultures, and so on. They have examined these issues both conceptually

and empirically. They have investigated environmental, technological, and economic constituents of
cultural similarities. Some have pointed out that
social life is molded by the same dynamic forces as
those thousands of years ago, that there are cultural constraints of family, religion, war, communication, and the like, which are biopsychological
frames variably filled with cultural content, that
there is a fundamental uniformity underlying the
diversity of cultural patterns, that the likenesses
are primarily conceptual and variations exist concerning details of prescribed behavior, instrumentalities, and sanctions, and so on.

Thus, while there are cultural differences there
are similarities as well. These may provide certain universal yardsticks. Therefore, by rejecting
the *a priori* universals of the natural law we are
not condemned to the radical relativism that precludes moral criticism of other people and compels
acceptance of anything that goes.

9. Problems With the Criterion of Truth

The natural law theory discovers a norm by such
procedures as insight, intuition, evident contemplation, or reason. There may be some psychological
satisfaction in this feeling of evidence. However,
at issue is the criterion of truth. The feeling of
evidence cannot be that criterion. Evidence guarantees the truth of a proposition only when the
feeling of evidence is accompanied by a state of
affairs that makes the proposition true. A feeling

of evidence may very well accompany a fallacy, considering it as a true assertion. Belief in the truth of a proposition is not enough. What is needed is justification. Belief cannot be its own justification. The natural law theory contains no objective criterion of truth other than faith.

Therefore, it is necessarily amenable to any interpretation inspired by any insight, intuition, or evident contemplation. In fact, the history of natural law amply demonstrates this. Natural law has justified slavery in Plato, Aristotle, and the southern states of an earlier America. It has also justified equality of humans in the Sophists and in Rousseau. For conservative legitimatists it has rationalized the existing legal order (Bodin, Hobbes). For reformist monarchomachs it has justified the overthrow of the existing order (Buchanan, Languet, Althusius, Milton, Sidney). While it has justified the moral individuality of man to the effect that his personal rights become the final limitation of all political power, as in the Sophists, the Stoics, and the Epicureans, or in the revived nominalism and voluntarism of Occam, Marsilius of Padua, and Duns Scotus' followers in the fourteenth century, or in the revived Epicurean thought of Laurentius, Buchanan, and Gassendi in the fifteenth, sixteenth, and seventeenth centuries, it has also justified the social nature of man to the effect that social solidarity becomes preeminent even to the extent of abolishing man's personal rights, as in Plato's interpretation of natural law as an organic teleological harmony in which each

individual and each class has an appointed function, or in Aristotle's identification of natural law
with the established order of society necessitated
by man's physical or moral nature, or in the
Church Fathers' (particularly St. Augustine's)
placement of natural law in the spiritual unity of
man through Christ (*corpus mysticum*), or in the
subsequent reformulation of it in the solidarity of
corpus mysticum by Auguste Comte and others
when natural law became secularized.

Moreover, since the claim to universality is *a
priori* in nature and not sociologically observed, it
has made possible for merely provincial philosophies of nature and culture to generalize for the
entire world. Witness, for example, the claim to
universality made by the Hindu *dharma,* or by the
Chinese Confucianism, or by the Roman Catholic
natural law.

If norms of natural law are deduced from an
absolutely uniform natural law, there arises a need
in the theory to account for variations in these
normative catalogs. The theory fails to account
for these variations, except to admit that they
exist, whether such admission be in terms of Aristotle's distinction between universal justice and
particular justice or in terms of Aquinas' distinction between reason and reason led astray by passions. When we raise the question as to which
position is the example of reason and which the
example of reason led astray by passions, we find
no objective criterion of truth in this theory to

settle the issue. All we come down to is faith, and if faith is held as justification of itself, as indeed seems to be the essential nature of faith, then we return starkly to the dogmatism made possible by this theory.

10. Undue Distrust of That Which is Man– Made

The natural law theory believes that what is man-made is wholly arbitrary, that convention implies arbitrariness, that freedom given to man in choosing a system of norms would mean that one system is equally valid as another so that anything goes. This is a mistake. Man has created normative standards, and he lives by them. These may be the artifice of man, but that does not deprive them of normativity. Nor does that make these norms necessarily arbitrary. There even exist transcultural standards, not presumed *a priori* but evident empirically, as mentioned above, and these standards test the rightness or wrongness of other people and their systems as well, such as, for example, extermination of Slavs, Jews, and gypsies of Indian origin in gas chambers of the Third Reich.

This, of course, does not mean that man has not produced arbitrary or capricious values, but he has also produced the standards by which we can call them arbitrary or capricious.

11. Mistaken Mixture of the Metaethical With the Normative

The natural law theory finds it necessary to mix the metaethical with the normative. Metaethically, it gives ontological description of moral concepts. Normatively, it prescribes conduct. However, it insists that the metaethical is necessary for the normative. This seems to be a mistake. For it is quite possible to accept a normative prescription without having to accept its metaethical description. There is no logically necessary linkage between the two. Conversely, other metaethical theories (e.g., utilitarianism) can be quite compatible with the same normative ethics.

Natural law theory affirms the metaethical theory of value-cognitivism that claims that intrinsic value judgments can be objectively validated. However, it is possible to affirm value-cognitivism and deny natural law. For example, the utilitarians (Bentham, Mill) do it in regarding utility as a demonstrably valid principle of morals and legislation. The natural law theorist, having committed himself to value-cognitivism, has the burden of proving the validity of his norms but, instead, he merely proclaims them.

12. Problems With the Nature of Nature

There are several difficulties with the use of nature in the natural law theory. Firstly, its exponents have used nature to denote a variety of things, such as something original, objective, not man-made which exists by itself and for itself, or the inner essence of man and things, or the harmonious totality of all that exists. Secondly, whichever way nature is conceived, a further difficulty arises as to whether this nature is to be regarded as the paradigm of order yielding ethical imperatives or a set of limitations upon man's capacities within which he must build his normative structure. Thirdly, there is the problem of distinguishing between those aspects of nature to which normative significance can be attached from those to which it can not be attached. Aristotle suggested a solution to this difficulty by invoking nature in a more specific sense. In this sense, every kind of species has its own end. Its characteristic excellence is realized in performing that which is conducive to this end. Aquinas grasped upon this teleological concept of nature and proposed the solution, namely, that the laws of nature are known equally to all through their use of reason. However, there are metaphysical assumptions in this solution that are outside the scope of common-sense belief, namely, that phenomena are divided into natural kinds, that each of these possess an essence, that this essence stipulates an end, and that virtue lies in realizing that end.

13. Difficulties With Purpose of Human Life as Evidence of Natural Law

Sometimes the purposive behavior of man is given as an evidence of natural law. It is suggested that one can comprehend natural law by discovering the need of human life. It is argued that human life has purpose and, therefore, we must accept that there is natural law.

This is a very dubious evidence for natural law. While it is true that there exists purposive behavior of man inasmuch as he acts for an end, goal, or aim, it is not at all clear that there is a purpose to his life, that there is an end to it, and that virtue lies in realizing that end.

14. Difficulties With the Position Assigned to Human Nature

Natural law sometimes makes an appeal to the concept of human nature and it judges the morality of acts by their relationship to a common human nature. Every man is human by nature. An essential human nature determines his natural status. Norms follow from this status.

There are several difficulties with this sort of thinking. Firstly, there is a circularity in this reasoning. Essential human nature is coextensive in this theory with human being. That is to say, it is constituted by the properties expressed in the concept of human being. The argument of the theory is not that its concept of human nature is a preferable one among many others but that this concept has as its ultimate basis the real essence of man. In order to show that this concept is the real concept, it must be shown that certain activities are essentially human. Here lies the circularity, for reference cannot be made for this purpose to the criteria used for applying the concept of human being because whether these criteria should be used is precisely the question at issue. Secondly, the presupposition of the theory is that human being is a natural being from which norms can be derived. However, although he is part of nature to the extent he is actual to himself, he is not identical with his natural being since this being awaits upon him to give it its meaning. Therefore, his being not being a natural being it cannot constitute that nature from which the theory derives norms. Thirdly, human nature is not a specific quality possessed by man but a potentiality for a certain range of qualities and activities. His perceptual apparatus and his potential ability for reasoning make it possible for him to possess this potentiality. However, nothing normative can follow from this potentiality.

Such, then, are the difficulties with the classical natural law theory.

B. MODERN THEORIES OF NATURAL LAW

There has been a resurgence in natural law thinking in the past few decades. The modern formulations of natural law include viewing this law as objectively given value (Gény), as morals (Dabin), as deontology (D'Entréves), as related to sociology (Selznick), as based on anthropology (Mead, and Edel and Edel), as ethical jurisprudence

(Cohen), as a relationship between moral truths and general facts (Brown), and as the inner morality of law (Fuller).

It must be pointed out that not all of these theories are based on the metaphysical-rational epistemology. For example, the anthropological or sociological theories are based on the empiricist epistemology.

THEORIES

1. Natural Law as Objectively Given Value: François Gény (1861-1944)

Gény views judicial interpretation of law as an activity much more creative than applying strict logical principles to the code. It, for him, requires an investigation of the reality of social life. The sources of law are not limited to the written law. They include, in addition, custom, authority and tradition as developed by judicial decisions and doctrine, and free scientific research. Free scientific research is based on three principles, namely, autonomy of will, public order and interest, and just balance of conflicting interests.

There are principles of justice in Gény's views that are higher than the contingency of facts. Beyond the positive nature of things there are rational principles and immutable moral elements. This absolute justice is necessary to give strength to legal interpretation. However, it can indicate only a direction, which can be specified only by consideration of facts and the positive nature of things. For Gény, it is an illusion to think that the interpreter of law can find a ready solution for the problems of life in the revelations of reason and conscience, since the just in itself cannot be applied directly and immediately. The just is a goal and the interpreter has to discover the means for materializing it under the given conditions.

Thus, while there are principles of justice revealed by reason or conscience that exist outside the world of phenomena and contingencies, they acquire their positive imprint only from the various dynamic factors in the life of the community.

Gény adopts the classical distinction between thought and will, or knowledge and action, or science and technique, and he applies this distinction to law. Science is the objective knowledge of those social realities that furnish law with its social material. Technique is the specific art of the lawyer. Consequently, it is a field of creative action. Law is not restricted to the form that regulates change but includes the social situation in which the lawyer operates.

Gény's theory of natural law is thus placed within the framework of the social, which provides the material for legal action. Natural law consists of those immutable and universal factors with which the law operates. These factors are divided into four categories, which Gény calls givens (donnés):

one, the environmental data (donné réelle), which
consist of physical and psychological realities, such
as sex, climate, religious traditions, social habits,
and so on.   Two, the rules of law are historically
shaped by the environmental data (donné histo-
rique), which are the facts, traditions, and circumstances that give a particular shape to the physical
or psychological facts of the environmental data.
Three, the universal principles of justice that can
be rationally derived from the historical-positive
norms (donné rationnel), which consist of principles derived from the reasonable consideration of
human relations.   These embody most of the principles of the classical natural law.   Four, the total
ideals underlying a legal system (donné ideal),
which are based on all the physical, psychological,
moral, religious, economic, and political considerations.   These embody the moral aspirations of a
particular civilization at a particular period.

Gény admits that his distinctions do not operate
so neatly in reality but he offers them in a general
way as an explanation of the unfolding of the legal
process.   At every stage of this process there must
be creative activity.

In a conflict between natural law and positive
law, he believes that the lawyer is bound by positive law but he provides for disobedience in those
extreme cases where the law is contrary to good
sense so as to result in flagrant injustice.

2. Natural Law as Morals: Jean Dabin (b. 1889)

For Dabin natural law is natural moral rule. Historically, what one has always sought of natural law are principles of moral conduct. Treatises applying natural law to different matters have, according to him, been nothing but treatises on special ethics. Natural law and special morals dictate the same rule and provide the foundation for the same institutions. There is no difference between inter-individual natural law and inter-individual morals, or between family natural law or family morals, or between political natural law and political morals. Even in its most narrow sense of being the expression of requirements of nature, natural law represents the source for the solution of moral problems in various matters. Furthermore, he argues, there is no distinction between morals of individual action and institutional morals of social life, since morals govern everything human, including social arrangements.

Thus, natural law is the moral rule taken in its homogeneous totality.

Thus defined, it is related to the law established by the state in two ways. On the one hand, civil law comes to the aid of natural law in order to force people from engaging in evil and it completes natural law by providing conclusions derived from first principles. On the other hand, natural law gives civil laws their foundation as well as the justification for obedience to them.

Civil laws contrary to natural law are bad laws. From the fact that civil law borrows a number of its precepts from natural law it does not follow either that natural law does not belong to the category of morals or that the civil law has lost its own nature.

Therefore, for Dabin, there exists a moral natural law which is fundamental to all domains of moral conduct, whether of individuals or of social institutions. There also exists a political natural law based upon the political instinct of man, which is dependent upon moral natural law because morals govern everything human. However, there exists no juridical natural law in the sense of solutions or directions given to the authority charged with the establishment of the civil law.

According to Dabin, there may be principles commonly accepted in the laws of certain countries at the same level of civilization, but these are not principles of natural law for two reasons. Firstly, they are heterogeneous, commingled rules of morals, common sense, and social utility. Secondly, they lack the necessity and universality inherent in the idea of nature.

Based upon this analysis, Dabin claims that one must not speak of relationships between natural law and positive law but between morals and law (i.e., civil law). Natural law signifies morals but does not cover all values.

3. Natural Law as Deontology: A.P. D'Entrèves (1902–1985)

D'Entrèves borrows some of his basic ideas from Giambattista Vico and argues that every law has two facets, *certum* (the element of authority) and *verum* (the element of truth, which is discoverable by reason). The basis of obligation of law lies in the interplay of *verum* and *certum*. Thus, in every law there is the ideal principle at work despite its material circumstances. Each law is a normative translation of a particular value. The ultimate ground of its validity, that is its *verum* as distinguished from its *certum*, lies in values and not in facts.

The notion of natural law as a deontology (i.e., a theory of duty or moral obligation) consists in the ascertainment of the element of obligation that makes us feel that we are obeying the law because of the element of truth it contains and not merely because of its certitude. The problem of natural law is to determine where the grounds of obligations ultimately lie. According to D'Entrèves, there are certain ultimate values in human nature that determine our judgment as to whether a law is just or unjust and, consequently, whether we are bound in our conscience to obey it or not.

This, for D'Entrèves, does not mean that no rational argumentation of ultimate values is possible because these are believed in. Nor does it mean that if a principle of justice has been denied

somewhere at some point in history, that denial is
justified.

He believes that the fear that the claim of values
to absoluteness might lead to fanaticism or hypoc-
risy can be met by professing humility and sincerity. He points to history to show that recourse to
natural law has indicated an earnest desire for
mutual understanding.

4. Natural Law as Related to Sociology: Phil-
ip Selznick (b. 1919)

Positive law includes an arbitrary element that
is repugnant to the ideal of legality. According to
Selznick, the proper aim of the legal order is to
reduce the degree of arbitrariness. He argues that
a science of natural law can be constructed
through scientific inquiry about proper ends and
values, since the basic aim of the natural law
philosophy is to ground law in reason.

The chief tenet of natural law is that arbitrary
will is not legally final. Consequently, principles
of legality and justice can always be appealed to.
The conclusions of natural law are no more eternal
or sacrosanct than scientific generalizations but,
Selznick points out, the fact that a conclusion is
subject to correction does not mean that it is not
grounded in theory supported by evidence. Natural law presumes inquiry, since its effort is to draw
conclusions about nature. These conclusions are
based upon scientific generalizations and grounded
in warranted assertions about men, groups, and

effects of law. Accordingly, most concepts of law, such as equality, reasonableness, fairness, etc., are subject to criticism on the basis of scientific investigation.

As he sees it, natural law inquiry presumes a set of ideals or values and the legal order is studied as a normative system with a view to discovering how that system can be brought closer to its inherent ideals. Law is, therefore, tested against conclusions regarding human needs as well as against tested generalizations as to the requirements of a legal order.

Arguing from the functionalist viewpoint in sociology, he maintains that it is not necessary for natural law supporters to prove that man has any inherent duties. Since functionalism identifies what is essential to the system and determines what is needed to sustain it at a particular level of achievement, it is sufficient that natural law is a system that has duties. In studying the distinctive structure of a society, its capabilities, and the forces that transform it, it is not necessary to show that all participants have a duty to uphold it.

The authority of natural law depends, according to Selznick, on the progress in the social sciences. Where social knowledge is weak, natural law is limited in its authority.

The quest of natural law is for universals. Its basic commitment is to a governing ideal, not to a specific set of injunctions, and that ideal is realized in history. Therefore, it presumes changing legal

norms. There are two ways for Selznick in which
these changes occur. Firstly, basic premises about
legality and its underlying assumptions about human nature and social life are revised as inquiry
proceeds. Secondly, the natural law principles are
adapted to the new demands, circumstances, and
opportunities as society changes. Thus, he maintains, natural law is neither eternally stable nor is
it like a directly applicable code.

Since natural law belongs to an interdependent
whole, Selznick cautions that it is not to be applied
in isolation from other legal materials. This interdependence creates a rebuttable presumption in
favor of positive law. This presumption helps sustain the authority of law-creation necessary to the
effectiveness of the legal order. Since it recognizes
the merit of the funded experience of the political
community, it thereby contributes to the development of natural law.

5. Natural Law as Based on Anthropology: Margaret Mead (1901–1978); and May Edel (1909–1964) and Abraham Edel (b. 1908)

Margaret Mead defines natural law as those
rules of behavior that have developed from a spe-
cies-specific capacity to ethicalize, and as manifested in all known societies. All known cultures
exhibit constancies. A systematic observation of
these constancies would probably show that the
kinds of cultural behavior found in all of them

have been an integral part of their survival systems up to the present time. Such universal constancies include rules concerning the sacredness of
life under some circumstances, rules concerning
the prohibition of incest in the primary familial
relationships in most circumstances, and rules concerning an individual's rights over some differentiated physical or cultural items. The fact that such
recognitions have been universal in the past does
not necessarily mean their continuance in the future, but she observes that they seem to have
provided ethical principles without which human
societies did not exist viably.

Edel and Edel point out that the anthropologist
does not look for common moral perceptions and
instinctive moral reactions. Instead, he looks for
universal moral rules and understands differences
through a mode of analysis that combines psychological with biosocial and historical factors. This
is so because anthropology has revealed an enormous range of differences in people's rules of behavior, their ideals of character, their concepts of
virtue and vice, and their goals of life. For the
anthropologist, then, the patterns of human social
interaction represent distinct answers to essentially the same question posed by human biology and
the generalities of the human situation. Thus,
these experiments in living are not simply direct
instinctual expression.

The success of these experiments in living requires certain minimal standards. Thus, each cul-

ture must provide patterns of motor habits, social relations, knowledge, and beliefs with which it is possible for people to survive. Common needs, social tasks, and psychological processes provide some common framework for the variegated human behaviors of different cultures. This framework includes conformity in the behavior of the members of any society. Therefore, amid all the historically developed cultural diversity there is morality.

Morality includes common structural patterns, common mechanisms, and, in parallel social institutions, common content. This, according to the Edels, suggests a guide to formulating a hypothesis about morality in relation to human needs. They do not reduce morality to a statement of biological, psychological, or social needs. Instead, they propose that the need-solution element be made explicit or realistic. Such a realistic morality is not made any less moral by the fact that its quality may be more rational and more open to reassessment and change. Moreover, the very idea of need-fulfillment has a value content. What does this approach do to absolutes in morals? The Edels argue that, in the first place, there is a great deal of vagueness in the general appeal to moral absolutes. Do these absolutes refer to fixed goals for all people, or fixed goals for all conditions, or unqualified rules, or completely established answers? In any case, appeal to absolutes does not remove the problem of further evaluation. A clear understanding is likely only if the study of absolutes is itself conducted in context.

6. Natural Law as Ethical Jurisprudence: Morris Raphael Cohen (1880–1947)

From the point of view of the requirements of a scientific theory, Cohen asks, what is the character of the principles of natural law and how are they to be established? The traditional answer has been that they are axioms whose self-evidence is revealed to us by natural reason. However, what must be shown is that, like other scientific principles, principles of natural law yield a body or system of propositions. These, therefore, are to be tested for their certainty, accuracy, universality, and coherency. We must ask, as in all normative sciences, that if our ultimate standards are to be formulated in terms of desire, what do the people of a given time and place do desire and what limitation does law, as an instrument of social contract, impose upon the ideal it serves? Natural law, Cohen argues, is dependent upon ultimate ethical principles. It cannot claim a greater degree of certainty and completeness than attaches to the basic ethical principles presupposed by it.

Cohen points out that the possibility of natural law must face three problems: (a) the indeterminateness of jural ideals, (b) the intractability of the human materials with which law works, and (c) the inherent limitation of general rules. As to the indeterminateness of our jural ideals, he suggests that it is an illusion to think that our ideal of justice determines a specific answer for all questions that can possibly arise. An examination of various ideals leads him to conclude that no ideal is both formally necessary and materially adequate to determine definitely which of our actually conflicting interests should justly prevail. That being so, law has to be the technique for determining what would otherwise be uncertain and subject to conflict. This need for certainty enforces human inertia, which makes the law lag behind the best moral insight.

As to the intractability of human materials, he shows that the elaboration of legal ideals is obstructed by the inevitable imperfections in the human beings who make, enforce, and obey the law. Therefore, it is wicked to insist on justice regardless of consequences.

As to the abstractness of legal rules, he points out that legal justice has to operate with abstract general rules, but this abstract uniformity works injustice in particular cases. Therefore, one cannot put an uncritical reliance on the abstract universality of legal justice.

The possibility of natural law, thus, faces these three problems. Cohen, on his part, proposes a normative or ethical legal science.

He maintains that while the scientific study of the social facts that law must take into account is necessary, it is not sufficient for a complete legal science. Law can be viewed as setting up rules that serve as norms, in the sense of commanding obedience and controlling conduct. These norms can be studied as legal history (i.e., what was actually decided at a given time and place), legal sociology (i.e., uniformities or abstract patterns that repeat themselves), and normative jurisprudence (i.e., questions concerning what law ought to be).

Normative jurisprudence depends upon ethics. Ethics is an attempt to organize all our judgments of approval or preference into a coherent system. It includes not only judgments concerning the traditional issues of individual morals but also questions concerning the ultimate values of all human activities. The relation of technical standards to human life and welfare necessarily involves ethics. Hence the dependence of normative jurisprudence upon ethics.

Cohen argues that an attempt to dispute the normative point of view in legal science by insisting on the study of empirical facts confuses the necessary with the sufficient conditions of a complete legal science. A normative legal science is not possible without a thorough knowledge of the actual facts of human conduct, but such a knowledge is not sufficient for all purposes.

7. Natural Law as the Inner Morality of Law: Lon L. Fuller (1902–1978)

Fuller believes that an understanding of a purposive human behavior or activity, such as law, cannot be achieved without the knowledge of the purpose of that activity. Therefore, in a purposive interpretation of human behavior, the distinction between fact (is) and value (ought) disappears. The value element is intrinsic to the facts of a purposive activity.

Law, for Fuller, is the collaborative articulation of shared purposes. Therefore, it is a purposive activity. Accordingly, facts and value merge into it. It has an inner morality that is deduced from the very nature of the legal system.

He elaborates upon the principles of this inner morality of law. These principles are: (1) generality; (2) promulgation (availability of the law to the party affected); (3) prospective legal operation (the general prohibition of retroactive laws); (4) intelligibility and clarity; (5) avoidance of contradictions; (6) avoidance of impossible demands; (7) constancy through time (avoidance of frequent changes); and (8) congruence between official action and declared rule. He clarifies that these eight principles are not maxims of substantive natural law in the sense of ideals inspiring a society. Instead, he points out, these constitute a procedural natural law.

CRITICISMS

The modern theories of natural law have attempted to avoid the metaphysical trappings of the early theories. However, there are other difficulties with these.

Gény's theory of natural law has aspects which cause problems.

Firstly, his belief in natural law seems to be grounded in an intuitive religious belief. His appeal to some kind of existential natural law shows the influence of Thomism upon him. This makes his theory subject to the problems of knowledge and the criterion of truth discussed in the preceding section on the classical theories of natural law. His claim is that natural law is established apart from the religious elements, but he has failed to lay down its specific content.

Secondly, there is an incongruity in his treatment of natural law While he rejects the notion of a physical, biological, economic, or sociological natural law, he, at the same time, urges recognition of natural law not as an ideal formulation but as a prototype of positive law that is possessed of the same kind of objectivity as positive law.

Thirdly, he makes a fundamental distinction between science and technique. According to him, science deals with what is given and technique deals with what is constructed. However, the distinction lacks clarity in his work, as, for example, when he regards technique the result of arbitrary will.

Fourthly, in emphasizing the role of intuition in grasping reality he denies the power of reason to solve the problems of the universe. However, he does not show how to draw detailed rules from such an approach.

Fifthly, he believes that one could arrive at solutions that will be universally accepted. This is too unrealistic.

Sixthly, his givens (donnés) are changeable factors. However, it is difficult to understand how that which is changeable can be given as well.

Dabin is quite ambiguous on the relationship of natural law with positive law. While, on the one hand, he claims that many positive laws have no moral significance even though they serve society, he claims, on the other hand, that positive law is prohibited from contradicting natural law. Moreover, since positive law in his view always includes a legal sanction that natural law does not, it is not clear how positive law can logically contradict natural law.

He also seems uncertain on the question of whether a positive law contrary to natural law is not law at all or whether it is a law but does not bind the conscience.

Moreover, when he calls for condemnation of immoral legal rules as contrary to the public good, it is not clear what that condemnation means. Should those rules be disobeyed, repealed, or what?

Cohen's ethical jurisprudence seems inadequate without laying down its basic assumptions. Only when these assumptions are laid down in detail with content that a judge would have a criterion for choosing one normative principle over another.

Furthermore, this jurisprudence, in order to be adequate, must include the scientific method for specifying the ethical content. However, this is impossible if the ethical is taken, as Cohen does, as a primitive (irreducible) concept.

D'Entrèves' theory suffers from the naiveté that humility and sincerity are sufficient guarantees against the fanaticism that natural law makes possible.

Fuller claims disappearance of the is-ought distinction in a purposive activity such as law, so that law has its own inner morality as intrinsic to it, which is specified in eight principles. There are several problems with this theory.

Firstly, it is doubtful if that distinction disappears. There are three major reasons for this doubt. One, the argument of disappearance is predicated upon the very distinction it denies. In order to judge whether an activity possesses the value attributed to it, it is necessary to know what the value being attributed is. This value ascription made upon something otherwise valueless is possible only after identifying that thing in non-evaluative terms. Thus, the distinction remains between the value (ought) and the fact (is) to which the value is being attributed. Two, the interpretation of purposive behavior necessitates an inquiry into whether specific acts achieve certain goals. In such an inquiry, value judgments necessarily occur that are in addition to those intrinsic to the behavior under examination. Not only are such judgments initially made on the basis of values, but, furthermore, these values are not limited by those claimed to be intrinsic to the facts of the particular behavior. Three, the fact that some behavior is purposive in nature implies only that the actor has the purpose, not that he ought to have it. Ought is not merged with is merely because the purpose in fact exists.

Secondly, when law is represented as a purposive activity under this theory, the meaning of purpose is not clear. It may mean several things. For example, it may mean something of which one must be conscious, or the forces determining one's conduct, or intentional acts, or the pursuing of a specific end, or the determinant of the means-end relationship, or the proximate or ulterior considerations, or something to be discerned from observable behavior alone. In any case, whatever meaning is ascribed to it, it does not follow from the fact of purpose that the purpose is an ought. A purpose may be as it is or as it ought to be.

Thirdly, when the activity is purposive, there at best may be a merging of purpose and action. This does not mean that ought and is have thereby been merged.

Fourthly, the theory seems to confuse the judgments about the purpose of an activity with judgments about its morality. The two are not the same.

Fifthly, the knowledge of the actor's purpose might assist the observer in organizing the observational data in a certain manner. However, it reveals nothing about the moral quality of that purpose. It may disclose his dispositional characteristics, his permanent possibilities of performance, or even purposive criteria for evaluating his actions. However, it does not reveal the oughtness of his purpose.

Sixthly, it is true that the adequacy of a description can be judged only with reference to the purpose for which the descriptive account is made. However, the account itself does not thereby become intrinsically evaluative. What is evaluative here is not the account itself but the judgment on the adequacy of the account rendered.

Finally, the moral claim for the theory's eight principles of the inner morality of law is hard to accept. These eight principles appear to be no more than the minimum components of an efficiently functioning modern legal system. Not only that, the formula seems to omit other conditions that may very well be regarded as additional minimum requirements. For example, such conditions may include establishing authoritative law-making procedures at the outset, complying with these procedures, providing institutions for the authoritative interpretation of law, providing for the execution of a law by a public official or a private citizen, and so on. In any case, to assert that this formula of efficacy is a statement of moral principles in any substantial sense of morality appears to claim too much. While infringement of any of these eight requirements may result in a less effective legal system, it would hardly arouse a sense of moral culpability. On the other hand, violations of moral principles may occur from a law-making which may have fulfilled all of these requirements. The issue of morality remains untouched by these eight principles.

Moreover, a mere violation of any of these requirements does not, in itself, result in official wrongdoing. Rather, such wrongdoing arises from the unjust consequences that result from the official's action.

The moral claim for these eight principles has, nevertheless, been defended on the following six grounds:

One, *only through these principles can substantially moral laws be achieved.* However, while law is admittedly a precondition to good law, it is also clear that the adoption of these eight principles can result in immoral as well as moral laws.

Two, *the requirement of generality, publicity, and congruent administration tend to assure morally good laws.* However, while this may indeed be the tendency, morally good laws do not necessarily follow from these requirements. Also, the fact that these requirements may tend to achieve moral laws does not prove that the requirements themselves are moral.

Three, *the requirement of clarity is a moral principle, since some evil purposes cannot be clearly articulated in law.* However, some good purposes are as difficult to articulate as some evil ones. Conversely, some morally repugnant laws are as clearly articulated as some morally laudable ones. Moreover, a law concerning a matter upon which there is a general moral agreement in society makes no great demands for clear and precise articulation.

Four, *the inner morality is moral because it implicitly views man as a responsible agent*. However, one need not conclude that because a proposition implies a view of man as responsible the implication itself is moral. Secondly, by adopting these eight requirements, one may become responsible for the efficacy of the law but not for its morality. Thirdly, the fact that a man is responsible does not ensure that he is thereby morally good in any substantive sense.

Five, *because these eight requirements are principles of institutional or political morality, or the morality of the officials acting in that capacity, they constitute morality*. No one questions that the political morality or the morality of official conduct is properly called morality. However, the issue is whether these eight requirements are determinative of the moral character of the official act. For reasons stated above, the moral question remains untouched by these requirements. Nothing morally commendable follows from adherence to these principles. Nothing morally reprehensible follows from nonadherence to them. It is possible to inflict a moral wrong by laws that are general, prospective, and clear, just as it is possible to correct a moral abuse by a retroactive law.

Six, *violation of any of these requirements undermines the integrity of the law itself.* Again, the concept of integrity of law defined in terms of these eight principles cannot determine whether that law itself is moral.

It has been further argued in defense of the moral claim of Fuller's eight principles that: (1) the requirement of consistency is a moral condition, since it would be morally unsatisfactory to impose sanctions where it is impossible to comply with inconsistent directives; (2) the requirement of not making impossible demands is a moral condition, since it reflects the Kantian principle that ought implies can; and (3) the requirements of promulgation, understandability, and prospectiveness are moral conditions, since it would be morally unsatisfactory to be punished for directives of which one is unaware, or which cannot be understood, or which are not prospective. However, since the application of these principles can achieve a morally perverse law, it can be said, consistently with the purposive theory, that although a morally bad law has been achieved, the morality of law, nevertheless, remains intact because the eight conditions have been met. This is a very curious position.

It might be argued that this criticism relates to the substance of law, which is a matter of extrinsic

morality, while this theory is concerned with the
form of law, which is a matter of intrinsic morality.   However, this argument brings to focus the
very point that the morality of law cannot be
apprehended by including things claimed by this
theory to be intrinsic while excluding things
claimed to be extrinsic.   The theory fails to account fully for the morality of law because a moral
accounting of law must do more than limit itself to
matters of form.   It must take recourse to that
which is of substance, to that which is external to
its form.   The theory, in the end, fails to establish
a logically necessary connection between moral
principles and law.

PART II

THEORIES OF LAW IN IDEALIST EPISTEMOLOGY

CHAPTER 5

IDEALIST THEORIES OF LAW

The idealist theories differ significantly from each other, but they all discover their fundamental principles through an inquiry into the human mind, as discussed above in Chapter 2.

THEORIES

1. Law as Harmonizing Voluntary Actions: Immanuel Kant (1724–1804)

For Kant, the rational character of life and the world in which man lives his life are found in human consciousness and not in the observation of fact and matter. The method of philosophy is not psychological and empirical but critical. Therefore, he makes a systematic inquiry into the functions of human reason.

He discovers three functions of human consciousness: thinking, volition, and feeling. These correspond to perception (which is the subject matter of his book, *Critique of Pure Reason*), morality (*Critique of Practical Reason*), and aesthetics (*Critique of the Power of Judgment*). His legal philosophy rests in volition (morality). Volition is derived from principles entirely different from the principles of perception (knowledge). Knowledge and volition are sharply distinguished in Kant because there is a fundamental opposition between nature and mind. Nature follows necessity. The mind, in contrast, has a free will whereby it can set purposes for itself. Things appear to man in a chaos. Human mind brings order into that chaos but he cannot determine their course. However, he can freely set aims for himself. The realization of these aims is a matter of belief, not knowledge.

In the area of knowledge general principles are arrived at. Likewise, Kant asks, whether there exist general principles that can be laid down as a basis of volition and, therefore, of ethical action. He maintains that such a basis must be given *a priori*. It cannot be had from experience and laid as logical necessity. It can only be given as a postulate.

The ethical postulate is possible only because man has freedom. The conception of freedom is a conception of pure reason. It is, therefore, transcendent, in that no corresponding instance can be found in any possible experience. It is not an object of any possible theoretical knowledge.

Thus, for Kant, there exists a pure will in us that is the source of all moral conceptions and laws.

In the practical sphere of reason, the reality of freedom may be demonstrated by certain practical principles that prove a causality of the pure reason in the process of determining the activity of the will. On this conception of freedom are founded certain unconditional practical laws, especially moral laws. These moral laws appear as imperatives which command or prohibit certain actions. As such, these imperatives are categorical or unconditional, according to which certain actions are allowed or disallowed as being morally possible or impossible. They are not in the form of the technical or hypothetical imperative which says if you want this then do that.

This gives rise to the conception of a duty. The observance or transgression of this duty is accompanied by a moral feeling, a pleasure or pain of a peculiar kind. However, moral feelings are only the subjective effects and not the foundation of these laws. The possibility of categorical imperatives arises from the fact that they refer not to a determination of the activity of the will but to its freedom.

A categorical imperative presents the action to the mind as objectively necessary. It expresses generally what constitutes obligation. Kant renders it in this formula: act according to a maxim that can be adopted at the same time as a universal law. This he claims to be the supreme principle of the science of morals. A maxim not thus qualified is, therefore, contrary to morality.

The science of right has for its object the principles of all the laws whose promulgation is possible by external act of legislation. By applying legislation to it, it becomes a system of positive right and law. The theoretical knowledge of right and law, as distinguished from positive laws, belongs to the pure science of law. This science designates the philosophical and systematic knowledge of the principles of natural right. It is from this science that the immutable principles of all positive legislation must be derived.

The conception of right, for Kant, has three characteristics. One, it relates only to the external relation of one person to another through actions. Two, it does not indicate the relation of an individual to the mere wish or desire of another. Three, in this reciprocal relation of voluntary actions it does not consider the matter of the act of will but only the form of the transaction. Right, thus, comprehends the whole of the conditions under which the voluntary actions of any one person can be harmonized in reality with the voluntary actions of every other person, according to a universal law of freedom.

Accordingly, every action is right which can coexist along with the freedom of the will of each and all in action. Ethics, as distinguished from the knowledge of positive laws, imposes upon one the obligation to make the fulfillment of right a maxim of his conduct. Kant, thus, arrives at the universal law of right, namely, that one would act externally in such a manner that the free exercise of one's will may be able to co-exist with the freedom of all others, according to a universal law.

This, he warns, is not to be taken as a motive-principle of action that one ought to limit one's freedom to these conditions merely because this law of right imposes obligation upon one. His objective, he clarifies, is to explain what is right, not to teach virtue.

Right is accompanied with an implied warrant to bring compulsion to bear upon a violator of it. That exercise of freedom which hinders the freedom that is in accordance with the universal law is wrong. Therefore, compulsion opposed to it is right. In this manner, the conception of right consists in the possibility of a universal reciprocal compulsion in harmony with the freedom of all. In this sense, right and the title to compel indicate the same thing. The law of right can thus be stated as a reciprocal compulsion in accordance with the freedom of every one, under the principle of a universal freedom.

As is consistent with his primary assumption of the individual's freedom, political power is conditioned by the need to render each man's right effective and to limit it through the right of others. Security for all can result only from the collective universal will armed with absolute power. The social contract that makes this transfer of power is not an empirical or historical fact but an idea of reason. For Kant, there is an absolute duty to obey the existing legislative power. Rebellion is never justified. The state is the protector and guardian of the law. The political ideal of the state is achieved when the spirit of freedom is united with obedience to law and loyalty to the state. The citizen may criticize but he cannot resist.

2. Law as the Idea of Freedom: Georg Wilhelm Friedrich Hegel (1770–1831)

Hegel sets out to give a complete theory of the universe. He presents a comprehensive system of thought. The starting point of this system is the Idea. The Idea is Reason and Spirit. It contains everything about the universe.

The Idea unfolds by means of the dialectical process that proceeds through the triads of thesis, antithesis, and synthesis. Any concept (thesis) contains its own opposite (antithesis), and the passage from one to the other occurs through a third category of synthesis. For example, the conception of being (thesis) contains its opposite nothing (antithesis) and passes through becoming (synthesis). Or, essence (thesis) and appearance (antithesis) find their synthesis in actuality. And so on.

A synthesis, in turn, becomes the starting point of a new triad. In this way, the entire universe unfolds in all its aspects.

This process, according to Hegel, is a logical process. Each part has a necessary logical connection with any other. Any aspect of reality is thus based on reason. It is the task of philosophy to show that what is reasonable is real and what is real is reasonable. Consequently, there is no conflict between idea and experience or between reason and reality. What matters is to perceive the immanent and eternal substance in the temporal and transitory appearance.

Hegel's dialectical process of unfolding of the Idea may be presented as follows:

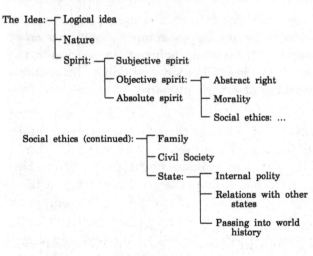

The Idea: — Logical idea
— Nature
— Spirit: — Subjective spirit
— Objective spirit: — Abstract right
— Absolute spirit — Morality
— Social ethics: ...

Social ethics (continued): — Family
— Civil Society
— State: — Internal polity
— Relations with other states
— Passing into world history

[303A]

The Idea, which contains all reality as well as the idea itself (i.e., the logical idea), contains as its antithesis the idea outside itself (i.e., nature), and the synthesis of logic and nature is the idea in and for itself (i.e., spirit). Subjective spirit (i.e., the categories of feeling, thinking, and consciousness) has its antithesis in the objective spirit (i.e., legal and social institutions), and their synthesis is provided by the absolute spirit (i.e., art, religion, and philosophy) which, as well, constitutes the full realization of the Idea. Thus, absolute spirit is at the beginning as well as at the end of all things.

Law falls within the scope of the objective spirit. The dialectic triad of the objective spirit is (1) abstract right (thesis), (2) morality (antithesis), and (3) social ethics (synthesis).

Abstract right includes those rights and duties that belong to human beings not because they are citizens but simply because they are persons. These rights are of three categories, namely, property, contract, and wrong (tort and crime). Right to property results from the free will, since a thing may be appropriated by the person as a means to his satisfaction. Appropriation is manifestation of the majesty of one's will toward things by demonstrating that they have no purpose of their own. However, for Hegel, the consequence of the right to property being a result of the free will is not that property should be equally divided among persons but, rather, that it should be divided differently upon people's differing capacities and abilities. The antithesis of property is contract, whereby one can relinquish his property by a voluntary act. Wrong results from the individual opposing himself to the universal will. Crime is, thus, a negation of the right. The objective of punishment is to restore right, or, that is to say, to restore the true will of the criminal, which will is in accordance with the universal will.

Morality is the antithesis of abstract right. Morality, for Hegel, is a rational factor and not a subjective sentiment. It results from a wrong of the individual will when this will becomes different from the universal will. Morality consists in doing the universal when the will discovers through a dialectical process that any will opposing itself to the universal will is wicked.

Social ethics is the synthesis of abstract right and morality. It, in turn, unfolds in the triad of (a) family, (b) civil society, and (c) the state. These are institutions in which the will of the individual finds itself in concordance with the universal will. *Family* is an institution based on feelings. However, in marriage two independent personalities are given up to become one person, so that marriage is an institution based on reason, to which being-in-love is irrelevant. *Civil society* results when the members of the family acquire an independent status and no longer remain part of the family. The society is thus conceived as a society of individuals pursuing respective self-interests and is divided into estates. These estates are three: the agricultural class that depends on nature, the industrial and commercial class that depends on its work and reflection, and the universal or the governing class that depends on reason. Civil society demands an administration of justice that defines mutual relations through promulgated laws and courts, protection of the right to well-being through the police, and formation of groups of individuals into associations that promote the universal end of the society, since their aims are more universal than the aims of the individual.

The *state* is the synthesis of family and civil society. It unfolds in the triad of (i) the relation of the state to its members (internal polity or constitution), (ii) the relation of the state to other states, and (iii) the passing of the state into world history. In its *internal polity,* the state is the embodiment both of the individual freedom and the universal. Therefore, it has three aspects: the universal (laws), the particular (application of laws to specific cases), and the individual (the monarch). Thus, the state is not the external authority imposed upon the individual but the realization of the individual's true universal self. The state is thus conceived as freedom. It is the manifestation of the rational will and not the common (or the majority) will. In the *relation of the state with other states,* states have no objective sphere of universal right among them. Their perpetually shifting relations are ultimately settled by war. In the synthesis of *the passing of the state into world history,* the actual mind of a single nation that actualizes itself through the inter-relation of the particular rational minds actualizes itself as the universal mind in the process of world history. The right of the universal world-mind is supreme.

By right, therefore, Hegel means not merely civil law but also morality, ethical life, and world history. This is because this concept of right brings thoughts together into what he calls a true system. Having examined the dialectical stages, he concludes that the right of the state stands above the preceding stages and is freedom in its most concrete shape, subordinate only to the supreme absolute truth of the world-mind.

3. Law as the Adjustment of Purposes: Rudolph Stammler (1856–1938)

Like Kant, Stammler finds a fundamental distinction between perception and volition. Law is not concerned with perceiving the world but with relating means and purposes to each other. Therefore, it belongs to volition. The concept of law is the universally valid element common to all legal phenomena, regardless of their content. Such an element, according to Stammler, can only be formal. It can only be a method whereby the necessarily changing material of the empirically conditioned legal rules may be so worked out, judged, and determined that they shall have the quality of objective justice.

Therefore, Stammler is concerned with a universal method as such in the sense of a formal process with absolute system. He is not concerned with any specific content of particular cases that may be worked out by this method. His quest is for the process of arranging. He is searching for a method of absolute validity, since it is not affected by the changeable material of historical fact.

A universally valid concept of law serves two purposes, one philosophical, the other practical. Philosophically, it responds to the mind's desire to reduce all phenomena to a unity, which is a peculiar ultimate of ordering the contents of our consciousness. Practically, it distinguishes law from religion, morality, history, etc.

Law is combining sovereign and inviolable volition. Therefore, its elements are: (a) volition, since it is a mode of ordering acts to the relation of means and purposes; (b) volition of men in their mutual relations, which is combined in law; (c) sovereign volition, as distinguished from arbitrary volition of an individual, not in the sense of political sovereignty of one will over another; and (d) permanency of the bond created by law, since it is inviolable.

Thus, the question of the possibility of realizing a purpose is distinct from that of the justice of its content. This is so, according to Stammler, because the realization of purpose considers an occurrence according to the laws of experience but the realization of justice aims at a systematic insight into the content of the volitional consciousness.

A universal element of legal propositions is the idea of adjusting the individual desire to the purposes of the community. Community, for

Stammler, is the formal unity of the individual purposes, not a concrete association having certain conditioned aims. It is a method of combining into an absolute unit the isolated desires of the individuals with a common and final purpose. The idea of just law means the unity of the methodical adjustment of individual purposes in accordance with the one final purpose of the community.

In this sense, his idea of law corresponds to the practical reason of Kant. Where it departs from Kant is that in Kant pure reason (critical knowledge of things) is opposed to practical reason (purposes set by belief and volition), but in Stammler the critical knowledge of law is the analysis of purposes and not the knowledge of a physical phenomenon.

The purpose of Stammler's just law is to assist in the formulation of a fundamental conception of life. Just law is the highest point in the study of social life of men, the only thing that makes it possible to think of social existence as a unitary whole, the way to unite with other fundamental endeavors aimed at right consciousness.

Thus, we have in Stammler the concept of law and the idea of law. The concept of law provides the universal elements of law. The idea of law directs means and purposes to one aim. The idea, too, has to be a formal one for the reasons mentioned above and it has to give expression to the idea of free will. This formal idea is the social ideal of a free-willing community of men. The notion of community thus conjoins with the notion of man being an end in himself.

From this analysis, he derives maxims concerning respect and participation. The maxims as to respect are (a) that a person's volition must not be subject to the arbitrary desire of another, and (b) that any legal demand must be of such a nature that the addressee can be his own neighbor. The maxims as to participation are (a) that a member of a legal community cannot be excluded from the community, and (b) that a legal power may be exclusive only to the extent that the excluded person can still be his own neighbor. It is in accordance with these maxims of right law that the adjustment is made of volitions in the community.

As to the validity of law, Stammler makes the admission that critical knowledge in this area needs to be assisted by a psychological supplement. Thereby, he introduces an empirical element into his purely formal theory.

4. Law as the Principle of Legal Evolution: Georgio Del Vecchio (1878–1970)

A neo-Kantian, Del Vecchio distinguishes between the concept of law and the ideal of law. He maintains that it is a mistake to take an ideal for a definition. The concept of law is its logical form, which embraces that ideal as well as all other possible juridical systems. Since juridical evaluations imply an inter-subjective or trans-subjective

reference as to what a subject can juridically do
with regard to another, law is the objective coordination of possible actions between several subjects
according to an ethical principle that determines
them and excludes impediments thereto.

Moral evaluations are subjective and unilateral.
Juridical evaluations are objective and bilateral.
These two kinds of ethical determinations are related in a fundamental way, namely, that what is a
duty is always right and that what cannot be a
duty is not right. Thus, if in a given system a
certain action is proper, then an impediment to
that action by others must not be possible, or else
it would not be an ethical system.

Law, according to Del Vecchio, is characterized
by bilateralness, generality, imperativeness, and
coercibility. (1) Bilateralness is the key element of
law, since law brings together at least two subjects
and gives a norm for both. Therefore, it is unlike
morality, since morality directs itself to the subject
per se and imposes upon him a choice between
actions which he can perform. In law, what is
possible for one party is not impedible by the other.
(2) The juridical norm is general, since it must
serve as a basis for regulating future relationships.
That regulation can only be done in a general way.
However, he concedes that generality is not absolutely necessary, since it is possible, though rare, to
establish a juridical norm by a relationship that is
individually determined, such as a provision in the
Italian Constitution of his times that the former

kings of the House of Savoy cannot enter and live in the national territory. (3) Law, like morals, is an imperative. (4) But law's distinction is the characteristic way in which the imperative is manifested. Law is coercible, so that it can be made to prevail by force in case of non-observance. He deduces this coercibility from the logical nature of law. That logic goes thus: since in law there is always a relationship between several subjects and a limitation between them, if the limitation is not observed (as when one invades the sphere of juridical power of another), the possibility of coercion against that transgression arises necessarily.

Del Vecchio believes that the confusion between the concept of law and the ideal of law has led to two errors. On the one hand, it has led the natural law jurists to identify the metaphysical concept with the physical concept of nature. On the other hand, it has led the positive law jurists to consider only the existence of positive law and to deny an ideal criterion of the positive law. The error of the natural law jurists lies in thinking that in order to assert the validity of an ideal they need to rely upon historical reality. The positive law jurists erred in deducing the non-existence of law as an ideal from the fact that it does not always exist as a verifiable phenomenon.

However, for Del Vecchio, the correspondence between the ideal and the empirical must be sought in more advance phases of reality. Man has a predetermined purpose. He must progress toward it in experience, in order to become in appearance what he in himself already is. The ideal of law designates the goal of its historical evolution. That evolution, even though frequently interrupted, conduces to an increasing recognition of the autonomy of the human being as the fulfill-ment of a supreme exigency of reason in its univer-sality. Thus, a juridical coordination of all human-ity in a worldwide human law tends to be consti-tuted positively.

The principles of that universal law are prede-termined in nature. Reason deduces those princi-ples *a priori* before they are verified *a posteriori* and actualized in contingencies of fact. He finds the evidence of this evolutionary process in exist-ing law of the more progressed states, as distin-guished from the primitive juridical systems.

Although justice rests in a formal idea, it also has a substantial meaning and it implies a faculty of evaluation. Consciousness postulates reciprocity in a formal sense, but it also produces a definite valuation. According to Del Vecchio, the senti-ment of justice (*sentimento giuridico*) has the abili-ty instinctively to evaluate legal phenomena.

CRITICISM

1. Kant

There is an exciting originality to Kant's theory. However, there are several troubling propositions in it:

1.   He defines law as the whole of conditions under which the will of each can coexist with the will of others in accordance with a universal law of freedom.   However, this may give us an ideal, but it certainly does not give us a logical definition of law that can summarize all possible juridical experience.   It excludes all those juridical systems that do not recognize equal liberty of all persons.   That would exclude so many systems that it would appear that perhaps law has never existed.

2.   Moral rules, for him, are absolutely imperative.   His categorical imperative is the basis of his moral as well as legal philosophy.   The principle of law and morality is the same, although his theory no doubt distinguishes between law and morality in that it considers morality as a matter of internal motives of the individual and legality a matter of action in conformity with an external standard set by law.   Morals, for him, cannot rest on experience, history, prudence, or expediency.   However, it seems that there do exist moral duties, such as not telling lies, which might be enforced by law but, instead, are left to individual conscience or social pressure for the reason that their legal enforcement would be too inconvenient or too expensive.   Kant would not admit of this, since this would be a matter of expediency.

3.   Moreover, there do exist duties that are legal but not moral, such as unintentional wrongs, and they do invite legal penalties.

4. Kant insists that justification for obedience to the legislators lies in natural or moral law. However, actual laws are not always just. His insistence removes all possibility of disobeying laws that are contrary to nature or principles of justice. It, thus, renders the struggle for justice meaningless.

5. For Kant, each rule of morality is absolute in its own right. However, the truth seems to be that people obey laws because they balance advantages and disadvantages in respect to the main body of law. They tolerate its imperfections not because each specific rule is absolute in its own right but because of lack of a feasible alternative.

6. Kant's categorical imperative, being the supreme principle of morals, cannot yield specific moral duties, since his objective is to explain right and not to teach virtue. These duties result, according to him, from dictates of conscience. These dictates of conscience, to him, are universal, clear, and absolutely certain. However, two problems arise in this reliance upon conscience. Firstly, conscience varies from holder to holder. It is very much uncertain. Secondly, this variability would result in a number of diverse rules dictated by the variety of conscience, but, logically, there cannot be diverse rules each of which is absolute.

7. Human existence is an empirical matter. Therefore, it is neither possible in fact nor persuasive in thought that rules for its moral conduct can be prescribed *a priori,* without empirical

knowledge, merely by an exercise of some pure reason. In fact, Kant's theory signifies nothing until its meaning is disclosed by empiricism.

8. The formalistic conception of justice, as in Kant's theory, does not yield justice. Firstly, its form cannot be satisfactory if developed by a technique which is uninformed by the empirical facts of living. Secondly, it cannot do justice without facts.

9. The origin of right in Kant is purely rational. This means that the actual content of laws can be determined from purely logical or formal principles. But he does not show how it is possible to do so.

10. In matters of law, the role of the transcendental free will is a suspect. Law deals with external acts of human beings in time and place. The freedom that is at issue is empirical, not transcendental or metaphysical. The cruelty of deflecting the issue into the transcendental is evident in Kant himself who, while elaborating magnificently on the transcendental free will, denies us the freedom to resist or disobey unjust laws.

11. Law is necessarily a matter that resides in the context of plurality. If that is so, it is untenable to begin with a proposition of the absolute freedom of the individual.

12. It is not logically possible for the transcendental freedom to explain the moral life of humans. In order to even know what a human being

is, you need the non-transcendental, or the phenomenal.

13.   Kant claims for his transcendental a purely
rational and non-temporal character.   However,
there is an interaction between the transcendental
and the temporal in that the moral determination
of pure reason has practical effects in time and,
conversely, temporal social arrangements are
judged unjust when they conflict with the transcendental freedom.

14.   Kant's ideal of freedom is only one of the
social ideals, either as a possibility in thought or as
a practice in history.   There have been other social
ideals, such as, for example, right embodied in law,
right embodied in force, power, supremacy of dynasties, nationalism, self-government, and so on.

15.   There are problems with Kant's proposition
that law concerns only external acts.   The proposition is not entirely true to fact.   There are counter
examples in legal history, such as laws punishing a
person for merely imagining or intending to kill
the king.   There is nothing inherent in the nature
of law that precludes it from concerning itself with
the non-external, psychic life.   Moreover, it is not
clear what is an external act.   Is remaining silent
and external act?   Yet, remaining silent has legal
consequences of liability, say, in torts, when the
defendant landowner does not warn his invitee of a
hidden danger.

16.   Kant's justification of compulsion proceeds
from the premise that in society there exist free-

willing individuals and that compulsion is right
since and insofar as it hinders the hindrance of
freedom. However, it is not possible for completely freewilling individuals to live in society. If one
dismisses this premise, so goes Kant's justification
for compulsion or authority.

17. Kant's test of rightness is so general that it
can allow numerous possibilities. He gives no test
for choosing between them. If we look for guidance in his own application of his theory, we find
utter arbitrariness. For example, he is quite arbitrary in choosing the definition of marriage as a
union of two persons of different sexes for reciprocal possession of their sexual faculties throughout
their lives over any other definition of marriage.

18. Although Kant's categorical imperative is
not intended to yield specific rules, it is unconvinc-
ing even as a general ethical guide. It impresses
as no more than an intuitive and dogmatic hunch.
Moreover, in the reciprocity of relations, one cannot be sure that the other person is proceeding in
accordance with the moral maxim formulated in
accordance with the categorical imperative so that
one, in turn, can proceed accordingly.

19. Kant laudably constructs the individual as
a person simply, as distinguished from a person as
a citizen, and he makes the state bound to follow
the law that results as its consequence. However,
he fails to show how the state must do so necessarily. His original construction is further lost when

he denies the individual any right to revolt against the state.

2. Hegel

1. The dialectical system of Hegel is remarkable indeed. However, he seems to have confused opposites with distinctions. Many of the concepts and institutions in his triads are not opposites or antitheticals of each other but, rather, different aspects of the social life. There may even have been some progressive development among them, but not necessarily through opposition of one to the other.

2. He purports to use his dialectical method for drawing logical deductions. However, he has in fact used it very arbitrarily. Consequently, we find in his theory such fantastic propositions as, for example, property being the antithesis of contract, wrong (tort and crime) being the synthesis of property and contract, the police being an institution of civil society rather than of the state, and so on.

3. He claims that only a rational and moral will is free. This is so because the arbitrary will is moved only by impulses and appetites and it wants incompatible things, so that it is necessarily frustrated. He further claims that man is free only when he desires and is able to do what he ought to do. However, from the fact that man must have a rational will in order to attain freedom it does not follow that an action that is inconsistent with his own principles is not free. This action may even

frustrate or reduce his freedom, but the action may, nevertheless, be free. Hegel seems to confuse the attributes of a free action with the requirements for attaining freedom. Conversely, a man may be entirely rational and yet not free, as when his principles are inconsistent with the established laws.

4. There seems to be an assumption in Hegel that in order for man to be fully rational, there must be a fully rational universal will, or a self-consistent moral system. However, man's rationality does not depend upon a moral or legal system.

5. There is also the assumption in Hegel that there is a continual development toward harmony between the individual will and the universal will in which his conception of world history represents the necessary progress of spirit toward rationality. Consequently, his system cannot admit of a plurality of legal or moral systems and universal wills, all of which could be equally rational. The danger lies in the fact that the denial of this plurality tends to foster dogmatism.

6. In Hegel, there is a close connection between the individual's rational will and the universal will. A man's rational will is the universal will manifest in him. All reality is universal spirit manifest. However, such an identity of the universal will with the individual's rational will does not exist. The universal will is found in laws and conventions that are not the same thing as the individual's will.

7. For Hegel it is a necessary and logical development from the concept of will that it be realized in the communities of free persons. However, it seem that will implies deliberate choice. The will is realized whenever that choice is made. This realization of the will does not have to be located only in the communities of free persons. Alternatively, if by realization of the will is meant happening of this event when people capable of making choice constitute a community of free persons, there is no logical necessity for such occurrence.

8. Observing Hegel's development of will from concept to Idea, it seems that people conceive of freedom, ascribe to it the supreme value, and attain it under certain conditions, and all of this is logically deducible from the will. However, the dynamics of freedom and its attainment are not so tightly connected in logic.

9. There is an incipient political doctrine in his philosophy of right. That doctrine consists in maintaining that freedom and the type of community in which freedom is realized are good and, therefore, desirable. Man is free under this doctrine when he accepts the established order conscientiously and not merely from habit. In fact, it is only from this political doctrine, and not from the nature of freedom, that Hegel's condemnation of disobedience can possibly flow.

10. According to Hegel, the state in which freedom is realized is desirable and it is desirable to the extent freedom is realized. That he did not

preach blind obedience to an actual state is clear from his philosophy of history, where he praises Socrates and Luther for defying authority and raising humanity to a higher level. However, his theory lends itself to the danger of being used as an argument for absorption of the individual in the state. In fact, it has been used to justify such a supremacy of actual state, as in Fascism, a responsibility which perhaps is not that of his theory if carefully understood. Nevertheless, the danger exists.

11. There is a great deal of equivocation in his use of the term contradiction that exists between thesis and antithesis. He uses it (a) as denoting distinct but inseparable aspects of a whole, which makes his dialectical process logical; (b) as denoting a logical exclusion of one concept by another so that if one applies the other cannot, the contradiction being resolved when both can apply to the same thing; (c) as denoting contrast of one with the other, the contradiction being resolved when they are superseded by something that combines their contrasted characteristics; (d) as denoting a necessary incompatibility between them, their contradiction being resolved when they are superseded by something in which the incompatibility is removed; and (e) as denoting one implying the other in the sense either that they are inseparable aspects of a whole or that they are stages in a necessary process.

12. Looking closely at his contradiction between abstract right and morality, it seems that he

means them (a) to imply each other, (b) to contrast with each other, and (c) to be necessarily incompatible with each other. Now, one cannot dispute that there can be incompatibilities between abstract right and morality, but it is not necessary that there be this conflict and its resolution.

13. Examining his contradiction between family and civil society, it seem that he is using the term contradiction in the sense of negation, a sense quite different from that used in connection with abstract right and morality. Civil society negates the family, since civil society arises from the breakup of the family, and this happens as of logical necessity. However, such a proposition is hard to accept. There may be a certain type of family, such as the extended family or kinship group, whose breakup has given rise to civil society, but that has happened not because of a necessity internal to it but because of external, sociological, causes. It is not necessary that the family should so break up. Furthermore, in the emergence of civil society, one type of family might give way to another, instead of the family breaking up, and even that is not logically necessary. There is no necessary contradiction between the family and the civil society that is resolved in the state.

3. Stammler

1. Stammler's theory proceeds upon the assumption that purely formal categories exist. However, it seems that the categories which are

claimed as formal are not really formal. They are categories of progressive generalization. More general categories are more formal. Less general categories are less formal. It is very doubtful whether in social matters it is possible for purely formal categories to exist.

2. Granting the existence of formal categories for the sake of analysis, there are still problems in proceeding with these categories. Stammler, like Kant, attempts to derive specific conclusions of justice from purely formal principles. However, in logic, no particular existential propositions can be derived from pure universals. Thus, from his ideal of a community of freewilling men the particular conclusions derived by him do not necessarily follow. Other, and different, conclusions can equally be drawn from it. There is nothing in his concept to disprove the compatibility of opposing claims with the ideal. For example, he claims that most societies condemn an agreement by couples to live together without marriage, but he does not show how in logic this is contrary to the ideal of a community of freewilling men. Or, he maintains that one volition must not be arbitrarily made subject to another volition, but by use of the meaningless term arbitrary one could approve or disapprove anything. No material guidance can be provided by formal categories.

3. Stammler determines the external form of all just law on the basis of the Kantian distinction between form and content. In doing so, he rejects

all material ends as empirical. Instead, he sets up
the pure form of the community of freewilling men
as the absolute end which is valid for all times and
places. However, he fails to show how a purely
logical form can determine the actual content of a
law without material premises.

4. Stammler attempts to extend knowledge
through analysis of concepts. However, such an
analysis can yield only analytic judgments (i.e.,
uninformative judgments that merely elucidate the
concept under which the subject falls, as distinguished from synthetic judgments, which are in-
formative judgments that tell us something about
the subject by connecting or synthesizing two different concepts under which the subject is sub-
sumed), not knowledge.

5. There is an extreme logicism in his theory
under which noncontradiction of a concept is the
only criterion of its truth. The difficulty with this
procedure is that it relegates the intrinsic value of
the concept to the extraneous or the irrelevant.

6. The predominance of pure idea over reality
necessarily compels the follower of that method to
ignore actual moral values. This is disastrous in
studying such a subject as law, which is fraught
with these values.

7. Stammler's conclusions of just law do not
logically follow from his premises. They seem to
result from his particular biases and social values.
Moreover, there is a discomforting vagueness that
leaves one unsure what are the relations of his just

law to the positive law of a given place and time.
For example, he does not tell us whether the just
law imposes itself on the lawmaker and becomes
the basis of positive law. Nor is it clear how his
ideal is to be adapted to the practical exigencies of
social life. Furthermore, his exclusively formalistic approach makes it logically impossible to move
from concepts to realities of social life. His formulae may possess formal virtues of unity, generality,
and universal validity, but they are incapable of
relating to facts of life. Moreover, his principles of
just law, like Kant's maxims of moral law, are not
proven in any way but are affirmed simply and
dogmatically. Again, it is hard to see how they
apply to social life. His own solutions seem to be
independent of his formulae, rather necessitated by
them. He has not solved the relationship of just
law and law. He has only propagated his own
particular ideological preference.

8.   His ideal of justice demonstrates the defect of
his theory. This ideal is clearly a mixture of his
formal proposition and his definite social ideal.
Thus, his solutions depend on the very factors of
ethical valuations that he meant to exclude from
his formal idea.

9.   Finally, we have the basic question whether
the legal systems of the world follow any *a priori*
logic. We can agree with Stammler that the notion of purpose inheres in law, but it is hard to
agree that such purpose is determined by *a priori*
concepts. Moreover, while logic is a valuable tool

of analysis, it alone cannot create principles of justice.

4. Del Vecchio

Here again, it is doubtful if an *a priori* method of arriving at the concept of law can provide the needed insights into matters of law. Such an approach dangerously separates law from the context of social life. Thus, deductions from Del Vecchio's concept of law would tell us that law deals with will-acts, but in law a person is both responsible for acts not willed by him and reaps the benefits of acts not willed by him. For example, a person is held liable in torts under the doctrine of *respondeat superior* for acts which are not willed by him but are the acts of his servants, and he inherits property under the laws of inheritance and succession as a result of acts not willed by him.

Del Vecchio's analysis that law is always determined by some ethical principle is erroneous. Firstly, iniquitous laws are found both in the consciousness of humans as well as in the body of laws. Secondly, there are laws that do not have anything to do with ethics but are only a convenient way of doing things.

Del Vecchio offers his concept of juridical sentiment (*sentimento giuridico*) as an intuitive test for evaluating legal phenomena. However, this concept is so mystical that it can be used to justify anything.

In the end, the idealist perception of law, too, seems quite metaphysical, as was the case with classical natural law in Chapter 4. Therefore, it too is capable of justifying whatever ideological position its user wishes to justify.

*

PART III

THEORIES OF LAW IN EMPIRICIST EPISTEMOLOGY

The theories about law that are based in the empiricist epistemology believe that the source of knowledge lies in experience, not in reason, nor in mind. These theories include the positivist theories, the historical theories, the sociological theories, the psychological theory, the American Realist theories, the Scandinavian Realist theories, and the phenomenological theories. Modern movements such as the Critical Legal Studies and its offshoots of the feminist jurisprudence and the critical race theory, too, proceed from the empiricist epistemology.

CHAPTER 6

POSITIVIST THEORIES OF LAW

A. EARLY POSITIVIST THEORIES OF LAW

THEORIES

1. Kautilya (India, Fourth Century B.C.)

Kautilya seems to be the first propounder of the positivist theory of law in history.

In Indian tradition, philosophy came to be associated with the concern for the release of the individual soul from the cycle of reincarnation and the union of that individual soul with the absolute soul. This union is called *moksha,* or, roughly translated, salvation. Values fall under the categories of law of virtue (*dharma*), wealth (*artha*), pleasure (*kama*), and the release of soul (*moksha*). The first three, known as the group of three (*trivanga*), were generally treated as separate from the *moksha* and were usually bypassed in most metaphysical systems. As a result, separate treatises arose for *dharma, artha,* and *kama. Artha* is viewed not merely as economic power but political as well. Its most elaborate treatment is found in Kautilya's *Arthashastra.* He was the minister of the Emperor Chandragupta in the fourth century B.C.

Kautilya believes that monarchy has advantages over other forms of government. He identifies the welfare of the people with the welfare of the monarch. The Rod of the king is the means for ensuring the pursuit of philosophy, the duties established by the Vedas, and economics.

The purposes of wielding the Rod are four. One, the acquisition of things not possessed. Two, the preservation of things possessed. Three, the augmentation of things possessed. Four, the bestowing of things augmented on a worthy recipient.

The maintenance of worldly order depends upon the wielding of the king's Rod. In order to maintain this order, the king should always hold the Rod up to strike, since there is no better means for the subjugation of human being than the Rod. A king without the Rod is a source of terror to human beings; a king mild with the Rod is despised; and a king just with the Rod is honored. When used after full consideration, the Rod endows the subjects with spiritual good, material well-being, and pleasures of the senses. When used unjustly, i.e., in passion, anger, or contempt, it enrages people. If not used at all, it gives rise to the law of the fish wherein the stronger swallows the weak. Administration of the Rod brings security and well-being to people when it is rooted in discipline. Discipline is both inborn and acquired, since training gives discipline only to one suited to it.

2. Shang Iang (China, ?–338 B.C.)

The Chinese politics of the fourth and third centuries B.C. were marked by the tendency for consolidation of power through absorption of small states by larger ones, elimination of the authority of the nobles over their peasants, administration of justice directly by the officials of the central government, and centralized tax collection. Legalism grew from such political ethos. While the earlier Confucianism dealt with ethical norms, Legalism analyzed the realities of power. It expressed the positivist view of law. It emphasized state power rather than popular welfare. Its concern, in fact, was not so much the law as the increase in the power of the state governments at home and in inter-state relations.

The contention between the Confucianism and the Legalism focused upon the scope of official judgment as against fixed and impersonal laws. The Confucianists contended that laws must be enforced by men. If the ruler and his officials were upright, a permanent body of laws would be unnecessary. The Legalists contended that a uniform set of standards ought to apply to the entire population. Law ought not to be subject to the discretion of magistrates. Furthermore, they conceived of law as self-operative in the sense that the ruler publishes his decrees and a fixed penalty is imposed for each offense, without any exceptions for rank or extenuating circumstances.

The Chinese Legalism was propounded notably by Shang Iang, Shuen Tao, and Han Fei Tzu. Han Fei Tzu is regarded as the leading exponent of this theory.

Kung-sun Iang, the later Lord Shang, or Shang Iang, is ranked among the most prominent statesmen of ancient China. He speaks of the supremacy of law and maintains that a country is governed through three instrumentalities, namely, (a) laws, (b) the certainty that the laws will be enforced, and (c) the power to carry the laws in effect. The king alone is the custodian of power. The administration of law rests jointly with him and his ministers. In order to establish the supremacy of law, it is their joint duty to apply it strictly.

Laws, according to him, are fixed standards of justice. The ever-changing minds cannot be trusted as guides. Thus, his argument goes, we cannot do away with laws. Although once in a rare while a generation may produce a perfectly wise and unselfish ruler, it is better to be content with a government by fixed laws, in spite of its defects, than wait for a wise governor and meanwhile suffer the evils of a commonplace ruler who is neither wise nor restrained by laws.

Laws, thus, are necessary in the community as it exists. Those who behave within legal bounds must be protected and rewarded by the government. Those who defy the laws must be punished without mercy. People will find an unfailing guide of legality in the system of rewards and punish-

ments when that system is well settled and promulgated, in which case they will have no occasion
for disputes.

According to Shang Iang, the ruler does not have
the right to treat his power as a personal monopoly. He must exercise it for the national welfare.
Maintaining the supremacy of law results in justice and avoidance of mischiefs of personal judgment. Justice is thus achieved since it is the
consummation of unselfishness and laws are the
very means for bringing it about. An unselfish
ruler necessarily maintains the supremacy of law.
Avoidance of mischiefs of personal judgment is
achieved, since placing transitory opinions before
laws would give rise to deceptive and oppressive
practices of the magistrates.

3. Shuen Tao (China, Contemporary of Shang Iang)

Shuen Tao defines law as a body of uniform and
impartial rules of civil conduct designed to regulate the activities of a nation. He maintains that
within the definite limits of law there is no room
for the cunning and the wicked. Therefore, he
argues, law should never be violated. Laws tend to
unify the minds of the people. Therefore, even a
legal system that is not perfect is better than
lawlessness. Statutes and sanctioned customs are
intended to work out justice and equity, just as the
standard weight is designed to establish fair dealing.

4. Han Fei Tzu (China 280?–233 B.C.)

Han Fei Tzu partly opposes Confucianism and partly reinterprets it in accordance with his ways of thinking. Like his teacher Hsun Tzu, he regards human nature as fundamentally evil. But unlike Hsun Tzu, he does not believe that education and culture are capable of redeeming it. He disputes the Confucian argument that government ministers should be selected on the basis of their upright character. He believes that all officials are potentially dishonest so that each should be made to act as a check upon the others. The masses are ignorant and incapable of seeing beyond their own immediate interests. The government should direct itself to them. Therefore, he concludes, a strict set of laws and penalties, impartially enforced, is indispensable to public order.

He likens the sovereign to the helmsman of a ship. The sovereign makes slight movements with the two handles of reward and punishment and the whole state follows his dictates. While statecraft keeps the sovereign in power, the laws are to be obeyed by the people. The intelligent ruler makes sure that his subjects do not let their minds wander beyond the scope of the law. Once laws have been established, everyone should obey them. In the state of the intelligent ruler, only the laws serve as teachings. There are no other books and records fit for such teachings. This, incidentally, led the first emperor of the Chin Empire to burn the books, especially the Confucianist texts.

CRITICISMS

Kautilya seems to suffer from a naive belief that the Rod of the king has the power of ensuring the pursuit of philosophy, the duties established by the Vedas, and economics. He ignores the role of the intrinsic worth of these particular matters as an account for their realization.

Chinese Legalism avoids the naive idealism of some of the Confucianists, but its own ethical deficiencies issue from at least three sources, namely, firstly, its emphasis on the state power almost to the exclusion of popular welfare; secondly, its condemnation of the people as necessarily possessed of evil nature; and, thirdly, its almost blind trust in the government.

Moreover, its trust in the self-operativeness of law is mistaken inasmuch as it views operation of law strictly as a matter of promulgating decrees and imposing penalties for their violation, without any exception or any regard to extenuating circumstances.

Its explanation for obedience of law as exclusively a matter of rewards and punishment ignores the fact that laws are obeyed in a general sense because values are achieved thereby.

To regard laws posited by the ruler as the only source of wisdom to the exclusion of all other sources, as Han Fei Tzu does, is clearly mistaken. Sovereign's laws have no monopoly on wisdom.

Often, contrary is the case. We need other sources of wisdom to evaluate the sovereign's laws.

Finally, the Legalist theory ignores the fact that at least a minimal tacit consent of the populace is required for any government to function.

B. LATER POSITIVIST THEORIES OF LAW

THEORIES

1. **The Command Theory of Law of the Utilitarians: Jeremy Bentham (1748–1832), John Stuart Mill (1806–1873), John Austin (1790–1859)**

The command theory of law takes utility as the foundation of morals.

The concept of utility is primarily propounded by Jeremy Bentham and John Stuart Mill.

Bentham maintains that the public good ought to be the object of the legislator and general utility ought to be the foundation of the legislator's reasoning. From this point of view, therefore, the science of legislation consists in knowing the true good of the community and its art lies in finding the means to realize that good.

Nature, according to Bentham, has placed man under the empire of pleasure and pain, to which we refer all life's determinations and judgments. He defines utility as the attribute of a thing to prevent some evil or procure some good. That

which conforms to the utility for an individual is
that which tends to augment the total sum of his
happiness. That which conforms to the utility for
a community is that which tends to augment the
total sum of the happiness of the individuals that
compose that community. Good is pleasure, evil is
pain. The purpose of law is to attain good and to
avoid evil, or, in other words, to serve utility.

Bentham uses pain and pleasure in their ordinary signification. He excludes metaphysics from
his consideration of them. Moral good or moral
evil are so because of their tendency to produce
physical good or evil, respectively, although the
physical includes the senses as well as the soul.

Bentham's utilitarianism is clearly individualistic and egalitarian. However, this leads him not to
anarchism but to law. Law must serve the totality
of individuals in a community. As a result, he
conceives of the end of legislation as the greatest
happiness of the greatest number. The logical
result of this is the subordination of the individual's right to the need of the community. Accordingly, he is opposed to any theory of inalienable
rights.

For Bentham, any particular legal or political
philosophy is a matter of faith. Its premises in
themselves are not capable of deduction. He
claims no more for his own utilitarianism. He
concedes that its rectitude cannot be either formally tested or directly proved, since that which is

used to prove everything else cannot itself be proved.

The happiness of the greatest number has to be reconciled with the sum of the pleasures of each individual. Bentham uses sympathy as the means to obtain this reconciliation, since amidst unhappiness no one would be happy. It is pain, therefore evil, therefore not in conformity with utility, to be among unhappy people. For unrestrained behavior of one would justify unrestrained behavior of others and thereby reduce everyone's happiness. This appears quite like Kant's definition of law, discussed above, except that while Kant derives this result from his categorical imperative, Bentham derives it from his principle of pleasure.

John Stuart Mill, who was Bentham's disciple as well as critic, recognizes the naiveté of Bentham's belief that there does not exist a conflict between the individual utility and the general utility. He attempts to relate justice to utility.

According to him, the meaning of justice is exceedingly unstable and controversial. Moreover, the eternal notions of justice are incompatible with the changing notions of utility and interest. Therefore, he provides the notion of the sentiment of justice as the means for reconciling justice with utility. The sentiment of justice is the feeling of right within an individual that would in itself lead him to resent anything disagreeable to him, which feeling is tempered by the social feeling. He conceives of just persons resenting a hurt to society even though that is not a hurt to themselves and, conversely, not resenting a hurt to themselves unless it is such that the society has a common interest in repressing it. The sentiment of justice thus combines individual self-assertion with consciousness of the general good. This, too, incidentally, is reminiscent of Kant's categorical imperative. Furthermore, through the individual's will and his sentiment for justice, Mill, like Hegel, has resolved the individual with the social interest to the point of eliminating any dualism between the two.

As to law, Bentham regards it as a collection of signs declaring the sovereign will of the state concerning the conduct to be observed by its subjects, which observance is achieved by means of expectation of certain events to occur with the intent of making the possibility of such occurrence a motive for that conduct. Thus, law has eight constituents: (1) source (person whose will it expresses), (2) subjects (persons or things whereupon it applies), (3) extent (the generality of its application), (4) aspects (various manners in which it applies to its object acts and circumstances), (5) force (motives it relies on to bring the desired effect), (6) means (corroborative appendages upon which it relies to bring those motives into play), (7) expression (nature of the signs by which the sovereign's will is declared), and (8) its remedial appendages, which may occasionally be used to obviate mischief.

John Austin's theory provides the most comprehensive formulation of a modern system of analytical positivism in law, although his definition of law is substantially similar to Bentham's and is reminiscent of Chinese Legalism, above.

As Austin explains, law is a rule laid down for the guidance of an intelligent being by an intelligent being having power over him. In this way, law is defined as completely apart from justice. According to Austin, there are laws properly so-called and improperly so-called. There are four kinds of laws: (1) divine laws or laws of God, (2) positive laws, (3) positive morality, and (4) laws merely metaphorical or figurative. Broadly speaking, there are laws of God and human laws. Laws of God have no juristic significance and are comprised of the principle of utility. Human laws are divided into (a) positive laws, which are laws properly so-called, and (b) positive morality, which are laws improperly so-called.

Laws properly so-called, or positive laws, are either set by political superiors to political subordinates or are set by subjects in pursuance of legal rights given to them. Laws improperly so-called, or positive morality, or moral laws, are not set by a political superior to a political subordinate and include such rules as rules of club, laws of fashion, international law, and the like.

Law, then, is a command. It is a signification of a desire. What distinguishes it from other significations of desire is the fact that the party to whom it is addressed is liable to evil from the party issuing it in case of non-compliance. Being liable to evil means to be bound or obliged or to be under a duty to obey the command. The evil that will probably be incurred for its disobedience is sanction or enforcement of obedience. Reward is not a sanction, since it does not oblige one to render service called for by the command. Command, duty, and sanction are thus inseparably connected.

Austin distinguishes law from a command that is occasional or particular. Law is a command that obliges a person or persons generally to acts or forbearance of a class.

Again, while both laws and other commands proceed from a superior to a subordinate in that one who can oblige another to comply with his wishes is the superior and the one who is obnoxious to the impending evil is the subordinate, the distinction of law is that it is set by a sovereign. That sovereign could be either a person or a body of persons. And it is addressed to the members of the independent political society wherein that person or body is sovereign. Customs, when turned into legal rules by judicial decisions, are tacit commands of the sovereign.

The sovereign is a determinate human superior who is not in a habit of obedience to a superior and who receives habitual obedience from the bulk of the political and independent society. An independent political society or an independent and sovereign nation is a political society that consists of a sovereign and subjects. It is, therefore, not a body that consists entirely of subjects.

Thus, law is characterized by command, sanction, duty, and sovereignty.

2. The Normative Theory of Law: Hans Kelsen (1881–1973)

While the philosophical basis of Austin is utilitarianism, the philosophical basis of Kelsen and the Vienna School to which he belongs is neo-Kantianism. However, unlike the neo-Kantian Stammler, Kelsen makes a complete break in his pure theory of law from any theory of justice.

The objective of his pure theory is knowledge of that which is essential to law. Therefore, it has nothing to do with that which is changing and accidental, such as ideals of justice. Accordingly, Kelsen completely rejects the legal idealism of the neo-Kantians like Stammler and Del Vecchio. He rejects Stammler's attempt, seen above, to combine the Kantian distinction of content and form with an ideal of law, and he also rejects Del Vecchio's intuitive idea of justice, discussed above. Instead, he insists on the theory of law being purely formal in its entirety.

The starting point of his pure theory of law is the Kantian distinction between the realms of cognition and volition, or is and ought. Science is knowledge, not volition. However, legal theory, for him, unlike Kant, is science, not volition. It is the knowledge of what law is, not what it ought to be.

Kelsen divides all sciences into causal sciences and normative sciences. The causal sciences deal with reality, i.e., the is of actual events. The normative sciences deal with ideality, i.e., the ethical, legal, esthetic, or other oughts. Law is a normative science, the normative here meaning knowing the norm and not constructing it. Being normative, law deals not with the actual world of events (is) but with norms (ought). The realms of is and ought being logically separate, the inquiry into the sanction of an ought can lead only to another ought. The content of the is may or may not coincide with the content of the ought, but a coincidence of content does not affect the logical separation of the two spheres of knowledge.

Kelsen's pure theory of law is a formal and universal theory. Therefore, its concern is essentials of law of any kind, at any time, and under any conditions, without being mixed with the alien elements of morality and ethics.

The legal relation contains the threat of a sanction from an authority in response to a certain act. The legal norm is a relation of condition and sequence. That is to say, if a certain act is done, a certain consequence ought to follow, and only in this sense is law an ought.

A legal system is made of a hierarchy of norms. Each norm is derived from its superior norm. The ultimate norm from which every legal norm deduces its validity is the highest basic norm, the *Grundnorm*. The *Grundnorm* is not deduced from anything else but is assumed as an initial hypothesis. A norm is a valid legal norm only by virtue of the fact that it has been created according to a definite rule, with the basic norm of the legal order being the postulated ultimate rule from which the legal norms are created or annulled. Therefore, by validity of a norm is meant its existence and not its efficacy.

Thus, law is created or annulled by acts of human beings. Therefore, it is positive.

It is independent of morality. The task of legal theory is only to clarify the relations between the basic norm and other legal norms and not to evaluate the goodness or badness of the basic norm. For Kelsen's theory, it does not matter which particular norm is adopted by a legal order. All that matters is that such basic norm has a minimum of effectiveness, that is, it commands a certain amount of obedience, since the efficacy of the total legal order is necessary for the validity of its norms.

State and legal order are the same, since the compulsive order of the state is the same thing as the legal order and only one compulsive order can be valid at a time within one community.

3. The Rule Theory of Law: H.L.A. Hart (b. 1907)

Hart explains his theory by positing a society corresponding to primitive communities, whose structure is one of primary rules of obligations. These rules contain restrictions on the free use of violence, theft, and deception. While in such a society there are tensions between those who accept the rules and those who reject them, the rejecters must be a minority in order for the society to endure.

Such a simple form of social control, he points out, suffers from three defects: uncertainty of the social structure, static character of the rules, and inefficiency of the diffuse social pressure by which the rules are maintained. The remedy for these defects lies in supplementing the primary rules with three secondary rules: the rule of recognition, the rule of change, and the rule of adjudication. The defect of uncertainty of structure is remedied by the rule of recognition, whereby the rules of behavior are acknowledged as authoritative. This rule, therefore, provides a proper way of disposing doubts as to the existence of the rule. The defect of static character of rules is remedied by the rule of change, which empowers a person or a group of persons to introduce new primary rules for the conduct of the life of the community. Finally, the defect of inefficiency of diffuse social pressure is remedied by the rules of adjudication which empower individuals to make authoritative determination of the breach of a primary rule in a particular situation.

Thus, the primary rules impose duties and the secondary rules confer powers. The heart of the legal system, according to Hart, lies in the combination of primary rules of obligation with secondary rules of recognition, change, and adjudication.

In this way, his analytical positivist theory of law performs the feat of combining the matters of recognition and social obedience, which are claimed as the essential element of law by the historical (Savigny) and the sociological (Ehrlich) theories, discussed below, with the matters of authority, command, and sanction which are claimed as the essential elements by other analytical positivist theories (Austin and Kelsen, above).

CRITICISMS

The basic criticism that the non-positivists make of the positivists is that by divorcing itself from the content of the law, the analytical positivism loses its usefulness in promoting peace and order. Therefore, the critics wonder if there is any value to the purely formal conclusions delivered by legal positivism.

In addition, there are other specific criticisms of Bentham, Austin, Kelsen, and Hart.

A. BENTHAM

1. Bentham equates good with pleasure and right with conduciveness to pleasure. This subverts the moral content of the terms good and right. If an act is good because it gives pleasure to the actor, then that excludes all possibility of its

moral evaluation. To say that it is right because it pleases the actor is to eliminate the very moral question we raise when we ask if the conduct is right even though it gives pleasure. The morality of an act consists not in its tendency to promote pleasure but in a moral judgment of it.

2. Bentham is not merely describing what is good or right but also prescribing that we should attain it. For him, the purpose of law is to serve utility. In doing so, what he is really doing is proposing the acceptance of the ethics of the greatest-happiness-of-the-greatest-number princi- ple. This ethics or ideology is neither universally accepted nor derived as a logical necessity from his definitions. Or, more precisely, it derives only from the falsity of his definitional propositions. Once you accept those premises, then, of course, the conclusion follows syllogistically.

3. He exaggerates the role of rationality in mor- al matters. He believes that, in order to persuade someone to a particular moral viewpoint, all you need to do is to show that it promotes happiness.

4. For Bentham, the greatest happiness princi- ple is the only absolute or universal rule. Since this is the only rule that promotes happiness, he argues, it ought therefore to be followed. How- ever, in doing so he commits the logical fallacy of deriving ought from is, discussed above, for he suggests that from something that is universally desired it follows that we ought to aim at it.

5.   Although it is true that a feeling of pleasure accompanies a person's success in achieving what he or she desires, it seems that he or she is satisfied when he or she attains the object of his or her desire. Therefore, the person's object is not pleasure but the attainment of something. A person does not desire pleasure for its own sake.

6.   Bentham assumes it to be a clearly understandable proposition that we desire only pleasure for its own sake. However, it is not clear either in Bentham or Mill whether pleasure is a feeling about the experiences called pleasant, or a quality inherent in the experiences, or something inherent in pleasant sensations, or a quality that varies in intensity and not in kind, or merely a desire to continue having the pleasantness of a sensation, or a separate feeling annexed to the experiences called pleasant in the sense that the experience comes first and then comes a feeling of pleasure. With so many distinctions left unclarified, Bentham's proposition cannot possess the claimed understandability by all.

7.   Bentham and Mill do admit that we can quite possibly desire the means of something as much as the thing itself and that we can even continue to desire the means when we have forgotten the end. However, if that is so, then it is not the case, as claimed, that the only thing that we desire is pleasure for its own sake.

8.   Bentham's felicific calculus is both too fanciful and impossible. It is too fanciful in that the

properties of pleasure (its amount, its intensity, its
duration, its likelihood of being enjoyed, and so on)
are not capable of being put to a single standard of
measurement and put together in some quantity of
happiness.   It is impossible in that we cannot get
this kind of information for our calculation.

9.   Bentham excludes ideals from his account of
what people want.   However, it seems that ideals
go a long way in determining what people want.
What they want depends in large measure upon
what they think is worth having.   There is more to
a human than merely the satisfaction of one desire
after another.

10.   Bentham believes that the interests of the
individuals composing a community automatically
promote the interests of the community.   However,
he fails to explain why this should be so.   He fails
to grasp the problem of balancing the interests of
the individual with the interests of the community.

11.   It seems that there is in Bentham a concept
of society that necessarily develops to a certain
goal.   However, this is an illusion.   Neither history
nor contemporary times illustrate such neat development of society to a certain neat goal.

B.   AUSTIN

1.   Sometimes a criticism is made of analytical
positivism that it takes ideals out of consideration
of law, that positivists do not think that matters of
ideals are of any concern to the lawyer.   This is an

unfair criticism. Austin himself instructs magistrates to apply utility in deciding cases. It is not
his position that ideals are of no concern to the
lawyer's entire task. However, it is true that in
identifying the essential elements of law his theory
does exclude the matter of ideals altogether.

One might argue in defense of Austin that his
concept of habitual obedience of the subjects to the
sovereign takes care of the concerns of ideals or
morals of the society, since a sovereign who flaunts
those ideals in a major way would not enjoy the
habitual obedience of the subjects. However, that
seems to be too remote, too indirect, and too diffuse
to be relied upon for ensuring the moral integrity
of law.

2. As pointed out by Maine, Austin unduly gen-
eralizes from the particular. His identification of
law with the product of legislation, along with a
coherent explanation for custom, is a characteristic
of only the western societies of his times. From
this he constructs a universal explanation of law
itself. Moreover, as Bryce has shown, Austin's
confusion between the notions of unlimited power
and final authority obscures the essential features
of even the legal order that was his prototype,
namely, the United Kingdom.

3. Austin's focus on command and sanction as
the essential elements of law is criticized by the
proponents of the historical and sociological theories of law who maintain that law exists independently of authoritative commands.

However, it is possible to argue that the two viewpoints are talking about two different things. While Austin is talking about the nature of authority in law, the historical and sociological jurists are talking about the source of such authority in society, which could very well be done without dismissing Austin's position on authority and command.

4. Legal relations include legal powers, rights, privileges, and so on. Austin describes these relations as commands of the sovereign. However, it does not seem quite congruous to characterize private rights, administrative acts, and declaratory laws as commands made by one having superiority over the addressee.

5. Austin's sovereign has given rise to many problems, some of which have been pointed by other analytical jurists themselves. Thus, Gray believes that the real rulers of a political society cannot be discovered. Moreover, while the state must be accepted as fundamental in law to which the machinery of government attaches, the interposition of another entity, namely the sovereign, is quite irrelevant. Hart thinks that the notion of sovereign oversimplifies the character of a political society, for it is the notion of rule that is the ultimate test for identifying law. Being set by the sovereign is not its defining characteristic. Hart further points out that the habit of obedience to a sovereign with unlimited powers, which is a defining characteristic of Austin's sovereign, does not account for the continuity of the law-making au-

thority possessed by a succession of different legislators. Nor does it account for the persistence of laws long after their maker and those who accorded him habitual obedience have disappeared. Nor, again, does it account for legal limitations on legislative power.

6. Austin does not seem quite clear about the meaning of the sovereign in his theory. It could be a real or actual thing, as when he says that it is a determinate person or group of persons, or it could be a juristic construction arising out of his interpretation of facts.

7. Austin's view of law as a command has been the source of a lot of intellectual anxiety. Even other analytical jurists have found it a sore point. Thus, Kelsen considers that the analytical purity of a theory of law is compromised by introducing into it this psychological element. Or, Hart points out that laws are to be defined in terms of the notion of rule so that it is dogmatic to insist that the status of a law as law is derived from a prescription, whether express or tacit.

8. Austin defines law in terms of the state. This has the merit of distinguishing the legal order from other orders. However, the historical jurists have argued that, far from being the distinguishing characteristic of all law, the state is only an incident of mature systems of law. Anthropologists have argued that we should look for the essence of law in its function and not in its form, so that law should be defined by what it does in society rather

than by the fact that it is commanded by a sovereign.

9.   One of the essential elements of law in Austin's theory is sanction, since it naturally follows from the notion of command that there be a fear of evil.   However, this does not account for the bulk of law that is enabling in nature rather than restrictive, such as the powers given to a testator over the distribution of his estate after his death. Moreover, sanction is not a satisfactory explanation for obedience to law.   It seems that while sanction has its own role to play for those who do not wish to obey the law, there are other factors, such as respect for law as such or the desire to have the advantage of a system of legal protection of acts, that significantly explain the phenomenon of obedience to law.

10.   The basic question is whether the source of validity of law lies in the command of the sovereign.   This view of validity is in sharp contrast with the view, as seen in preceding chapters, that law is valid because it is the expression of natural justice or some other ideal, or the view, discussed in the next chapter, that law is valid because it is the embodiment of the spirit of a people.

C. KELSEN

Kelsen's theory suffers from the criticisms made of the analytical positivism in law, above.   In addition, there are some particular difficulties with it.

1. Kelsen makes the methodological dichotomy between natural (causal) sciences, which operate by the method of causality, and social (normative) sciences, which employ the volitional method. He, thereupon, posits that law is a normative science concerned with ought rather than a natural science concerned with is. However, the truth seems to be neither that the method of natural sciences is purely causal and rigidly deterministic, nor that the method of social sciences is rigidly volitional. In natural sciences, the choice between alternative hypotheses is often one of convenience, wherein identical conclusions may even be derived from different premises. Experiments cannot possibly be made without preconceived ideas. Conversely, each experiment yields generalizations that serve as predictions for other experiments. For example, in physics, this interaction between speculative assumptions and experiment is well demonstrated by the persistent inquiries and continually changing theories concerning the structure of the atom, the theory of relativity, and the interchangeability of matter and energy. Likewise, the method used in the social sciences is not exclusively volitional. An increasing emphasis is being placed on certainty and measurability. Even in law, the American realist movement, discussed below, has emphasized fact research and analysis in the legal decision-making process. In more recent times, behavioral research, which employs quantitative techniques in the analysis of factual data, has been put to significant use in law. Therefore, a closer examination

of the methods of science does not confirm the methodological dichotomy claimed by the pure theory of law.

2. The descriptive function of this theory is problematic. According to this theory, rules of law formulated by the science of law are descriptive, while legal norms enacted by the law-creating authorities are prescriptive, and that the task of the science of law, as a general theory, is not to describe a particular legal system but merely to show how a particular legal system should be described, i.e., which concepts should and should not be used in making this description. The resulting description must take the form of rules (or ought statements) in a descriptive sense. However, this conclusion is puzzling. For, at this point of inquiry, the description would not be a set of rules or ought statements but, instead, a set of statements explaining the meaning of the rules.

Indeed, it may be a mistaken belief that law, a science of norms, can be explored using norms as tools, for then law becomes a science with conclusions of law, not a science with norms or legal rules as its objects of inquiry.

Perhaps Kelsen simply means that his purely scientific statements explaining the meaning of a law mention certain rules of ought statements as the equivalent in meaning of that law. However, this interpretation of Kelsen's theory seems to be overly generous. Nevertheless, it has been argued in Kelsen's defense that the use of words differs from the mention of them, the latter being descriptive. Thus, although the law-creating authority within a particular legal system may employ certain words to enact a law, the formulation of the meaning of the law by the science of law merely mentions these words in conjunction with other words that explain the meaning of the law.

3. The pure theory separates reality (causal sciences) from ideality (normative sciences). Law and morality belong to ideality. It views positive law as a system of valid norms. Morality cannot also be a system of valid norms. Therefore, a valid rule of law cannot be contradicted by a valid moral rule, since, in Kelsen's words, "[n]either the jurist nor the moralist asserts that both normative systems are valid. The jurist ignores morality as a system of valid norms, just as the moralist ignores positive law as such a system. Neither from the one nor from the other point of view do there exist duties simultaneously that contradict one another. And there is no third point of view." The collision of moral and legal duty in the mind of an individual is explained as the psychological result of his being under the influence of two ideas that pull him in different directions, not as the simultaneous validity of two contradictory norms. Therefore, for the pure theory, this collision is one of factuality rather than of normativity. This position would seemingly apply both to the case of the individual involved in the conflict and, *mutatis mutandis*, to the case of an observer who considers the law in question to be valid but in conflict with morality.

However, the difficulty lies in the fact that when an individual experiences this conflict, he believes not only in the existence of the conflict but also in the impossibility of discharging both the duties. Thus, the requirements of a valid law conflict with the requirements of a moral principle. This finding is clearly of normativity, not of factuality. Moreover, even if one accepts Kelsen's claim that neither the jurist nor the moralist asserts the validity of both normative systems, it does not follow that such assertions of conflict between law and morality cannot be made meaningfully.

4.   The is-ought dichotomy in this theory results in separate, unconnected worlds of nature and validity. However, this result seems unsatisfactory because if the purpose of the system of norms is to interpret the social reality by revealing its consonance with the normative system, then the two systems must have something in common. Only the synthetic association of reality and validity makes the normative system a meaningful referent of social reality to the category of validity.

5.   The theory fails to maintain its claimed purity of the is-ought dichotomy. Under it, the legal norms derive their validity from the basic norm but the validity of the basic norm is presupposed. However, if this means that there are basic procedures that are accepted in a particular society for identifying authoritative rules, then they are not presupposed but experienced, and thus are found in the realm of factuality, not normativity.

Moreover, the determination of the valid basic norm under this theory is founded upon its principle of the minimum of effectiveness, which is conformity of man's actual behavior to the legal order. The proof of this minimum of effectiveness obviously requires an inquiry into political and social facts. That proof is a matter of is, not ought.

6. There are at least six admissions within the theory that infuse factuality (is) into a structure of normativity (ought), which is contrary to the claimed dichotomy of is and ought. These admissions are: (1) the admission that the efficacy of the legal order taken as a whole is a condition of the validity of individual norms; (2) the recognition that legal norms may be created by a revolution; (3) the acceptance of the fact that an individual norm may lose its validity due to the inefficacy of the legal order; (4) the assertion that the basic norm is not an arbitrary creation, since its content is determined by facts; (5) the view that the basic norm effects the transformation of power into law; and (6) the suggestion that law is a specific technique of social organization.

Moreover, the very hierarchy of legal norms involves ranking various manifestations of legal will, such as statutory enactments and judicial decisions, and thus implies a certain evaluation of state activity. This ranking cannot be achieved by separating the realm of facts from the realm of norms. Thus, contrary to this theory's claim, law is bound to include in its structure certain ontological elements that give content to the concepts that formalize it.

7. The claimed universality of this theory is dubious, too. The hierarchy elaborated by this theory purports to express the pure and universal form of law. In order for that claim to be valid, no possible legal system must fall outside it, but that is not the case in reality.

8. Finally, a basic question arises whether it is possible to have a true picture of law merely through observing the formal hierarchy of norms and ignoring the social forces (including ethics) that create law.

D. HART

1. Hart defines law as the union of primary rules of obligation and secondary rules of recognition, change, and adjudication. However, this does not help in distinguishing the legal order from any other order, such as a social club or a religious order, which may very well have primary and secondary rules of this kind.

2. Hart excludes morality from his rule of recognition. This has led some critics, such as Dias, to say that Hart cannot possibly exclude morality from this rule of recognition since social and moral considerations go into the making of law and prevent it from validating abuse of power.

However, it seems that this criticism of Hart's theory is not warranted. An assertion that the rule of recognition is an analytic element of law does not mean that it cannot have a content that is determined by social and moral considerations. Morality is excluded only from the analytic elements of law.

2.   Hart makes a rather sharp distinction between his primary rules that create duties and his secondary rules that create powers. However, it seem that the same rule can possibly do both. Its interpretation as to whether it is creating a duty or creating a power depends not on the rule but on the circumstances to which it is applied.

4.   Hart does not clarify what he means by rules. He does not distinguish rules from principles, standards, and policies that possess the quality of law. If he means to exclude these, then he is excluding too much of the legal phenomena from his definition of law. If he means to include these, then he is eliminating the distinctions that do exist between rules and principles, standards, and policies. He does not give reasons why these distinctions do not or should not exist.

5.   Primary rules create duties under this theory and secondary rules confer public and private powers. Thus, the term power is applied to comprehend everything that is regulated by law that is not a duty. However, in doing so, he uses the term to signify things that cannot in ordinary legal usage be properly called power, such as, for example, capacity or competence.

6. Finally, in this theory the transition from the primitive or prelegal societies is made by addition of the secondary rules. However, it seems that the primitive or prelegal societies do have the secondary or power-conferring rules, as seen in their institutions of marriage, promise, and so on. It might be argued in Hart's defense that the secondary rules of recognition, change, and adjudication are meant to denote not such things as marriage, promise, and the like, but such things as rules of legislation, administration, and jurisdiction. However, in that case, it appears that these are hardly the most important factors, as claimed, in the transition of a prelegal society to a legal society.

CHAPTER 7

HISTORICAL THEORIES
OF LAW

The historical theories arose as a revolt against two factors: one, the rationalism of the eighteenth century which paid no attention to the historicity of social conditions and propagated its belief in natural law, first principles, and power of reason to deduce the theory of law, and, two, the premises of the French Revolution which believed in the power of human will over traditions and circumstances.

THEORIES

1. Law as a Manifestation of the Spirit of the People in History: Friedrich Karl von Savigny (1719–1861)

Savigny regards history not merely a collection of examples but the only way to acquire true knowledge of the human condition. Accordingly, in history he gains his knowledge about law.

He likens law to a people's language, manner, and constitution. In his view, the law of a people has already attained a fixed character peculiar to that people in the earliest times of history. These phenomena do not exist separately from each other but, instead, are united in nature and represent the particular tendencies and faculties of a people. The common conviction of the people binds them into one whole. Therefore, law excludes all notions of an accidental and arbitrary origin. It is located in the consciousness of an inward necessity. It grows with a people and dies when a nation loses its nationality. It is developed first by custom and popular faith and next by jurisprudence.

Thus, it is developed not by the arbitrary will of a law giver but by internal, silently operating powers.

Consequently, it is not made but found. Its growth is essentially an unconscious and organic process. The organic connection of law with the being and character of the people is manifested in the progress of the times. The spirit of the people (*Volksgeist*) manifests itself in the law of the people.

In primitive communities, law is a matter of a few easily grasped legal relations. In modern societies, it grows to a greater complexity in which the *Volksgeist* can no longer manifest itself directly. Instead, it is represented by lawyers who formulate the technical legal principles. The task of the lawyers is not to create law but to bring into legal shape that which exists in the *Volksgeist*. In this process, legislation is merely a last stage.

Since law is the manifestation of the peculiar character of a people, it is not of universal validity. Like the language of a people, it cannot apply to other peoples. Legal institutions must, therefore, be studied with reference to their particular time and place and not with reference to general or abstract principles.

2. Law as the Development in History of Personal Conditions From Status to Contract: Sir Henry Sumner Maine (1822–1888)

Maine studies legal evolution in different societies in history. From this he concludes that there are two kinds of societies: static and progressive. The static societies include the greatest part of mankind, including India and China, whose social and legal development stops at a certain stage and which show not a particle of desire to improve beyond that point. In contrast, the progressive societies include an extremely few societies of Europe which represent a rare achievement of civilization in the history of the world and are propelled by a desire to improve and develop.

According to him, there are three successive stages of legal evolution in static societies. The first stage is that of law-making by personal command of the rulers who are believed to be acting under a divine inspiration. This is succeeded by the second stage of the epoch of customary law, which is marked by a gradual crystallization of habits into customs. An aristocratic minority replaces the original law-makers of the theocratic power and formulates the legal customs. The third stage in this evolution is the era of codes.

The evolution of the static societies is arrested at this stage and is characterized by a fixed legal condition dominated by family dependency. He calls this condition status. In the condition of status, the member of a household is tied to the family dominated by its head. Laws still have an extremely limited application and are binding not on individuals but on families. Legislation and adjudication reach only to the heads of the families. The rule of conduct for the individual remains the law of his home, as distinguished from civil law. His legislator is his parent.

Only the progressive societies, represented by the few societies of Europe, are characterized by a desire to improve and develop. Therefore, they move beyond the stage where the static societies stop. The sphere of civil law tends to enlarge itself. The agents of legal change become active. At every point of the progress a greater number of personal and property rights are removed from the domestic forum to the public tribunal.

These agents of change or development are, in historical order, (a) legal fiction, (b) equity, and (c) legislation. Legal fictions change the law in accordance with the changing needs and signify assumptions that conceal the fact of alteration of a law by keeping its letter unchanged but modifying its operation. Equity exists alongside the original civil law due to a superior sanctity inherent in its principles. Legislation represents an increased law-making power of the state and its obligatory force is independent of its principles.

As Maine sees it, the distinguishing feature in the movement of the progressive societies through these instrumentalities of change has been the gradual dissolution of family dependency and its replacement by individual obligation. The civil law increasingly applies to the individual. The movement, according to him, has been from personal conditions to agreement, or, in other words, from status to contract.

3. Law as an Auxiliary in a Stage of Economic Determinism: Karl Marx (1818–1883) and Friedrich Engels (1820–1895)

Marx and Engels observe that the history of all human society has been the history of class struggle, in which the oppressor and the oppressed stood in sharp opposition to each other. Political power is the organized use of force by one class in order to subjugate another class. Social evolution, according to them, moves toward the disappearance of class distinctions.

People carry on social production. In this production they enter into definite relations. These relations are independent of their will and correspond to a definite stage of development of their material powers of production. These relations of production in their totality constitute the society's economic structure.

Definite forms of social consciousness correspond to this economic structure. People's social existence determines their consciousness, not the other way around. It is the mode of production in material life that determines the general character of the social, political, and spiritual processes of life. When material forces of production conflict with the existing relations of production, as they do at a certain stage of their development, social revolution follows and changes the economic foundations. It thereby transforms the entire superstructure.

The broad epochs in the progress of the economic formation of society are the Asiatic, the ancient, the feudal, and the modern bourgeois methods of production. The bourgeois relations of production are the last antagonistic form of the social process of production. The material conditions for the solution of that antagonism are created by the productive forces developing in the bourgeois society.

The materialist conception of history thus begins with the principle that production and exchange of its products are the basis of every social order. The distribution of the products and the division of society into classes are determined by the features of production, i.e., what is produced, how it is produced, who produced it, and how the product is exchanged. Therefore, according to Marx and Engels, the causes of social changes and political revolutions are to be found not in the minds of men (philosophy) but in the mode of production and exchange (economics).

Injustice in social institutions indicates that the social order has not kept up with the changes that have been quietly taking place in the methods of production and forms of exchange. The means to get rid of the abuses are also present in the altered conditions of production, or, in other words, in the existing material facts of production. Thus, the capitalist means of production transform the great majority of population into proletarians and thereby bring forth the force that carries out the revolution.

The process proceeds in the following manner. The proletariat seizes state power and transforms the means of production into state property, but in doing so it puts an end to itself as the proletariat. Class differences and antagonisms are ended. So is the state. The state, being an organization of the exploitative class, was needed to forcibly hold down the exploited class in the oppressive conditions determined by the existing mode of production. It is, consequently, rendered unnecessary when there is no longer any class of society to be subjugated. State interference becomes superfluous in social relations. The state withers away with the replacement of the government of persons by the administration of things and common direction of the processes of production.

Law has little to contribute in this scheme of things, except to exist, like the state, as means whereby those controlling the production maintain their control over those who are oppressed. Law, too, would wither away with the withering away of the state.

CRITICISMS

1. Savigny

1. Some of the suppositions of the historical theory are not supported by history. The theory makes an organic connection of all social institutions in the spirit of a people (*Volksgeist*). Law is an expression of this *Volksgeist*. This would mean that one people cannot borrow the law of another. However, such has not been the case in history. Examples abound of instances when law or custom of another has been imported by conquest, invasion, or peaceful penetration.

2. Under this theory history determines the present. Law, thus, is not a matter of conscious human effort. However, such a view deprives historical knowledge of all its practical importance.

3. The deterministic view of law taken by this theory discourages all efforts at consciously improving the legal condition.

4. Since law in this theory is an expression of the conviction of righteousness of a people, an evaluation of its justness is made impossible. Although Savigny himself accepts the possibility of a bad law being opposed to the spirit of the people,

his theory cannot do so consistently with the positivistic or empirical claim made of the *Volksgeist*.

5. It seems that a historical study may tell us how a particular proposition of law fared in its own circumstances, how it was interpreted and applied then. However, it cannot help us evaluate present laws under present conditions.

6. Savigny's approach denies the abstract methods of evaluation. However, it becomes unconsciously metaphysical when it attempts to govern modern life by ancient texts. Furthermore, it presupposes the values of conservation as opposed to the values of change. These processes are not empirical and their method not historical.

7. Custom is regarded by this theory as a manifestation of the *Volksgeist*. However, there are several problems with this view. Firstly, it is difficult to say that all customs carry with them the general conviction of rightness inherent in a notion of *Volksgeist*. Look, for example, at the custom of slavery in domestic laws or the custom of war in international law. Secondly, there are customs that are so local in their origin that they cannot be said to have arisen from any widespread conviction, as, for example, the cosmopolitanism of many commercial customs. Thirdly, many customs arise from convenience or imitation rather than a conviction of their righteousness. Finally, custom is a combination of the inner manifestation of social tendencies (feelings, desires, consciousness) and their external manifestation in conduct.

Savigny focuses only upon the inner aspect. To that extent, his is a deficient account of custom.

8. Savigny assigns to the jurist only the role to make an exposition of the existing law from the characteristic customs of the community, not to add anything creative to it. This account of juristic activity is not persuasive for several reasons. Firstly, judicial decision-making is not such a non-creative, mechanical process as conceived by Savigny's theory. Laws are not apprehended by all men and women in a like manner. Therefore, they need to be interpreted. This interpretation is a creative activity and is much influenced by the judge's own values, as pointed by the American realists, discussed below. Secondly, great advances have been made in law by the great expositors of law who have projected in it their personal genius. This is not the same thing as mechanically stating the customs of the society or representing the *Volksgeist*.

9. Germany of Savigny's times was characterized by a growing feeling of nationhood. He was, therefore, probably correct in detecting an idea of the spirit of the people in that period of German history. However, he extends that idea to all societies. He thus uses an *a priori* conception in claiming the universal validity for his idea. In doing so, he no longer remains true to his own historical method.

10. His theory considerably exaggerates the creative role assigned to the *Volksgeist*. That

there is some interaction between traditions and legislation is not disputed. However, traditions are not all-controlling of the emergent law. Sometimes they are even deliberately changed by new law. Far from reflecting the *Volksgeist*, law sometimes changes it.

11. This theory has failed to provide us the means for discovering the *Volksgeist* or proving it. It seems impossible to ascertain the existence of a national mind. Therefore, this concept, like natural law, is also very mystical and quite capable of supporting any ideology.

2. Maine

1. Maine claims a cultural superiority of the European societies over the rest of the mankind. This is not only too chauvinistic, it is also unsupported by the history of non-European societies. As pointed out in Chapter 2, above, law's particular role in the social organization of European societies has been the result of the particular historicity of European cultural experience, which is not shared by other cultures. Maine is thoroughly mistaken in regarding this as an evidence of the inferiority of other cultures to the culture of Europe.

2. His generalizations about primitive law and primitive societies, too, are dubious in many respects. For example, he maintains that law and religion are indistinguishable in these societies.

However, anthropologists are divided on this issue. While some believe that such is the case, others point out that the association of law with religion is only a late development among primitive societies.

In fact, primitive societies might well be argued to possess a phenomenon called law, if by law is meant the function performed by it and the attitude of people toward it. Many anthropologists hold that law is found in such features. Such features are evident in primitive societies, as seen in rules of behavior regulating relations of individuals and groups, reciprocity of services characterized by their obligatory character, obedience, machinery for dispute resolution such as reconciliation, compensation, sanctioned vengeance on part of the person wronged, and so on.

According to Maine, the early development of societies occurred through the successive stages of personal judgments, oligarchic monopoly, and code. However, primitive societies have been more complex than the simple, single pattern given by Maine. They exhibit a wide range of institutions. On the basis of this range, some anthropologists have classified them as First Hunters, Second Hunters, First Agriculturalists, First Pastorals, and Second Pastorals. Other classifications have been proposed, as well. In any case, Maine's simple model is much too deficient.

Maine maintains that the later development in progressive societies has been in the sequence of legal fiction, equity, and legislation. However, legislation came first in these societies. After that, fiction and equity played their part.

Nor is primitive law as rigid and inflexible as Maine supposes it to be. Primitive societies are not characterized by a blind obedience to law, without regard to the dynamics of human behavior in its interaction with the purposes that people pursue and with the social structure within which they pursue them.

One might attempt a defense of Maine, as has been done, by arguing that the above knowledge about primitive societies is the result of the anthropological investigations undertaken only since his times, so that criticizing him on these grounds is not fair. That may be so. However, at best, this is a tribute to the genius of the man and not an argument for the validity of his theory.

3. Maine's most important conclusion is that the movement in progressive societies has been from status to contract. This is not borne out by a closer observations of these societies. Developments in these societies suggest movement toward status and erosion of contract.

In the first place, his own examples of this movement are faulty. He observes, for example, that the status of the slave had been superseded by the contractual relation of the servant to his master. However, if one is not deluded by the seduction of the contractual form, one can see that what had happened was not that the fetters of status were

superseded by the freedom released by contract but
that the old slavery was replaced by a new slavery
which, as Wolfgang Friedmann points out, was
founded not on legal incapacity but on the economic helplessness of the worker. The change that ·
came about in this type of status was the result of
factors which have nothing to do with contract.
These factors have been, one, the association of
workers in trade unions and, two, state interference against horrible injustices of the freedom of
contract. Therefore, the case is not that there has
been a movement from status to contract, as
claimed by Maine, but, rather, that there has been
a reform from contract to status.

Secondly, a further erosion of the freedom of
contract is seen in social legislation that compulso-
rily provides for such things as workmen's compensation, minimum wages, safety in the workplace,
worker amenities in the workplace, social security,
and so on.

Thirdly, both the worker and the industrialist
have sought advantages through giving up individual freedom of contract by joining the trade union
and the business association or cartel, respectively,
and by taking recourse to long-term collective
agreements.

Fourthly, Maine's freedom of bargaining contem-
plated in his contract has been increasingly replaced by the status-like conditions in many areas
of economic life resulting from the standardized
contracts prevalent in these areas, which range

from government contracts to transportation, insurance, leases, mortgages, and so on.

Fifthly, the rise of totalitarian governments in Maine's progressive societies of Europe demonstrates a movement away from, and not toward, contract.

Finally, it is too simplistic to classify all legal relations into the categories of status and contract. It is even erroneous to put these relations on a progressive scale wherein status is left behind and contract is approached. Legal relations in modern society are complex, some of which may be in the nature of status, some in the nature of contract, and some quite indifferent to the concerns of either status or contract. Moreover, all of these converge upon the individual or the corporate legal entity at the same time, instead of exhibiting a movement from one to the other.

3. Marx and Engels

1. The Marxist theory gives a scientific form to social development. Since that development is scientific, this theory claims that it is inevitable. It also points to the method of production as the single cause of all cultural phenomena. However, it is incorrect to call this approach as the method of science. What characterizes the scientific method is probability, not necessity, and its quest is characterized not by a single all-comprehensive law but a plurality of these laws. It is true that

when science was still seeking its method, there may have been in it a search for an all-comprehensive law of causal necessity, but that is not the case in modern science. As Dewey has pointed out, science is not a competitor with theology for a single ultimate explanation. Therefore, while economic factors no doubt influence matters of social organization, they are not the sole cause of all developments in culture.

2.   Class conflict is a method of social progress under this theory. Therefore, one would conclude that if you aim at social progress you must intensify class conflict. However, it is quite possible to regard these conflicts as deleterious to progress, since they tend to waste or destroy resources needed for progress.

3.   Marx and Engels observed, probably accurately, the social conditions of a particular place in a particular time. However, it is a fallacy to claim from this anecdote a scientific, universal principle. Their conclusions are not based upon data that represent the conditions of all societies.

4.   It seems that the creative element of the process of social progress is crucial to the idea of progress. However, the Marxist theory's deterministic view deprives this process of that creative element. It promotes a fatalistic belief in recurrent cycles of history. This is both erroneous and dangerous. It is erroneous in that history does not repeat like that. It is dangerous in that it discour-

ages other elements of culture that play their role in improving the human condition.

5. Ideology, for Marx and Engels, is false consciousness or illusion. It is, therefore, condemned implicitly. However, this view is mistaken both historically and as a principle of action. Historically, ideologies have actually played their part in mobilizing people to certain goals. That is no illusion. As a principle of action, they represent commitments that move peoples to achieving that in which they believe. This, too, is not an illusion. It may very well be that the values that people attempt to realize through their ideologies are not necessarily materialistic and not controlled by the method of production, as Marx and Engels would have it, but that does not make them illusory.

What is objectionable here is not the existence of ideologies. As pointed out in Chapter 2, above, it is the confusion of ideology with philosophy that is objectionable, since this process passes off a value preference as the objective truth. We have seen this incipience in many philosophies examined above and we now see it in the Marxist theory as well. We shall see in the subsequent chapters, too. Values do exist, they do conflict, and a choice has to be made from among them. Acknowledging that choice as the ideological preference, rather than disguising it as philosophy, places the responsibility of making that choice on those who make it. Dismissing the whole issue as illusion, as this theory does, is misleading.

6. The political theory of Marx and Engels is fraught with many problems. We shall not analyze them within the scope of our inquiry here. We shall not examine, for example, whether in their classless society administration can possibly consist only of business management and adjudication of disputes, or whether group conflicts would not arise in such a society, and so on. We shall only point out that by conceiving law merely as an instrument of suppression, their theory prevents an inquiry into the useful roles that law might possibly play in society.

CHAPTER 8

SOCIOLOGICAL THEORIES OF LAW

THEORIES

The sociological theories about the nature of law may be classified into three categories: (A) law viewed in sociological aspects, (B) the jurisprudence of interests, and (C) the free law.

A. LAW IN SOCIOLOGICAL ASPECTS

Theories that view law in sociological aspects include, most prominently, those of Ihering (law in the social purpose), Ehrlich (law in the inner order of human associations), and Duguit (law in the objective conditions of social solidarity.

1. Law in the Social Purpose: Rudolf von Ihering (1818–1892)

Law, according to Ihering, is the sum of conditions of social life in the widest sense of the term, as secured by the power of the state through the means of external compulsion. Thus, there are three crucial elements to it: its dependence upon coercion, its norm, and its purpose (or the conditions of social life).

Coercion: Law consists of those rules laid down by society that have coercion. Since the state is the sole possessor of coercion in society, it is the only source of law. The other associations that have the right to make their own laws, such as the Church, have that right either by the express grant or tacit toleration of the state. The criterion that distinguishes law from ethics and morality is the recognition and realization of it by the force of the state. Ihering reconciles his insistence on coercion in law with the concept of international law and with the concept of that part of public law that concerns the duties of the monarch by maintaining that both of these are laws with coercion as an essential element and the only difficulty is that the organization of coercion in these instances meets with insurmountable obstructions.

Norm: Just as coercion is the outer side of law, norm is its inner element. It is an abstract imperative of human conduct. In that sense, it is a proposition of a practical kind inasmuch as it is a direction for human conduct. It is thus a rule, but it is distinguished from all other rules by virtue of its concern with conduct. It is distinguished from maxims by virtue of its binding and imperative character. Abstract imperatives in the ethical world order are social imperatives, since the subject of their purpose is society. These imperatives are of law, morality, and ethics. In law, they are regularly laid down by the state and realized exclusively by the state authorities. The legal imperatives are directed to the organs of the state that are entrusted with the management of coercion. Thus norm, like coercion, is a purely formal element.

Purpose: Ihering points out that norm and coercion being formal elements, they do not inform us of the content of law. It is through the content of law that we learn of the purpose served by law in society. This content is infinitely various. There is nothing universal about it. Law cannot make the same regulations for all the time and for all the people. It must adapt them to the conditions of the people, to their degree of civilization, and to the needs of the time. The standard of law is not truth, which is absolute, but purpose, which is relative. Certain legal principles found among all peoples have a resemblance to truth but to call them truths would be like calling the fundamental arrangements of human civilization (houses, streets, clothing, use of fire and light, etc.) truths. They are results of experience assuring attainment of certain purposes. Science may separate those institutions that have endured the test of history from those that have had only a temporary usefulness, but the institutions that have endured are nothing other than the useful placed beyond doubt.

According to Ihering, law exists to realize some purpose. It is to secure the conditions of social life. Conditions of life include the conditions of physical existence as well as those goods and pleasures that give one's life its true value in his judgment. All legal principles of any kind and wherever found can, for Ihering, be reduced to the security of conditions of social life.

The conditions of social life or the requirements for the existence of society, as related to the attitude of the law toward them, are of three types: (i) extra-legal, (ii) mixed legal, and (iii) purely legal. (i) The extra-legal conditions of life belong to nature and are offered to man with or without requiring his effort. Law has nothing to do with them. (ii) The mixed legal conditions belong exclusively to man and include preservation of life, reproduction, labor, and trade, corresponding to his instincts of self-preservation, sex, and acquisition. Their security does not depend upon law, but upon nature, and law comes to assist these three instincts only in the exceptional cases when they fail. (iii) The purely legal conditions are those that depend entirely on legal command, for example, the command to pay debts or taxes.

Ihering maintains that the realization of the law by the state enables the individual to desire the common interest as well as his own individual interest. He thus makes the individual interest part of a social purpose by connecting one's purpose with the interests of others.

The reconciliation between the interests of the individual and those of the society is achieved through the levers of social motion. Society acts upon individuals through two basic motives of egoism and altruism. Correspondingly, there are two kinds of levers of social motion: egoistic and altruistic. The egoistic levers are made up of reward and coercion. The altruistic levers are made up of the feelings of duty and love.

2. Law in the Inner Order of Human Associations: Eugen Ehrlich (1862–1922)

For Ehrlich, the center of gravity of legal development lies not in legislation, not in juristic science, not in judicial decision, but in society itself. It is the inner order of associations, not legal propositions, that determines the fate of man. The explanation for social phenomena comes not from their juristic construction but by inferring the underlying modes of thought from fact. Accordingly, people regard their rights as issuing from the relations of one person to another and not from legal propositions about those relations. Thus, the state precedes the constitution, the family precedes the order of the family, possession precedes ownership, contracts precede the law of contracts, the testament precedes the law of wills, and so on. The inner order of human associations not only comes temporally before legal propositions but is also the basic form of law from which legal propositions are derived.

Ehrlich explains that in a social association, human beings come together and recognize certain rules of conduct as binding. Generally speaking, they regulate their conduct in accordance with these rules, which are social facts produced by the forces operating in society. These rules are of various kinds. Examples include rules of law, work, religion, ethics, decorum, tact, etiquette, fashion, etc. Ehrlich maintains that the legal norm is of the same nature as all other rules of conduct. The essential compulsion behind the legal norm, just as behind other norms of conduct, is social compulsion, not state authority.

The state is merely one legal association among numerous others. Others include family, church, and corporate bodies. Consequently, there are many legal norms that have not been expressed in legal provisions of the state. The function of the state norms of compulsion is to protect norms formed in society and to protect the various institutions of the state.

There are social facts of law that exist in the conviction of an association of people. These facts are usage, domination, possession, and declaration of will. Norms of law are derived from these facts. State compulsion is not necessary to this process.

These facts of law affect legal relations in three ways: (a) they give enforcement to these relations; (b) they control, hinder, or invalidate these relations; and (c) they impute legal consequences to their relations that are not derived directly from them. Only one type of legal norms, namely, the norms of decision, is state-made.

The transformation of state norms into a fundamental legal norm takes place, if at all, when those norms become part of the living law. The living law, or the law as it actually exists in society, is always in a state of evolution and is always ahead of the state law. It is the task of jurisprudence, according to Ehrlich, to solve this tension between the two. It is thus a product of social developments, as well as a stimulus to them.

The norms of law regulate the relationship between the state law and the facts of law. This relationship exists in three modes: (a) there may be legal norms purely based on facts of law (e.g., contracts, bylaws of corporate associations, etc.) or they may be derived from them (e.g., remedies for damage, unjust enrichment, etc.); (b) there may be state commands that create or deny social facts, e.g., expropriation or nullification of contracts; and (c) there may be norms that are unconnected with social facts, e.g., taxation, trade concessions, etc. The task of the jurist is fairly technical where the social facts of the law are quite clear. However, where the social facts of the law are not so clear, Ehrlich instructs the jurist to seek guidance in the principles of justice. The static justice of the ideal forms, which tends to consolidate existing conditions, is mitigated by dynamic justice, which is characterized by the competitive forces of the individualistic and the collective ideals.

3. Law in the Objective Conditions of Social Solidarity: Leon Duguit (1859–1928)

Auguste Comte's scientific positivism and Durkheim's distinction between collective and individual consciousness have inspired Duguit's theory of law.

Comte opposes the empirical method to the metaphysical method and believes that all reflections must be derived not from preconceived ideas but from experience and observation. He applies this method to the evolution of mankind and discovers that human history has gone through three phases: first, the theological phase, wherein forces of nature are explained through personified deities; second, the metaphysical phase, wherein those personified forces are explained through causal relations; and, third, the scientific or the positivistic phase, wherein personification is expunged from nature so that nature is viewed experimentally and objectively. Corresponding to these phases of human history are the branches of human knowledge. Sociology builds a real science of human society based on facts and not ideology.

Durkheim follows this approach and discovers two kinds of needs and aptitudes of people that hold them together in societies: one, common needs, that are satisfied by mutual assistance and by bringing together of similar aptitudes; two, diverse needs, that are satisfied by an exchange of services wherein one utilizes his aptitudes to satisfy the needs of others. He argues that social cohesion is achieved by this division of labor and social solidarity will increase with energetic and free development of individual activities.

Duguit seizes upon social solidarity as a fact of social life. That, for him, is indisputable, non-ideological, and non-metaphysical. He believes that social norms, like biological laws of organism, are based on the fact that is society. Solidarity is the law of the social body according to which that body is maintained.

Law, too, is a fact, since it is an aspect of social solidarity. Law exists by virtue of facts, and not because of any higher principle of good, interest, or happiness, and these facts are that people do live and can only live in society.

The duty to maintain social solidarity is, for him, an indisputable fact. This prompts him to establish a rule of objective law that is free from the arbitrariness of human will. Therefore, he assails state sovereignty as a myth. The state is not a person distinct from individuals but only the individual will of those who govern. Those who govern are just the individuals who exercise preponderant force. Correspondingly, they have a duty of performing a social function, namely, organizing certain services, assuring the continuity of these services, and controlling their operation. The government and the state are, thus, a part of the social organism and have their own task to perform in the division of labor whereby social solidarity is attained.

He draws interesting consequences from this principle of social solidarity. He advocates strict principles of state responsibility to control abuse of state power. He recommends decentralization and group government. He rejects state intervention in transforming a social norm into a legal norm. He denies any division between public and private law, since both are parts of the social body with certain functions to fulfill. He rejects the necessity of individual rights, since everyone cooperates for a common end and fulfills a certain function. He, thus, manages to demolish both state sovereignty and individual rights.

B. JURISPRUDENCE OF INTERESTS: PHILIP HECK (1858–1943) AND ROSCOE POUND (1870–1964)

German jurist Philip Heck originally conceived of the jurisprudence of interests. American jurist Roscoe Pound elaborated it with striking similarity.

The jurisprudence of interests focuses upon the problem of legal interpretation.

As **Heck** points out, it is a method designed to serve the practical ends of law. Its aim is to discover principles that judges should follow in deciding cases. It attempts to replace the conceptualizations of the traditional jurisprudence with a maxim of analysis of interests or a theory of conflicts.

As Heck sees it, each command of law originates from a struggle between opposing interests, and the law determines this conflict of interests. Law, therefore, is the result of these opposing forces. The degree in which its purpose is achieved depends upon the weight of those interests that are superseded by it. The conflict of interests that underlie each rule of law must be analyzed. The judge has to adjust interests and decide their conflicts in the same way as the legislator does, although, in Heck's scheme, the legislative evaluations of interests has precedence over the judge's individual evaluation.

However, the judge's task is not only to apply a particular command but to protect the totality of interests, since the wealth and variety of the actual problems of daily life make laws inadequate, incomplete, and sometimes contradictory. For this purpose, it is necessary to adopt a method of systematic inquiry into the interests involved. This method must distinguish the function of framing rules from that of arranging them. The jurisprudence of interests grounds itself in the study of reality and the needs of practical life, and it frames rules with a view to balancing the competing interests. It, thus, explains given rules of law as the outcome of these competing interests.

Pound sets up social engineering as the crucial task of all thought about law. Toward that task, he formulates and classifies social interests. Legal progress is achieved by balancing these interests.

He classifies legally protected interests in three major categories: (a) public interests; (b) individual interests; and (c) social interests. (a) Public interests include the interests of the state (i) in subsisting as a state and (ii) in acting as a guardian of social interests. (b) Individual interests consist of (i) interests of personality, such as protection of physical integrity, freedom of will, reputation, privacy, and freedom of belief and opinion; (ii) interests of domestic relations, such as protection of marriage, maintenance claims, and legal relations between parents and children; and (iii) interests of substance, such as protection of property, freedom of testation, freedom of industry, and contract. (c) Social interests are composed of interests in (i) general security, (ii) security of social institutions, (iii) general morals, (iv) protection of social resources from waste, (v) general progress, and (vi) individual human life.

C. FREE LAW: EUGEN EHRLICH (1862–1922) AND HERMANN U. KANTOROWICZ (1877–1940)

The objective of the free law theories is not merely to analyze the legal process as a matter of social reality but also to instruct the judge to alter the statute law in accordance with the demands of justice.

Ehrlich explains that the basis of free decision lies in the fact that no rule is just for all times. Consequently, a great bulk of rules of decision are determined by the changing social conditions to which they are applied. However, he clarifies that the free decision is not arbitrary, since it grows out of the principles of judicial tradition. It is a characteristic of the judicial office that the judge's decision represents not his personal opinion but the law found primarily in past legal records, statutes, judicial decisions, and legal literature. The administration of justice has always contained the personal element of the judge, which is a welcome fact for Ehrlich, since the judge's personality must be great enough to be entrusted with the judicial function. Thus, the concern of the free decision is not with the substance of the law but with the proper selection of judges.

Kantorowicz presents two forms of law, namely, formal and free. Formal law is that which has completed a definite process of formation or interpretation. Free law is that which has not completed these processes.

Formal law is explicit or implicit. In its explicit form, it issues either from the original legislative authority (statutes), or from delegated legislative authority (orders-in-council, rules of court, bylaws, ordinances, regulations, etc.), or from customary authority (judge-made law). In its implicit form, it is customary law. Free law is either nascent, in the sense that it would be formal had it completed the process of formation after entering that process, or desired, in the sense that those who apply it desire it to become formal law. Both the nascent and the desired free law may be either explicit or implicit.

Free law is not only required by the incompleteness of the formal law but has to be accepted as existent, since judges create new formal law, and it cannot be the case that, prior to that, there was no law at all governing the matter. Sociological studies and concepts assist in the formation of the nascent law by providing the necessary knowledge of recent history of law and present social conditions. The formation of desired law proceeds through juristic relations, which means applying that particular interpretation of the statute among several possible interpretations that allows the realization of the purpose of the statute, but if that purpose cannot be ascertained, then it means applying the judicial ideal of the interpreter.

CRITICISMS

1. Ihering

1. Ihering locates law in the social purpose. However, when one proceeds with the idea of purpose in law, one faces the crucial question of deciding between conflicting purposes. Ihering is of no help in making this crucial determination as to purpose.

2. Nor has he succeeded in resolving the conflict between individual and collective interests. He attempts the reconciliation between the two through his levers of social motion, which consist of reward and coercion in the egoistic mode and feelings of duty and love in the altruistic mode.

However, reward and coercion can subjugate individual interests, not reconcile them. Moreover, to say that deeply abiding conflicts of interests can be eliminated simply by feelings of duty and love is nothing other than wishful thinking. These feelings are not an adequate method of reconciliation of the interests in conflict.

3. There are some contradictions between his fundamental assumptions and his conclusions. For example, he assumes conscious egoism as the motivating factor of human life so that its levers of reward and coercion build social institutions of commerce and law, but he ends up condemning legal egoism. Or, he makes his distinction between the point of view of sacrifice of the individual's purpose and the point of view of identifying the individual's purpose with social purpose, but such a distinction is inconsistent with conscious egoism.

4. He posits his law of causality as the principle of sufficient reason according to which everything that happens is the consequence of another antecedent change, and he maintains that this law is postulated by our thinking as well and is confirmed by our experience. This law, thus, asserts the unity of man and nature and regards man as a coherent part of nature. He then applies this law to human action and discovers that matter is different from life so that the type of causality that exists in physical nature (matter) is quite different from that which exists in the human will (life).

The causality of matter is characterized by mechanical or efficient causes and reacts to the past, whereas the causality of life is characterized by psychological or final causes and reaches for the future. Life, he concludes, is the application, through purpose, of the external world to one's existence, and purpose is the idea of a future event that the will attempts to realize. However, in so arguing he has lost the coherence and unity of man and nature that he earlier asserted, for human situation is now treated as unique and human behavior is referred to a distinct principle. In this way, his conclusion has lost its congruity with the principle that was fundamental in his scheme.

5. The main concern of his theory is to consider those conditions of man and society that are independent of law, that are prior to it, and that define law's functions and goals. Therefore, one would expect that this calls for an inquiry into extralegal sources of law. However, his own subsequent inquiry confines itself to analyzing concepts and techniques that law develops and uses in dealing with the issues of problems dealt by law, its purposes, and its values, instead of clarifying the objective conditions and purposes that call for the application of law and define its functions.

2. Ehrlich

1. Ehrlich's theory suffers from a basic difficulty that it fails to distinguish law from customs and morals. This is all the more disappointing for the

fact that he himself warns us that the lines between morals and law are shifting, from which one
would expect that the investigator has to be very
clear about the distinctive features of the law in
order to observe the shifting lines.

2.   He points to the basic elements governing
human communities that underlie law and are
expressed in fact before becoming precepts of law.
However, the basic problem of resolving conflicts,
which is law's calling, remains untouched.   His
sociological investigations do not give us any assistance in dealing with the problem of conflicting
interests.

3.   His conception of the living law does not take
an adequate account of the differences in social
institutions that exist in different societies.   For
example, the meaning of marriage is quite different in India from that in the United States.

4.   He treats the distinction between law and
custom too simply, in that he fails to analyze how
law and custom influence each other.   There is a
reciprocal relationship between the two, which he
has ignored.   For example, as Patterson has pointed out, the ritual and sanctity of the marriage
ceremony was brought about by the fact that the
law of property denied the right of inheritance to
an illegitimate child.

5.   Social institutions, for Ehrlich, arise spontaneously.   Thus, there is an automatic ordering of
various social relations, such as marriage, family
associations, possessions, contracts, succession, and

so on. However, such complex and far reaching forms of social relations do not sprout spontaneously. It seems more likely that these social institutions have emerged as a result of interplay between values cherished and modes of life pursued in society, not spontaneously.

6. The interplay of custom and law does not seem to be as pervasive as suggested by Ehrlich and his followers. There are important aspects of law that are in no way expressions of usage and custom of a people. A common example of such type of law is tax. Other examples include the law of social insurance or social security, workmen's compensation law, and the like.

7. Nor is the relationship between custom and law such that it could be said that the law is always an expression of the customs of those whom it governs, as is the case with infants, incompetent adults, and the unborn.

8. Law is often a deliberate and conscious act to alter certain practices found in customs and usages. This makes law far from being an expression of these customs. In fact, it makes law as something that contravenes these customs.

9. There are two aspects of custom that need to be distinguished, namely, custom as a source of law and custom as a type of law. This distinction is quite familiar in international law and primitive law. Ehrlich fails to make this distinction. The more formalistically tight legal systems of modern societies are characterized by a great amount of

specific law produced by the legislative process that may have usages, customs, and mores of the people as its source but whose validity is in no way derived from them.

10.   Ehrlich distinguishes between legal norms created by the state for specific state purposes, such as those needed to protect its constitution, finances, administrative structure, etc., and legal norms whereby the state contributes only its sanction to social facts.   However, contrary to his conclusions regarding the importance of custom, it seems that deliberately created state law for specific state purpose has been greatly expanding in response to modern social conditions that have called for greater state control.   This has increasingly pushed custom to its place of innocent irrelevance.

3. Duguit

1.   Duguit's method is scientific positivism. Thus, his theory is grounded in the premises of facts, not ideology.   Through this method he discovers social solidarity as a fact.   From this fact he derives three rules of conduct: one, that one ought not to prevent the accomplishment of the end of social solidarity and one ought to cooperate toward achieving that end; two, one ought to abstain from an act contrary to the end of social solidarity; and, three, one ought to do everything to increase social solidarity.   He thus claims to be able to derive his values (ought) from facts (is).   This is a fallacy.   As

discussed earlier, one cannot derive an ought conclusion from an is premise. He commits this fallacy again when he argues that courts should nullify
statutes that do not promote the public service.
These ought conclusions are issuing from enthymematically concealed ought premises.

2. Consequently, his conclusions are dogmatic
expressions, not logical derivations. Instead of respecting facts, as professed by scientific positivism,
he has replaced the dogmas of some of the earlier
theories of law with the dogmas favored by his own
theory. Specifically, he has replaced the dogmas of
individualism, subjectivism, and moralism with the
dogmas of collectivism, objectivism, and realism.
In doing so, he has marshalled the assistance of the
least discernible of all facts, namely, history, in
which facts can be found to support either of these
dogmatic sets.

3. Under Duguit's theory, laws are dictated by
the objective conditions of social cooperation.
However, congruence of laws with such objective
conditions may be a desirable goal to strive for, but
laws are in fact made by humans in accordance
with their perceptions, proclivities, and prejudices,
often either in ignorance of or disregard for the
objective conditions for good.

4. Duguit gives judges the power to nullify statutes that contravene social solidarity. This may be
dangerous. Giving such broad powers to the court,
with no restrictions other than the injunction to
apply social solidarity, can easily lead to judicial

despotism and defeat progress intended by reform legislation. In fact, this has many times been the case even in systems that have worked more under an idea of checks and balances than under an unbridled principle of social solidarity.

5. While Duguit is quite right in pointing out the fact that social tasks and needs increase as the society grows in its complexity, he underestimates the growth in governmental authority as the instrumentality possessed of the capability for meeting these needs. He may not have entirely ignored this rise in the strength of central authority, for he does suggest that a proof of the existence of a legal norm would be found in the rising of an active group against someone attacking social solidarity. However, such rising is not a reliable guarantee against the miscarriage of social solidarity by the central authority.

6. Duguit expunges ethics from law and infuses service in its place. Thereby, he claims to have avoided idealism and metaphysics. However, in postulating his own law of social solidarity, he has set up yet another idealist concept, the metaphysics of which are quite comparable to those of Kant's idealism of freedom or the precepts of the natural law philosophers.

7. Finally, Duguit's social solidarity, too, like the idealist and natural law methodologies, is capable of being filled with whatever content one wishes of it, ranging all the way from liberty to suppression of liberty, from social progress to social

reaction, and so on. As Friedmann has pointed out, Duguit's notion of function and duty has been used in Soviet jurisprudence to exclude individual rights, eliminate private law, and assimilate all law to administration, and his anti-revolutionary syndicalism has been used by the Fascist jurisprudence to combat Marxist conceptions, to frustrate organization of workers in trade unions, and to impose an all-powerful state.

4. Jurisprudence of Interests

1. The jurisprudence of interests suffers from the problems that exist in the sociological jurisprudence generally. In addition, the jurisprudence of interests points to the balancing of interests but does not give much assistance to the crucial question of how that balancing is to be done.

2. The classification and enumeration of interests with which Pound has filled volumes cannot give us a reliable guide to identifying conflicting interests in society, since these change from time to time and from society to society. Moreover, the classification scheme itself manifests the particular evaluative judgment of the classifier.

5. Free Law

1. The free law argument gives too much power to the judges with practically no restraints. Thereby, it paves an easy path to judicial despotism. To say, as Ehrlich does, that judicial decision is not

arbitrary because it is characterized by the principles of judicial tradition that heeds to the past
legal records, statutes, judicial decisions, and legal
literature, is to ignore the fact that all of these
have to be interpreted and applied as the judge
sees fit.

2. This theory shifts the concern altogether
from the substance of law to the proper selection of
judges. It thereby unduly minimizes the role that
law plays in expressing the collective and dominant values of a society.

CHAPTER 9

PSYCHOLOGICAL THEORY
OF LAW

THEORY

Leon Petrazycki is the most prominent exponent of the psychological theory of law.

According to him, realities consist only of physical objects and living organisms, on the one hand, and psychic phenomena, on the other. Imaginary, abstract, and verbal objects do not exist as independent realities.

Observation is the fundamental method of studying all phenomena, whether physical or spiritual.

Legal phenomena occur in the consciousness of one who is experiencing rights and duties at a particular point of time. Self-observation and introspection of the phenomena are necessary for one to have any cognition of them. We acquire knowledge of only those psychic phenomena that we have ourselves experienced. However, our inward, psychic acts may be observed externally in the bodily movements produced to communicate them, such as gesture, speech, and so on. By observing the same actions on the part of others, we suppose that they are based on the same psychic experiences.

Thus, as Petrazycki sees it, the scientific method of cognition is a joint method of inward and outward observation. Accordingly, the study of law is the study of different classes of external manifestations of legal experiences and of the differences between these experiences and the manifestation of related psychic processes. This method can be simple or experimental. The experimental method is just as applicable to this study as to the study of any field of psychic experiences of others.

These positivistic and empirical foundations lead him not to see legal rules and abstract legal principles as crucial to the understanding of the legal phenomena but to see the actual workings of the human mind that experiences the sense of duty and the rightfulness of a claim. Law and morality are to be observed in our experiences of obligation. They are psychological human experiences containing negative or positive valuation and a dynamic consciousness of duty. The negative valuation occurs when, in contemplating or observing certain action, we experience a restraint not to perform it or a repulsion against it issuing from a mystical authoritative pressure as if from some superior source. The positive valuation occurs when, in such contemplation or observation, we experience a feeling of approval and attraction accompanied by a prodding, impulse, or stimulation to perform

the action in question, which feeling, too, issues
from a mystical authoritative pressure from above.

Therefore, law or morality is a projection of our
legal or moral emotional experience. The meaning
of the term emotions in Petrazycki's theory is not
limited to the feeling of pleasure and pain but
extends to motoric drives or impulsive urges to
action. These drives or impulses are distinguished
from decisions based on will in that the latter are
deliberate choices made between alternative ways
of action. Emotions are of two kinds: one, emotions that have specific well defined objects, such
as the appetitive emotions wherein the objects attract us (e.g., hunger, thirst, sex) and the repulsive
emotions wherein the objects repel us (fear); and,
two, abstract or blank emotions that can be connected with a variety of actions as their stimuli
and objects. Legal, moral, and aesthetic emotions
are of the latter kind.

Thus, in Petrazycki's theory, both law and morality exist in the psychic realm. They are distinguished by difference in the kinds of emotion. In
moral experience, there is only the awareness of
duty, that is to say, an authoritative restraint
impending a certain action but unaccompanied by
the conviction that someone else has the right to
its non-performance, or an authoritative impulse to
perform a certain act but unaccompanied by the
conviction that someone else has the right to its
performance. An example would be giving alms to
a beggar. In legal experience, the sense of one's

own or someone else's duty is accompanied by the conviction that another person has a right to it.

Thus, legal emotions are imperative-attributive of claim or right at the same time. While, therefore, moral obligations remain general, legal obligations tend toward concreteness of what is due. Consequently, Petrazycki concludes that there are no moral rights. The entire field of justice (intuitive laws) belongs to law, since justice is a process that occurs within the realm of legal psychology. The case is not that moral sentiments influence and modify legal rules, as claimed by traditional theories, but that intuitive law emotions produce changes in positive and official law.

The consequence of regarding the imperative-attributive character as the distinguishing feature of law is that the realm of law is extended to a much broader area than traditionally understood. As Petrazycki points out, it includes games, sports, domestic behavior of children, parents and maids, behavior of teachers, behavior in social hospitality and etiquette, religious law, relations among members of criminal gangs, relations of lovers, friends and relatives, and so on.

On the basis of imperative-attributive experience, law is divided by Petrazycki into the categories of (1) intuitive and positive law, and (2) official and unofficial law.

The division of law into intuitive and positive comprises imperative-attributive experiences that are completely independent of the idea of any authoritatively normative facts, such as statute, customs, etc.

Intuitive law is distinguished from positive law not in the sense of intuitive law being the desired or ideal law and the positive law being the existing law but in the sense of whether or not the imperative-attributive experiences refer to normative facts. The content of intuitive law is intellectual and is characterized by the absence of ideas of normative facts. From this, four consequences follow.

One, the content of intuitive law is individually diverse, since that content is defined by each person's individual conditions, although it may very well be that these conditions are common to a number of individuals, which fact results in a congruity of their intuitive law. Positive law, however, has a uniform pattern of rules for larger or smaller masses of people, since its content is defined by perceptions of external facts.

Two, the directives of intuitive law conform with the individual circumstances of a given life situation, whereas the directives of positive law are constrained by a preordained pattern of precepts, customs, or decisions that ignore individual peculiarities.

Three, intuitive law develops gradually and symmetrically, with free variability and adaptability, whereas positive law lags behind the present spiritual and economic life due to the fixation of its content by normative facts, which are facts of the past.

It does not follow from the above that intuitive law is necessarily better in content or more perfect or ideal than positive law. In fact, the contrary is quite possible. Its content can be poorer than that of the corresponding positive law because the content of the intuitive law depends upon the conditions of individual development that may be lacking in the family's legal education, or because the intuitive law worked by mutual psychic communion in groups of persons with opposing common interests would prefer one set of interests to the prejudice of others, or because that part of society that directs legislation may be more enlightened than the intuitive law of the backward strata.

Four, the propositions of intuitive legal consciousness are infinite in scope and unlimited in applicability, whereas the rules of conduct are based on authoritative-normative facts and are, therefore, limited to the time subsequent to the publication of the command and prior to its abrogation, as well as to the place (state, city, or house) to which they relate and to the persons to whom they are related.

Thus, while rights and obligations of positive law are temporary and local, those of the intuitive law are universal. They exist always and everywhere. Moreover, intuitive norms are true and valid *per se,* since impulsions are connected to the ideas of certain conduct as such, regardless of anyone's commands or customs, whereas the significance of positive norms is conditional. In the legal mentality, therefore, they have a higher ranking.

Intuitive law is an essential factor of individual conduct and social phenomena. It operates exclusively in many areas of our relations, such as relations with neighbors, family members, lovers, friends, and so on. In those areas where problems of conduct are foreseen and decided by positive law, people are guided not by legal injunctions but by their intuitive law. Therefore, according to Petrazycki, it is not positive law but intuitive law that is the basis of legal order and the power that actuates the social life.

Petrazycki points out that there are certain causal tendencies that are found in the functioning of legal psychology but not in the functioning of moral psychology, namely, (a) the tendency to reach the implementation of law regardless of the obligor's wishes; (b) the tendency toward hate and repression in law because of its attributive character, as distinguished from the peaceful character of morality; (c) the tendency to construct a unitary, positive, and heteronomous pattern of general rules to prevent disputes and determine rights and duties, as distinguished from morality, which lacks such a unifying tendency; (d) the tendency toward concreteness of content and scope of legal duties and rights, as distinguished from moral duties, which remain mostly vague and general and indicate only a direction of an action but not its specific limits; (e) the tendency to anchor rights and duties in verifiable facts and not in facts that cannot be publicly scrutinized; and (f) the tendency for submitting legal conflicts to third-party judgment, state courts being one such means. These tendencies result in the establishment of a durable, well defined, and coordinated system of social behavior that we recognize as the legal order.

Law, for Petrazycki, performs two social functions, namely, the distributive function and the organizational function. The distributive function consists in the distribution of goods of economic value mainly through the concept of ownership. The organizational function consists in attributing to certain persons the right to issue orders and in attributing to other persons the duty to obey.

As Petrazycki sees it, the long-range history of law exhibits three evolutionary tendencies: one, a decrease in the motivational pressure (sanction and award) of the law; two, a shift from crude stimuli (fear) to subtler incentives (profit motive), from egoistic to the mixed to the altruistic motives; and, three, a steady increase in the demands of law.

CRITICISMS

1. Petrazycki distrusts the linguistic usage of words in ordinary language. Ordinary language, he maintains, is often misleading. Freed from it, he makes his inquiry into law and, as a result, expands the realm of law to such areas as games,

sports, etiquettes, relations of lovers, relations of criminal gangs, and so on. However, it is one thing not to let ordinary language restrict the scientific inquiry but quite another, and not a very satisfactory one, to use the term law for matters so far afield as relations between lovers or gangsters. There may very well be a common psychological element in all of the above relations and law as commonly understood in ordinary language, but is law of jurisprudence the correct notion to designate that element?

2. There is no scientific criterion in Petrazycki's theory for judging whether intuitive law is good or bad. Consequently, what is left of it is merely a formal system. In that respect, it is not unlike the purely legal positivism of Austin or Kelsen, discussed above, which Petrazycki criticizes. His own theory, inasmuch as it fails to provide a scientific method of distinguishing between the good content of legal impulsions and the bad, remains formal like the positivist theories and, to that extent, unsatisfactory. This is especially so for a theory that professes, as Petrazycki's theory does, to provide a scientific theory of legal reform.

CHAPTER 10

AMERICAN REALIST THEORIES

The realist theories about law are of two types: the American and the Scandinavian. The two are related only by the word realism. Other than that, there is no similarity between the two. American realism is a pragmatic and behavioral approach to social institutions. Scandinavian is a philosophical critique of the metaphysical foundations of law, a psychological approach to law, and sometimes a combination of the behavioral and psychological approaches.

In this chapter we shall examine the American realism. The Scandinavian realism will be examined in the next chapter.

THEORIES

John Chipman Gray (1839–1915) and Oliver Wendell Holmes, Jr. (1841–1935) were the founders of the American realist movement in law. The movement found its philosophical support in the logic of John Dewey (1859–1952) and the pragmatism of William James (1842–1910). It was elaborated by other exponents, prominently by Karl N. Llewellyn (1893–1962), Joseph W. Bingham (b. 1878), and Jerome Frank (1889–1957).

We shall first make a note of the philosophical underpinnings of American realism in Dewey's logic and James' pragmatism. Then we shall examine the various expressions of it.

A. PHILOSOPHICAL FRAMEWORK OF AMERICAN REALISM: JOHN DEWEY (1859–1952) AND WILLIAM JAMES (1842–1910)

Dewey develops an instrumental or experimental logic as a theory of inquiry. Its function is to study the methods used most successfully to gain and warrant our knowledge.

In this process of inquiry, there are three stages. An antecedent condition of these stages is the indeterminateness or internal conflict of a situation wherein the inquirer experiences a "felt difficulty." The first stage is the formulation of problems to be solved. This may be successively refined in the course of the inquiry. The second stage is the suggestion of a hypothesis relevant for solving the problem. Deductive reasoning may have to be resorted to in some complex inquiries in order to refine the hypotheses and ascertain their logical consequences. The final stage is experimental testing wherein the suggested hypotheses are confirmed or disconfirmed. If the inquiry is successful, the original indeterminate situation is transformed into a unified whole. The objective of inquiry is knowledge. Knowledge gained in a specific inquiry serves as the background for further inquiry.

This is a general schema for all inquiry. Its specific procedures will vary with different types of inquiry and different kinds of subject matter. Also, a specific inquiry cannot be completely isolated from the context of other inquiries, since its rules, procedures, and evidentiary requirements are derived from other successful inquiries. Moreover, all inquiry presupposes a social or public context that is the medium for finding the warranted conclusions and norms for further inquiry. Furthermore, inquiry is essentially a self-corrective process, so that a knowledge claim, norm, or rule may be criticized, revised, or abandoned in light of subsequent inquiry.

Therefore, for Dewey, there are not absolute first truths that are given or known with certainty. The rationality of inquiry and of its object (knowledge) arises from the fact that inquiry is a self-corrective process whereby we gradually become clearer about the epistemological status of both our starting points and our conclusions.

American legal realism follows this logic of inquiry.

It is also governed by the pragmatist philosophy.

William James is the principal exponent of pragmatism, although its origin must be ascribed to C.S. Peirce. James himself acknowledges that origin.

According to James, the pragmatic method is a method of settling otherwise interminable metaphysical disputes. It interprets each notion by tracing its respective practical consequences. If no practical difference can be traced from holding true one notion or another, then all dispute with respect thereto is idle, since the alternatives mean practically the same thing. In a serious dispute, we must be able to show some practical difference from the fact of one side or the other being right.

Under this thought, our whole conception of an object consists of our conception of the effects of a practical kind that the object may involve. Thus, pragmatism takes the empiricist attitude, rejects *a priori* reasoning, and turns to facts.

It is claimed only as a method. Therefore, it does not stand for any special results. It consists in the attitude of orientation that looks away from first things, principles, categories, and supposed necessities and that, instead, looks toward last things, fruits, consequences, and facts.

American realism developed within the philosophical framework of experimental logic and pragmatism. Of course, its propositions are not entirely original in legal philosophy. Such things have already been said by Han Fei Tzu (China, 280?–233 B.C.), discussed in Chapter 6, and the free law movement (Germany, early twentieth century).

B. EXPRESSIONS OF AMERICAN REALISM

1. Law as Rules of Conduct Laid Down by Judges: John Chipman Gray (1839–1915)

Gray believes that the state exists to protect and promote human interests. The state does so primarily through the means of rights and duties. However, there is no universal knowledge of these rights and duties. Consequently, no one knows perfectly his own rights and duties and those of others.

The state establishes judicial organs in order to determine the rights and duties of the state and its citizens in actual life. The judges determine those rights and duties by settling what facts exist and by laying down rules according to which they deduce legal consequences from facts. According to Gray, these rules are the law. Thus, he defines the law of the state or of any organized body of men as the rules that the judicial organs of that body lay down for the determination of legal rights and duties.

As he sees it, the courts, with the consent of the state, have been constantly applying rules that were not in existence and were, therefore, not knowable by parties when the causes of the controversy between them occurred. The courts are not willing to face this fact because they do not wish to call attention to the fact that they are making *ex post facto* law. However, the main function of a judge is not to declare the law but to maintain peace by deciding controversies. In a question that has never been decided, he must decide the case somehow and he lays down some rule that meets acceptance with the courts. That rule is the law, which was not known or knowable by the parties to the controversy.

2. Law as Prophecy of What the Courts Will Do: Oliver Wendell Holmes, Jr. (1841– 1935)

Holmes approaches the understanding about the nature of law from the point of view of results. Therefore, he takes the viewpoint of a bad man. This bad man cares nothing about good or evil or about praise or blame of his fellow men and is deterred only by tangible penalties. Holmes maintains that this bad man does not care for the axioms or deductions. He only wants to know what the courts are likely to do in fact. Therefore, Holmes defines law as the prophecies of what the courts will do in fact. This prediction is all that we are interested in knowing in matters of law.

Holmes believes that it is only in the broadest sense of logic that law is a logical development, like everything else, in as much as every part of the universe is effect and cause. However, a system of law cannot be worked out from some general axioms of conduct. Any conclusion can be given a logical form, but behind this form lies a judgment as to the relative importance of competing legisla-

tive grounds. Such judgments of relative importance vary with time and place.

3. Law as What Certain Officials Do About Disputes: Karl N. Llewellyn (1893–1962)

Llewellyn, too, concentrates on disputes in identifying the field of law. Actual disputes call for
somebody to do something about them so that
there may be peace for the disputants and for
others disturbed by the dispute and a solution may
be reached. It is the task of law to do something
reasonable about disputes. The persons who perform this function are officials of law, such as
judges, sheriffs, clerks, jailors, or lawyers. Accordingly, he defines law as what the officials of law do
about disputes.

He modifies this definition by pointing out that
the main thing is what the officials are going to do,
whether their actions relate to disputes or anything else. He admits that this definition is only a
partial statement of the whole truth in that it fails
to give an adequate account of law as a shaped
instrument that is changing or casting for the
ideal.

The essential aspect of the realist jurisprudence
is a movement in thought and work about law. He
enumerates nine features of this movement: (1)
the conception of law as a judicial creation and as
being constantly in flux; (2) the conception of law
as a means to social ends so that it needs be
continually examined for its purpose and effects;

Sinha—Jurisprudence NS—10

(3) the conception of the society changing faster than the law so that the law has to be reexamined for society's needs; (4) the temporary divorce of is (observation, description, and establishment of relations between the things described) and ought (value judgments) for purposes of study; (5) distrust of traditional rules and concepts to describe what courts or people are actually doing, and emphasis on rules as generalized predictions of what courts will do; (6) distrust of the theory that traditional prescriptive rule-formulations are the exclusive factors in judicial decisions; (7) the belief in grouping cases and legal situations into narrower categories than in the past; (8) the insistence on evaluating any part of law in terms of its effects; and (9) the insistence on sustained and programmatic attack on the problems of law along any of these lines.

Consequently, the movement follows the following lines of approach: (1) a rationalization that views opinions not as reflecting the process of deciding cases but as arguments made after the decision has been reached, in order to make the decision seem plausible; (2) a discrimination among rules as to their relative significance; (3) a replacement of general categories by specific correlations of fact-situations; and (4) a study of personal (personality of judges) as well as quantitative (statistical inquiries into available remedies) factors in the law.

4. Law as Generalization of Potential Legal Effect and Considerations Weighed by Courts in the Decision of Cases: Joseph W. Bingham (b. 1878)

Law, according to Bingham, is the field of a practical science and of a practical art. It partakes of a practical science inasmuch as lawyers try to forecast potential legal consequences of particular causal facts. It partakes of a practical art inasmuch as they try to influence the actual trend of concrete legal consequences.

There are three aspects to judicial generalizations. Firstly, they often make historical summaries of past decisions. These summaries are not important in solving a present legal problem and have no logical authoritative force upon future decisions. Secondly, they often predict legal consequences, thereby dictating or promising decisions. Thirdly, they may be considered as elements that cause decision. Accordingly, they must be weighed and analyzed with other facts to determine their causal efficiency in inducing the decision.

It is superstitious to believe that law necessarily preexists, that it is general and authoritative, and that judges do not have power to make the law but only to interpret and apply it. The judicial function lies in the orderly settlement of disputes between the parties, not in legislation. Adjudication concerns only concrete cases.

For Bingham, it would be illogical to settle most questions by generalizations that are broader than the concrete case. To dictate decisions in future cases not yet before the court is to legislate, and courts do not legislate. A generalization may be a material step in the court's reasoning toward a decision, but it does not thereby become a rule of law. Moreover, judicial generalizations have defects that are inherent in most reasoning, such as determinations by instinctive processes, lack of experiments to cover the entire field of generalizing in detail, and misapprehension and misinterpretation of controlling ideas and impulses. Due to these defects, judicial generalizations cannot be relied upon without thorough scrutiny, analysis, and corroboration.

Therefore, there is nothing authoritative in the existence of a rule or principle. A rule or principle is an abstract comprehension of considerations that would weigh with courts in deciding a concrete question. These generalizations are valid rules or principles of law only if they accurately indicate potential legal effect. It is the courts, according to Bingham, that produce these effects.

5. Law From a Psychoanalytical Point of View: Jerome Frank (1889–1957)

As Frank sees it, law is uncertain, indefinite, and subject to incalculable changes.

However, for him, this uncertainty is not an unfortunate accident but, rather, of immense social value, for otherwise the society would be straitjacketed and unable to adapt to the realities of the ever changing social, industrial, and political conditions.

From the point of view of the average man, law is a decision of a court with respect to a particular set of facts affecting a particular person. No law exists for those facts until a court has decided on them. Until then, there is only the opinion of lawyers, which is none other than a guess as to what a court will decide. As to a given situation, therefore, law is either actual as to a specific past situation or probable as to a specific future decision.

Psychologically, the process of judging seldom begins with a premise from which a conclusion is subsequently worked out. Instead, judgments, including judicial judgments, are worked out backward from tentatively formulated conclusions. Decisions are based on the judge's hunches. These hunch-producers, or the stimuli that prompt a judge to try to justify one conclusion rather than another, include rules and principles. But there are other hunch-producers as well. These are the hidden factors in the inferences and opinions of ordinary men, the judges being ordinary men. These factors depend upon the peculiarly individual traits of the persons whose inferences and opinions are to be explained. The peculiar traits, disposition, biases, and habits of a judge determine what he decides to be the law.

Therefore, in order to know the hunch-producers that make the law we must know the personality

of the judge. Law may vary with the personality
of the judge who happens to decide a given case.
This variation from judge to judge is not discoverable, at least not so at the time when Frank wrote,
due to the method of reporting cases and the verbal tricks used by judges to conceal disharmony
among them. Rules and principles do not constitute law, although they are among the causative
factors of the conduct of judges. Personality of the
judge is, for Frank, the pivotal factor in that conduct.

Thus, law is not certain.

The desire for certainty in law is a childish
emotion seeking a father-figure. Modern mind,
Frank argues, must grow out of this father complex. It must become pragmatic and eliminate the
childish dread of paternal omnipotence and respect
for it. This dread and this respect are strongholds
of resistance to change.

Frank's ideal is the 'completely adult lawyer'
who needs no external authority and who is possessed of a constructive doubt that enables him to
develop law in accord with advancing civilization.

CRITICISMS

1. One limitation of the American realist approach is that it can only be applied where the
judiciary is not intimidated by the legislative forces
and where the interaction of social forces is sufficiently free so as to enable their scientific weigh-

ing. Therefore, it fails for those who seek a universal definition of law.

2. Furthermore, it can apply only to a legal system whose method is case law. Only in such a system can one find judicial decisions as a body of facts.

3. In identifying the field of law as exclusively judicial, the American realists expunge rules and principles. However, this is an exaggeration of the unimportance of rules and principles. As shown below, these do have a role to play.

4. With respect to the question of ideals, there are four types of difficulties with American realism. One, it does not adequately deal with the question of ideals of law. The fact that these ideals do exist cannot be doubted. The realists themselves do not doubt it. However, by separating is from ought and concentrating only on is, they have ignored the problem of ideals from their theory. Two, as a result of this procedure, realism, too, becomes only a formalistic approach, incapable of the reform that its advocates seem to desire. Three, it allows a framework in which any preferred ideology can be promoted. Even at that, the range of idealogues permitted is limited to those who become judges or comparable officials. Four, it provides no means for distinguishing good law from bad law.

5. By reducing law to the fact of judicial behavior, American realism has eliminated any distinction between facts and law. However, such a dis-

tinction does exist both in the legal profession and in the ordinary usage of language. The distinction needs be clarified, not eliminated.

6. The method of legal rules, as distinguished from the realist method, consists both of formal rules and judicially formulated rules that fill gaps in the formal rules. Therefore, the realists' criticism of that regime as totally mechanistic does not accurately reflect that process.

7. The procedure of the American realists is to focus upon the wording of the law and then criticize it as being an inadequate statement of legal phenomena and therefore inappropriate for defining that phenomenon. However, this procedure misses the fact that it is not the wording or the text of a law that is operative in the decision but its meaning.

8. In maintaining that law would stand still if rules decided cases, the American realists ignore the fact that law adapts itself to the constantly changing conditions by asking what the legislator in a statute or the judge in an opinion would have meant, or, in other words, by discovering the objective meaning of the statute or the opinion.

9. When the realists point to the uniqueness of the concrete case and hold that the legislator could not have intended the inclusion of that which has not yet occurred, they overlook the fact that the statute refers to classes of things and not to individual objects.

10.   The realists believe that an institution exists in the fact that people behave in certain patterns.   However, a social institution cannot be studied without recourse to the rules that govern it.

11.   A great number of jural relations never make it to the court.   The realist approach would simply have to ignore them, since it looks at the courts as the exclusive field of law.

12.   The realists regard legal science in the model of natural science and claim that it is empirical and its purpose is prediction, as opposed to regarding it as a rational and normative science that attempts at transforming the given law into a generally consistent system of rules.   However, as Kantorowicz has pointed out, such an approach suffers from six confusions.   Firstly, it confuses natural science and cultural science.   Natural science deals with laws of nature that remain inviolable, whereas cultural sciences deal with human actions, governed by human laws, which actions can be lawful or unlawful.   Secondly, it confuses explanation with justification.   The method of natural science is explanation through cause and effect, whereas the method of a rational and normative science is justification through reason and consequence.   The judicial decision is not an explanation but a justification.   Thirdly, it confuses law and ethics.   It confuses legal with moral norms, since legal norms demand external behavior but the moral norms always take into account the

motive. Fourthly, it confuses realities with their meaning. Law is concerned with the meaning of observable realities, but meanings are not empirically observable. Fifthly, it confuses the concept with a constituent element of that concept. The case is not that law is what the courts administer but that courts are the institutions that administer the law. Finally, it confuses cases with case law. It is not the case that is binding but the case law that is binding, since only the *rationes decidendi* are binding. *Rationes decidendi* are not facts that could be put to empirical research. They are constructions of purposive interpretation.

13. The American realists call a decision the behavior of the judges. However, this does not seem correct. Behavior connotes those physical acts that are connected with the judge's organism. However, the legal effect of his decision is quite different from the physical effects of his behavior. While a legal decision relates remote situations through a purely logical connection, a judge's behavior relates to the physical world and operates continuously in time and space.

14. A legal decision does not follow the pattern of physical causation, either. Thus, obedience to the decision by one on whom it is legally binding depends on an independent judgment and will.

15. Holmes' bad man is not a very convincing character. Holmes makes him worry about judicial scorn but be totally indifferent to extralegal penalties. It is hard to conceive of a temperament

that would be so worried about judicial penalty but not at all worried about other penalties. Be that as it may, it seems that his calculus of whether it is worth risking the judicial penalty for his action would involve a moral evaluation of his act, and that is not a matter of fact.

16. Holmes maintains that rights and duties resolve themselves into nothing other than a prediction of what the courts will do about them. However, an inquiry into what the courts are going to do involves an investigation into the reasons underlying the institution that gives rise to these rights and duties, for only by such an inquiry is it possible to predict what the courts will do.

17. Bingham has substituted the behavior of the judge for the behavior of the people as the substance of the law. Rules, according to him, are not part of the law but are merely subjective ideas in the minds of those who think about the law. His dualistic metaphysics posit a mind and a world external to it. While the external expression of principles and rules exists outside of the mind, the principles and rules themselves cannot exist outside of the mind. Thus, according to him, meaning exists only in the mind of the speaker or writer.

However, that does not seem to be true. It seems that the meaning of things follows from the nature of the things considered, whereas its apprehension depends on the objective existence of such meaning and on our ability to apprehend it. Therefore, it is not correct to say that the meaning

of things depends on the mind of the speaker or
writer. Meanings are genuine parts of the objective world that we apprehend. As Morris Cohen
points out, the nominalist (denial of rules) thinking
in which Bingham engages confuses the existence
of particular images in individual minds with the
objective meaning of principles or rules in the
world that is common to us. Therefore, rules and
principles exist in objective reality, not, as claimed
by Bingham, in the minds of those who think about
the law. Even Bingham himself admits that
courts are and should be governed by constitutional provisions and legislative enactments, which are
clearly formulated in general rules.

18. Frank has ridiculed the craving for certainty as childish. However, denial of it would, in
Morris Cohen's elegant words, be "complete mad-
ness". As Cohen puts it, "[i]f I actually doubt that
stones will continue to lie on the ground if undisturbed, that my body is material, and that my
fellow beings continue to exist, the last named will
for their and my protection have to lock me up in
some asylum." Frank's objective in his theory is
to deny certainty of the law. However, his mistake
lies in not being able to see that the problem in law
is not the eradication of certainty but finding the
precise relation between the certain and uncertain
elements in the law.

CHAPTER 11

SCANDINAVIAN REALIST
THEORIES OF LAW

Scandinavian realism rejects natural law as well as analytical positivism and it introduces its own concepts as below. Its most prominent exponent is Axel Hagerström (1869-1939). It is further developed by his disciples, namely, Karl Olivecrona (b. 1897), A. Vilhelm Lundstedt (1882-1955), and Alf Ross (b. 1899).

THEORIES

1. Law as Conative Impulse: Axel Hagerström (1869-1939)

Hagerström examines the psychological implications of a command. According to him, the content of a command is different from the content of a threat accompanying that command. The imperative in a command is meant categorically and is not intended to arouse the idea that something ought to happen merely in the realization of a positive value or the avoidance of a negative value on the part of the person commanded.

Therefore, threat is only an appendix to the command. Its use consists in inducing the address-

ee to act in a certain way by means of additional
motives. Command does not refer to any value for
the recipient. The issuer of the command influences its receiver by his mere utterance of it, not
because the utterance is intended to arouse in the
recipient the idea that a certain wish or volition
exists in the issuer, or because it is a direct expression of a personal wish or volition of the issuer, or
because it arouses in the recipient a wish to act in
a certain way, without referring to the recipient's
scheme of values. Without arousing wishes as
motives, it effects an association between a feeling
of conative impulse and the idea of a certain action.

This mode of influence has the character of a
practical suggestion, since it does not use the motives of the person influenced, and has, as its
condition, the existence of special relations between the active and the passive party, such as a
superiority of power that makes the recipient sus-
ceptible to the issuer's influence.

The imperative form is explained by Hagerström
as something that functions merely as an auxiliary
to the power accruing to the mention of an action
when that mention makes the idea of that action
predominant. Its function is to break down the
resistance to the command arising from opposing
impulses, doing so by arousing a direct intention to
act in the way commanded. When that is not
necessary, all it does is to keep in check possible
opposing conative impulses.

The imperative form is concerned with the state of consciousness that is intention.

There are two factors in consciousness of intention, namely, a feeling of conative impulse and the idea of a certain action. The imperative form ("Thou shalt") represents the conative impulse. "I will" represents the idea of a certain action. An imperative does not express an already existing feeling of conative impulse in the issuer of the command. Rather, it arouses such a feeling in the recipient. Therefore, the question arises of how someone can have a consciousness of intention that refers to someone else's action. Hagerström resolves this question by arguing that one's consciousness of intention regarding someone else's action can be conceived as involving an idea in the former person of a certain intention in the latter person. Thus, in an imperative the issuer of the command has a feeling of conative impulse associated with the idea of a certain action on the recipient's part. The state of consciousness that the imperative aims at producing exists in this way also in the issuer.

The suggestion in a command, therefore, does not appeal to the recipient's system of values. Consequently, the consciousness of intention that it aims at producing does not attach any valuation to the feeling of conative impulse. It follows, then, that the command, in order to be effective without the assistance of threats, must cause in the recipient an intention that is devoid of valuation. This impulse is determined not by values that are significant for himself but by the imperative form. This explains why being influenced by a command is accompanied by a feeling of inward constraint.

Duty is connected with the imperative and consists in a feeling of inner compulsion toward a certain action. This feeling of duty, as Hagerström sees it, is also not a matter of valuation. Ascribing an inner value to a person who fulfills his duty is secondary to the feeling of duty itself. The feeling of duty is not determined either by valuation of the action as necessary to avoid unpleasantness or by reference to objective values. Rather, it is an impulse toward a certain action, and its compulsive feeling is determined by something external to the individual, regardless of his evaluatory attitude as to that action. The feeling of duty, thus, is a conative feeling, a feeling of being driven to act in a certain way.

Law, thus viewed, is a conative impulse.

2. Law as Independent Imperatives: Karl Olivecrona (b. 1897)

According to Olivecrona, a rule of law is concerned with people's conduct. Its purpose is to influence their actions. Its content is an idea of an imaginary action by a judge in an imaginary situation. Its form is imperative, not narrative. However, this imperative is neither a command nor is it something that is created by the state.

It is not a command for several reasons. A command is not a declaration of the will of the state, for command is an act through which one person seeks to influence the will of another, whereas a declaration of will is an assertion or a statement of fact intended to convey knowledge. Consequently, if rules were declarations of the will of the state they could not possibly be commands. Furthermore, a rule of law is not a command, since a command presupposes one person who commands and another to whom the command is addressed, which is not the case with an organization called the state whose machinery is run by an ever changing multitude of persons, such as heads of the government, members of the government, and members of the legislative body. These persons find rules of law in existence that are enforced on the whole. No one of them could think that the law consists of his commands, and each can only cause change in some part of the law.

Nor is law a creation of the state. The state is not an entity existing independently of law. Therefore, law cannot emanate from it. The misconception about the state being the creator of law is, for Olivecrona, due to the fact that the state organization provides a machinery for making rules psychologically effective through legislation.

Thus, according to Olivecrona, rules of law are given in the imperative form, but they are not commands, since a command in the proper sense implies a personal relationship.

They are independent imperatives. They are
nobody's commands, although the form of language
used to express them is characteristic of a command. They are imperative statements that function as guides for people's conduct and cause people to act in certain ways, independently of any
person commanding. Moreover, the imperative is
connected with such concepts as an idea for an
action, or an idea of entering into certain relationships, or the establishment of a right or duty, and
not with the concept of directing a person. The
laws of a country consist of ideas about human
behavior accumulated over centuries through the
contributions of innumerable collaborators, expressed in the imperative form by their originators
(especially through formal legislation), preserved
in the books of law, and continually revived in
human minds. There is no fundamental difference
between moral and legal rules. Their distinction
lies not in the objective character of the rule but in
the response it evokes in the mind.

Law, for Olivecrona, chiefly consists of rules
about force. The case is not that law is guaranteed
or protected by force, but that it consists chiefly of
rules about force that contain patterns of conduct
for the exercise of organized force. It is true,
Olivecrona admits, that rules contain patterns of
conduct for the private citizens but, he points out,
these patterns are only another aspect of the rules
about the use of force.

3. Law Determined by Social Welfare: Vilhelm Lundstedt (1882–1955)

Lundstedt believes that the only possible approach to coping empirically with questions of law is his method of social welfare. That method rejects the method of justice of the traditional jurisprudence. It is based on historic facts, logical criticism of legal ideology, and psychological experience.

For him, legal activities are indispensable for the existence of society. Preservation of society forms the incentive for the continued pursuit of legal activities. Therefore, the shaping of these activities by lawmakers and courts must be determined by the social organization, since social organization is the most frictionless and undisturbed functioning of the legal machinery.

Law is the very life of mankind in organized groups. It is the conditions that make it possible for individuals and social groups to coexist and to cooperate for ends other than mere existence and propagation.

As mentioned above, Lundstedt rejects the method of justice. Instead, he points to the importance of the feelings of justice in legal machinery. The feelings of justice are guided and directed by the laws as enforced (maintained). The common sense of justice would lose its ability to play its role in the legal machinery without the rules of law actually maintained. If the legal machinery stopped working, the feelings of justice would lose all bearing and control.

Lundstedt maintains that law is determined by social welfare. Social welfare, in his sense, has nothing to do with any absolute values. Instead, it involves actual evaluations of what is best for the society. It is something that is actually considered (evaluated) as useful to men in society at a certain time. It means the encouragement of that which people in society generally strive to attain. This includes all conceivable material comfort and spiritual interests.

Lundstedt notes the treatment of interests by the proponents of the jurisprudence of interests, discussed above, and denounces their categories as another legal ideology. He wishes to establish as a fact what can be observed in general, namely, that the overwhelming majority of people wish to live and develop their lives' possibilities. Thus, the area of social welfare comprises the general spirit of enterprise and a general sense of security. From this he derives such postulates as the common production and exchange of commodities, the reliability of promises, the sense of safety to life, limb, and so on.

4. Law as a Scheme of Interpretation for a Set of Social Facts That Constitute the Counterpart of Legal Norms: Alf Ross (b. 1899)

Ross presents a concept of the validity of law that combines behavioristic and psychological aspects. According to him, the concept of validity involves two factors: (a) the outward observable and regular compliance with the pattern of action; and (b) the experience of this pattern of action as being a socially binding norm.

Legal norms, for him, serve as a scheme of interpretation for a corresponding set of social acts in such a way as to make possible both (i) the comprehension of those actions as a coherent whole of meaning and motivation, and (ii) their prediction within certain limits.

The capacity of legal norms to serve as above is based on the fact that these norms are effectively complied with because they are felt to be socially binding. The body of norms known as a national legal system is distinguished from other bodies of norms by the fact that a national law system is the system of rules for the establishment and functioning of the state machinery of force.

The validity of a system of norms means that the system, because of its effectiveness, can serve as a scheme of interpretation. As applied to legal norms, this means a synthesis of psychological and behavioristic realisms. Psychological realism finds the reality of law in psychological facts, so that a norm is valid if accepted by popular legal consciousness. Behavioristic realism finds the reality of law in the actions of the courts. A tenable interpretation of the validity of the law lies in a synthesis of the psychological and the behavioristic views.

Law, then, is a process of reality, that has stabilized itself in an idea of validity as understood in the above fashion.

CRITICISMS

1. Lundstedt argues for a conception of law as the expression of a sociological probability. This is very difficult for the common human being to accept, on whom the law operates. The common person conceives of law as a binding norm. This conception is even more difficult for the judge to accept, since he cannot perform the task of law, which is his calling, by merely calculating the probable social reactions from his actions. The questions in law are not how people have decided and acted in the past or how they will probably act in the future, but how one ought or ought not to act.

2. The Scandinavian realists use such propositions as social welfare and, yet, claim to be staying away from the normative. It is difficult to see how they can do so. The conception of social welfare is claimed by Lundstedt to be based on observation of facts, but how do you merely observe facts and categorize them as welfare or its opposite? This activity necessarily involves a role for the normative. Welfare is not a category of fact but a category of evaluation.

3. Scandinavian realists fail to approach an essential problem in the realm of law, namely, the question of rightness or wrongness, goodness or

badness, or, in other words, the moral evaluation of posited laws. Even Lundstedt's concept of social welfare is fixed by its own premises of evaluation and does not admit of principle of ought other than what is. By dismissing these questions of rightness and wrongness as metaphysical, these realists are only avoiding the issue.

CHAPTER 12

PHENOMENOLOGICAL THEORIES OF LAW

We shall first attempt to understand what phenomenology is. Then we shall examine the theories about the nature of law that issue from this philosophy.

The German philosopher Johann Heinrich Lambert (1728–1777) was the first philosopher to mention phenomenology as a discipline. He viewed it as the theory of illusion, since phenomenon, to him, denoted the illusory features of human experience.

Immanuel Kant (1724–1804) gave it a broader meaning by classifying objects and events into noumena and phenomena. Noumena are things-in-themselves, or those objects and events that are as in themselves, independently of the cognitive forms that we examined in Chapter 2, above. Phenomena are objects and events as they appear in our experience. Consequently, Kant believed that only phenomena can possibly be known. Thereupon, he presented his transcendental idealist epistemology to gain knowledge thereof, as discussed above.

Hegel (1770–1831) disagreed with Kant and believed that the spirit (or mind) develops through various stages, from where it apprehends itself as phenomenon until, at the height of its full development, it is aware of itself as it is itself, or as noumenon.

Phenomenology, thus, attempts to know mind as it is in itself. It does so through studying the ways in which it makes its appearance to us.

In the mid-nineteenth century, phenomenon came to denote whatever is observed to be the case. Consequently, phenomenology became a purely descriptive study of a subject matter. Thus, William Hamilton (1788–1856) spoke of it as a purely descriptive study of mind. Eduard von Hartmann (1842–1906) thought its objective as rendering a complete description of moral consciousness. Charles Sanders Peirce (1839–1914) believed it to include not only a descriptive study of the observable but also of whatever is before the mind, real or illusionary. It was to address itself to whatever is "to be" in the widest possible meaning of the term.

The meaning of phenomena has thus grown from the middle of the eighteenth century when Lambert wrote (1764) to the early twentieth century when Peirce wrote (1902).

Although the meaning of phenomena thus changed, phenomenology itself remained one field of study related to philosophy, such as logic, ethics, or aesthetics.

However, with Edmund Husserl (1859–1938), who wrote in the early twentieth century, phenomenology became a way of doing philosophy, a method. Husserl believed that the phenomenological descriptions of intentional acts are distinguished from the descriptions of ordinary psychology by the transcendental-phenomenological reduction. This reduction is a methodological device. It consists in the transition from an ordinary attitude toward events and objects to a reflective attitude. By performing this reduction we discover the transcendental ego or pure consciousness, and we discover that whatever is in the world is so only as object for our pure consciousness.

By this method, phenomenology explores and describes a realm of being that is not accessible to empirical observation. It is accessible only to what Husserl called the eidetic intuition.

As Husserl's work progressed from 1907 to 1936, his concept of transcendental ego evolved and changed. The transcendental ego at first had an absolute character, so that everything else existed relative to it. Eventually, it lost its absolute status and became correlative to the world. Moreover, while the world earlier used to be what it is for any transcendental individual, it is now an intersubjective community of individuals.

Phenomenology, thus, changed from description of a separate realm of being to reflection upon (i) the ways in which our communal experiences come to be, (ii) the criteria for the coherence of different types of experiences, and (iii) the adequacy of these experiences.

Of course, there have been other phenomenologists since Husserl, such as Moritz Geiger, Alexander Pfander, Max Scheler, Oscar Becker, Adolf Reinach, Hedwig Conrad–Martins, and perhaps even Martin Heidegger, Jean–Paul Sartre, and Maurice Merleau–Ponty.

Looking at the overall phenomenological tendencies, it can be said that phenomenology indicates two things: one, a way of doing philosophy by using the phenomenological method as primarily outlined by Husserl; and, two, certain doctrinal themes developed by different phenomenologists, or the ontological, metaphysical, and anthropological consequences drawn by them through the use of the phenomenological method.

Thus, phenomenology appears as a variety of things. For example, it is an objective inquiry into the logic of essences and meanings, or a theory of abstraction, or a psychological description of consciousness, or a speculation on the transcendental ego, or a method of approaching concretely lived existence, or as existentialism itself. There are several kinds of phenomenology in the work of Husserl alone.

What gives a conceptual unity to this philosophical movement is its method. This method consists of a series of three reductions: (a) the philosophical reduction, which is achieved by bypassing all theories and explanatory concepts about things and thereby returning to things themselves; (b) the eidetic reduction, which is achieved by eliminating the factual elements of the object under investigation so as to perceive its essence (*eidos*) through discerning in it its typical structure; and (c) the transcendental reduction, which is achieved by bypassing other objects of consciousness so as to disclose the thing consciousness, or intentionality, thereby enabling the consciousness to perceive itself in pure transcendental ego.

According to one observer (H. Spiegelberg), there are seven steps of the phenomenological method, namely, (i) investigating particular phenomena; (ii) investigating general essences; (iii) apprehending essential relationships among essences; (iv) watching modes of appearing; (v) watching the constitution of phenomena in consciousness; (vi) suspending belief in the existence of the phenomena; and (vii) interpreting the meaning of phenomena.

THEORIES

Various attempts have been made to apply the phenomenological method to the description of law. This has resulted in various phenomenological theories of law.

These theories display three main approaches: (1) an approach that proceeds from the key concept of *Natur der Sache* (nature of the thing) and is seen in the works of certain German philosophers; (2) an approach that derives from the German phenomenological value philosophy (*Wertphilosophie*) and is adopted by certain Latin American philosophers; and (3) an approach that takes the positivist and existentialist viewpoint and is found in the works of certain French philosophers.

1. Nature of Thing Approach

The *Natur der Sache* (nature of the thing) approach believes that phenomena have certain immanent values. It translates the reality of phenomena into the world of legal institutions. This is seen in the philosophies of Gustav Radbruch, Helmut Coing, Gustav Fechner, and Werner Maihofer.

According to Radbruch, *Natur der Sache* is the moving force that transforms legal institutions in response to social change. It is a dynamic concept whereby law, being an instrument of change, responds to the changing social relationships. Thus, for example, the growth of trade unions and employer associations demanded the new institution of collective contracts to represent the new type of social relationship. Radbruch insists on the separation of the *Natur der Sache* from natural law thinking.

Coing, on the other hand, attempts to combine *Nature der Sache* with natural law. He derives certain highest principles of law from basic values and institutions. According to him, there are basic values (e.g., elementary feeling of justice) as well as institutional values (e.g., values represented by the state, economic institutions, and so on). Legal institutions have immanent values.

Fechner points to the physical factors of the *Natur der Sache* that determine legal rules, e.g., gestation, paternity, and so on.

Maihofer regards *Natur der Sache* as a source of law and a measure of justice that brings the abstract imperatives of the law in accord with the norms of conduct prescribed by the social situation of concrete legal condition. For example, this is seen in the concept of good faith or reasonableness as applied to statutory provisions.

2. Value Philosophy Approach

The value philosophy approach to law is derived from the phenomenological value philosophies (*Westphilosophie*) of the German philosophers Max Scheller and Nicolai Hartmann.

Scheller posits that values exist in a scale. Their hierarchy or ranking is determined by five criteria. One, the degree of detachment of the values from a temporal situation determines their durability. In that way, spiritual values are higher than material values. Two, the higher the values the less do they increase by extension and decrease by division. Three, lower values are founded in higher values. Four, the rank of a value is determined by the depth of satisfaction yielded by its realization. Five, the rank is determined by its relation to a specific experience, so that moral values have a more general quality than the sensual ones. Hartmann clarifies that the hierarchy of values is not an invariable and absolutely valid good. Everybody has a choice between good and evil. There is a range of actions between the two from which he has to choose.

Theories of law issuing from the value philosophy appear in the works of certain Latin–American philosophers, such as the Spanish–Mexican Luis Recasèns–Siches, the Mexican Eduardo Garcia–Meynez, the Uruguayan Juan Lambias de Asevedo, and the Argentinian Carlos Cossio.

Recasèns–Siches seeks to reconcile the objectivity of juridical values with the historicity of juridical ideals. According to him, there are five sources of this historicity: (a) the diversity and changeability of social reality; (b) the diversity of obstacles in the way of materializing a value; (c) the adequacy of the means to materialize it; (d) the priorities as determined by the social needs; and (e) the multiplicity of values that engender particular norms for a particular community in a particular situation. He argues that since individual consciousness is the center of all reality and since human life is the starting point of all philosophy, the values of humanism or personalism that regard the state and the law as subservient to the individual are higher than the values of transpersonalism that regard the individual subservient to the state.

Garcia–Meynez points out that while juridical values are objectively valid, they are not absolute.

They are characterized by various forms of relativity. This relativity arises (a) as to persons, (b) as to concrete situations, and (c) as to space and time.

Asevedo sees positive law as a mediation between the values of the community and human conduct.

Cossio presents his egological theory of law that regards law as an egological object, that is to say, as human conduct in its intersubjective interference. The judicial decision consists of (a) the logical structure given by a framework such as a constitution, (b) the contingent contents of a situation supplied by the circumstances of the case, and (c) the juridical evaluation imposed by the judge. Judges are obliged to make decisions in accordance with a conception of justice.

3. Positivist and Existentialist Approaches

Certain French philosophers have taken a positivist and existentialist approach to the phenomenological explanation of law. Most important of them is Paul Amselek.

Amselek reminds us that in order to return to law itself and to see it in its objectal purity, the phenomenological method calls for the method of reduction in both its philosophical and eidetic senses.

He finds that there are three series of irreducible elements in the *eidos* or the typical structure of the object law: (1) generic eidetic elements, wherein law presents itself as a set of norms and, therefore, belongs to the eidetic genus of the normative; (2) specific eidetic elements, wherein the norms that constitute law present themselves as ethical norms with the function of command; and (3) particular eidetic elements, wherein these commands that constitute law are part of the function of the public direction of human behavior.

These three elements constitute the *eidos* of law.

Amselek's aim is to establish a phenomenological positivism. His theory, therefore, is anti-metaphysical. He explains that the juridical phenomenon consists in the application of a norm to an object. The structure of the norm model rejects any order of values as an external model to which the norm must conform. There exist objectively observable juridical norms that are obligatory instruments of judgment. Since norms are models of occurrence in the course of things, they are models as existential content. They are, thus, opposed to concepts that are mental modes of structural content.

CRITICISMS

1. The phenomenological assertion is that facts constitute legal values *per se.* Thus, the theory claims a fusion of fact and value. According to it, human existence is a value by its very ontological structure in that man cannot exist or act without values. Therefore, these values are created because man must exist. The process of comprehen-

sion of juridical values must be perceived through
the practical activity of man at a given place and
moment of history. Values are, thus, objectively
realized in the factual activity of man. Ought does
not represent an autonomous sphere of phenomena
but only an essential particularity of the structure
of certain phenomena (such as law) that express a
thing to be realized. Instead of a dualism between
fact and value, there is an immanent sense of the
real, the totality of which is comprised of both fact
and value. In law, the identification of fact and
value is exhibited by the existence of certain factual relationships that have immanent legal value.
For example, the courts have been able to attribute
legal consequences to certain relationships that fall
outside the forms prescribed by the relevant statutes, thereby demonstrating a direct and immediate transposition of the practical situation into the
juridical universe.

However, it is difficult to accept this surfacing of
the immanent as either a fusion of fact and value
or as the abolition of the distinction between fact
and value. This may be one explanation of the
interrelationship of law and social change, and
there are others. But the mere adjustment of legal
values to new social values does not indicate fusion
of the two.

2. If fact and value merged in the nature of
things, certain inevitable values would surface.
This is an axiological fatalism. Such merging
would eliminate the crucial question of choice be-

tween different values or ideologies and would dismiss the conflict between them as non-existent. This is clearly not the case. The very issue of morality is predicated upon the existence of these choices. If one did not have these choices to make, there would be no need for moral judgment of such human acts as laws.

3. The phenomenological thesis provides a convenient disguise for any particular ideology. Thus, this thesis has led some of its adherents to believe in the development of human freedom as an existential role (Poulantzas), or in the progress toward human freedom and the classless society as essential realities of our times (Maihofer). To believe that human freedom or the classless society, or even progress toward these ends, are realities of our time is certainly too fanciful to accept. Even apart from the incredibility of this account of contemporary reality, the theoretical point remains that such a characterization is merely a disguise for a preferred ideology.

CHAPTER 13

THE CRITICAL LEGAL STUDIES MOVEMENT AND ITS OFFSHOOTS

In this chapter, we shall make a note of a jurisprudential movement called Critical Legal Studies (CLS) and its two offshoots, namely, the feminist jurisprudence and the critical race theory.

A. CRITICAL LEGAL STUDIES

The CLS movement does not compare in originality with the theories discussed in the preceding chapters, nor has it as yet presented a coherent theory. Nevertheless, it is of sufficient importance in contemporary jurisprudential thought to warrant us taking a note of it. The movement grew in the United States in the 1970s, primarily with the Conference on Critical Legal Studies, first held in 1977, and it has found a sympathetic chord in the *Critique du Droit* in France and the Critical Legal Conference in Britain. It grew in the period of disenchantment of the post-Vietnam era for the purpose of denouncing the established notions about law and legal institutions and creating an alternative view of law and society that would promote a substantive vision of human personality.

We shall observe the philosophical moorings of the CLS movement, examine major aspects of its thesis, and present its criticisms. We shall do so with an awareness that its scholarship is diverse (close to 200 scholars identify themselves with it in the United States alone) and that its positions have been shifting and even mellowing.

PHILOSOPHICAL MOORINGS

The philosophical moorings of the movement are found in the Critical Theory of the Frankfurt School, the Relativist Epistemology, and the American Legal Realism.

1. Critical Theory of the Frankfurt School

The Frankfurt School was a group of German intellectuals in the 1930s (primarily Georg Lukacs, Max Horkheimer, Theodor Adorno, Herbert Marcuse, and Jurgen Habermas) who, at the *Institut für Sozialforschung* (Institute of Social Research), reinterpreted Hegel and Marx and proposed a critical theory.

According to this School, it is a mistake to interpret Marx as a scientific social analyst giving an account of history. The appearance of being scientific arose from the idea that Marx's theory would confirm itself in social life along the scientific model. However, according to the Frankfurt School, Hegel and Marx must be understood as critics whose central claim consisted not in denouncing the naturalist philosophy and adopting the positivist philosophy but in putting the necessary distance between philosophy and critique.

To the extent Marx claimed to have delivered an objective and predictive analysis of social life, the critical theorists consider him wrong. They maintain that it is wrong to think that social theory can deliver scientific axioms. They posit two opposing tendencies: cognition and liberation. Cognition is established by dialectics of self-reflective criticism examining the resolution of theoretical conflict. Liberation is achieved by a series of assumptions about the consciousness of the agents who are being considered by the critical theory. The self-reflective nature of the theory induces the agents to liberation.

Thus, the critical theory is presented as a form of knowledge (cognition) that is inherently liberating. However, this claim in itself is not unique to the critical theory. What is unique to it is the claim that the critical theory simultaneously achieves cognition and liberation by avoiding what it considers the mistaken paths followed by positivism and naturalism. As the critical theory sees it, positivism achieves a liberating methodology by expunging the cognitive content from it but, at the same time, defining liberation in terms of a subjective empirical world. Naturalism achieves cognition by sacrificing a methodology that would confirm itself in social life. Consequently, the critical theory proposes a dialectic-of-criticism between its claims about the social world and its claims about the value of self-reflection.

Methodologically, the critical theory distinguishes itself from the empiricist method of science, from the method of theoretical consciousness (e.g., Marx), and from the method of hermeneutic inquiry or interpretation. Although it accepts the usefulness of these methods to the extent they contribute to a total method of the critical theory, it is conscious of the fact that the empirical method objectifies aspects of social life through theory or evidence, that the theoretical consciousness method attempts a similar control of social life through theory or analysis, and that the hermeneutic method of providing the best possible interpretation of the texts of theory and practice does not consider the separation of theory and action as fundamental. Therefore, none of these is considered by the critical theory as either liberating or cognitive to the full extent. The critical theory is suspicious of external control or external cognition. It adopts self-reflection.

The critical theory claims to be liberating. It is liberating because, on the one hand, it exists in the world of action, and, on the other hand, it acts as a theory for social change. To that end it seeks a critical distance from facts, a necessary distance that empiricism violated. It restricts the role of empiricism to that of elaborating the facts from which the critical distance must be kept. It considers liberal reform tendencies as wrong because they are grounded in social life and, therefore, cannot possibly comprehend the structure that contains and limits them.

The critical theory claims to be liberating not in the sense of either providing a strategy for achieving notions of freedom held by actors or persuading a set of reforms to the agents. Rather, it aims at the description of assumptions about social conditions, which assumptions could be altered by a process of theoretical and political enlightenment. When the theory produces those results, the claim is substantiated. Thus, the liberating claim becomes cognitive as well.

2. Relativist Epistemology

The CLS movement attempts to use for its purposes the relativist epistemology of the twentieth century. The tenets of this epistemology are the rejection of traditional certainties and the denial of objective truths.

Traditionally, truth was sought by relating to some permanent neutral framework, such as connecting the mutable world of appearances with the immutable realm of forms, as in Plato. Understanding is reached when language comprehends the form, or the essence, of an object. Objective reality exists and is mirrored by language. In medieval thought, the realm of forms became the work of the Christian God. By the eighteenth century, the Enlightenment resulted in a shift from theistic metaphysics. Thus, Descartes located the idea of certainty in the individual mind. Kant moved it from the individual mind to the transcendental realm of *a priori* universal mental structures. In the twentieth century, a new epistemology has emerged that rejects transcendence of any sort and confronts the absence of absolutes.

This relativist epistemology was brought forth by developments in mathematics and physics. Traditionally, mathematics and physics were thought to correspond to an objective reality. However, the mathematicians of the 1820s produced geometries based on postulates that were fundamentally different from those of Euclidean geometry. By the late nineteenth century, geometries became formal systems that were not necessarily connected with empirical reality. In the twentieth century, Einstein demonstrated a similar truth in physics, namely, that Euclidean geometry did not necessarily describe the physical universe. His relativity theory disproved that the universe is capable of a single objective description. It did so by rejecting the Newtonian concepts of absolute space and time and by claiming that both space and time constitute a four-dimensional continuum so that each must be measured against another. Quantum mechanics further separated science from transcendental reality by challenging the Newtonian physics that atoms are solid bodies moving in empty space. The quantum theory held that atomic events do not occur but only show tendencies to occur and the subatomic matter does not exist with certainty at definite places but only shows tendencies to occur. Consequently, instead of the epistemological case being that objective reality exists and is mirrored by language, the inadequacy of everyday language was exposed because quantum theory had now to redefine atoms. While traditionally atoms were viewed as particles, they now had to be redefined as both waves and particles. Moreover, Heisenberg's uncertainty principle, according to which any increase in the accuracy of the measurement of an electron's position in space decreases the probable accuracy of the measurement of its velocity, established that observers affect the phenomena observed. Furthermore, the mathematician Godel's incompleteness theorem proved that consistency in arithmetic cannot be shown by the formal deductions of arithmetic. This demonstrated the fact that the language of mathematics is necessarily an incomplete description of reality, a learning that was transferred to all languages.

The relativist epistemology resulted in two major critiques of the metaphysical or the transcendental. Firstly, the American pragmatists held that no objective *a priori* rationality existed that corresponded to experience. Secondly, the logical positivists, originating in the Vienna Circle, held that only those propositions are true that can be observationally or experimentally verified, so that all metaphysical, transcendental, and *a priori* concepts are meaningless.

One consequence of the rejection of absolutes was the embracing of ethical relativism. Sociologists argued that value systems could only be products of social, economic, and psychological pressures. Anthropologists demonstrated a range of human values. However, most American thinkers restrained relativism only to creating a dichotomy between fact and theory. They denied abstract logic as having a necessary connection with reality and they maintained that facts, not theories, describe objective reality. Facts, thus, became the source of certainty, despite Einstein's relativity theory and Heisenberg's uncertainty principle. In jurisprudence, the American Legal Realists rejected absolutes and trusted science to make objective reality accessible. They called for empirical studies of law, which they believed would yield the design for reform.

However, the objectivity of facts came to be challenged by developments in linguistics and visual arts. These developments demonstrated that facts and their perception are shaped by the preconceived categories of the observer. Linguists, such as Ferdinand de Sassure, Edward Sapir, and Benjamin Whorf, demonstrated the contingency of human categories, displacing the notion that language is governed by objective referents. Objective facts were shown to be inaccessible to human beings. Even perceptions were shown to be subject to the contingent categories of language. Artists and art historians, too, demonstrated that facts are dependent on the observer's interpretation.

The experience of certainty came to be reexamined, especially through the examination of languages by the linguists and the examination of culture by the anthropologists. Thus, among the linguists, Sapir contended that no two languages are sufficiently similar to be regarded as representing the same social reality. Whorf maintained that linguistic pattern determined perception as well as thought. Sassure argued that the meaning of signs issued from their relationship to other signs within a sign system and not from some actual relationship to referents in the world. For Sassure, therefore, knowledge depended on human beings alone, not upon fixed referents. This approach was applied to the study of culture. Thus, historians, such as Lucien Febvre, moved the historiographical focus from the history of ideas to the history of mental structures. Philosophers, such as Ludwig Wittgenstein, argued that no single reality existed independently of the observer's interpretations. According to him, the basis of cognition is human agreement and not a transcendent reality. He thus moved the relativist epistemology beyond ethical relativism by proposing the standard of human agreements.

In the 1970s, thinkers began to examine the relative status of science and literature and argued that all disciplines, whether scientific or nonscientific, provided only interpretations of texts and not access to objective truth. Science had no superior status to that of mere subjectivity. Thus, historians of science, such as Thomas Kuhn and Paul

Feyeraband, contended that scientific models did not describe outside reality objectively. Scientific models were interpretations dependent on the observer's perspective. Anthropologists, such as Clifford Geertz, substituted an interpretive theory of culture for the objective observations of behavioral facts. Any interpretation, Geertz maintained, is partial. The French post-structuralists, such as Roland Barthes, argued that a text could have a meaning only in terms of the interpretative framework chosen, so that no interpretation could be objective. Literature, according to them, institutionalized subjectivity. They also pointed to the pervasiveness of ideology or interpretation, so that no interpretation is innocent. Post-structuralist thought, thus, went beyond the classical structuralism developed by the French anthropologist Claude Levi–Straus after World War II, who had argued that culture generates meaning because of the relationships among its elements and not because these elements are inherently meaningful. The post-structuralists shifted their eyes to interpretation.

The post-structuralist discovery that no objective texts exist led to two interpretations in the 1970s and 1980s. On the one hand, critics such as Stanley Fish maintained that everything in the text is the product of interpretation. Therefore, a description of what the text does to the reader is a description of what the reader does to the text. However, this does not result in interpretive anarchy because there exist interpretive communities made up of those who share interpretive strategies not for reading but for writing texts. On the other hand, the deconstructionists, pioneered by the French philosopher Jacques Derrida, posit that all texts reflect the belief in objective truth. Therefore, he argues, the critic's role is to deconstruct this metaphysics by exposing how the text undermines its own claims to truth and how its meaning is in fact contingent.

3. American Realism

The CLS scholars claim their ancestry in the American Legal Realists of the 1920s and 1930s, discussed above in Chapter 10. They connect themselves to the critical tradition of the Realists, but they reject the Realist program. Thus, they accept the indeterminacy contention of the Realists that legal reasoning can rarely require, in an objective sense, a particular result. They accept the debunking of formalism in legal reasoning. However, they reject the social policy analysis of the Realists, whereunder decision-makers must identify social interests at issue in a particular controversy, balance them, and understand the consequences of legal decisions through studying the operation of the legal system with the help of concepts drawn from sociology and political science. They charge that the legal-policy arguments are similar in nature to the discredited formal-doctrinal arguments and that they result only in defending the *status quo*, since the policy choice under this methodology is not based on a vision of good and just life.

The CLS movement abhors liberalism and individualism, extols community, criticizes the legal order, challenges the social hierarchy, and calls for a fundamental change in human relations. It is reminiscent, therefore, of late eighteenth and early nineteenth century utopian socialism, particularly of Fourier and Owen, and the revolt of romanticism of the early nineteenth century in literature, religion, and philosophy against the rationalism of the eighteenth century.

MAJOR ASPECTS

The major aspects of the CLS thesis include the following:

1. *Rejection of Liberalism.* Liberalism is a tradition of political philosophy grounded in the social contract theories of Hobbes, Locke, and Hume, that believes that society consists of autonomous individuals entertaining values based on subjective desires, that society has common values, and that these values can be accommodated through social, economic, political, and legal institutions. Liberalism, thus, accommodates these values, rather than transforms them.

CLS rejects this tradition. In the first place, as CLS sees it, liberalism creates a false vision of human sociability. Its view of society as composed of right-bearing citizens engenders a rights-consciousness that isolates individuals and forces them to juxtapose their existence with that of others. Secondly, liberalism envisions the world into dualities, such as, for example, individualism and altruism, subjectivity and objectivity, freedom and necessity. These dualities lack a consistent normative theory and, thereby, enable decision makers to rationalize any result. Thirdly, liberalism offers legitimacy to capitalism and disguises exploitation with pretensions to freedom and individual rights. This disguise misleads the masses into supporting the system that oppresses them. The capitalist welfare state is, thus, a capitalist maneuver to deceive the oppressed.

2. *Exposing the Fundamental Contradiction.* CLS points to the fundamental contradiction of the liberal theory, which lies in the liberalist demand that the individual be free to pursue his or her self-interest, whereas this pursuit requires restraint of other individuals. It exposes liberalism's curious position that freedom is possible through its negation. That contradiction, it argues, is institutionalized in creating a political state to limit freedom.

3. *Other Contradictions.* CLS points out the fundamental contradiction of advanced capitalism with which the liberal tradition suffers. This contradiction, for CLS, denotes conflicting social forces in a Marxian dialectic. Concentration of economic power in the dominant class results in exploitation of the proletariat, which conflict engenders revolution for destroying capitalism.

The contradiction between procedure and justice means that in the liberal system a failure to follow the right procedures defeats a just cause.

Finally, there are contradictions between individual and community, between subjectivity of personal values and the hope for an objective moral truth, between rules and standards, between free will and determinism, between active rights of liberty and passive rights of security, and between democracy and the antidemocratic practice of judicial review.

4. Trashing or Delegitimation. According to CLS, liberalism must be trashed, delegitimized, demystified, and unmasked because merely tinkering with the system to improve it only reinforces the prevailing economic realities. By using the tinkering method, liberalism distorts reality, provides false hopes for a more humane society, and fails to change the fundamental structure of society. As CLS sees it, social institutions are socially created, contingent, and unjust while they appear natural, necessary, and just. Law legitimates the *status quo* by perpetuating the mass delusion about the naturalness of social institutions. This realization enables one to create a new society.

5. Deconstruction. As mentioned above, the intellectual source of CLS' deconstruction is Jacques Derrida's post-structuralist technique of interpretation of texts in which texts have no objective meaning. Meaning found in text is the result of an act of interpretation by the reader and not of an inherent objective quality of the text. Derrida's method would reveal in texts those points that are at odds with their ostensible thesis and, consequently, reveal meaningful, but not otherwise evident, tensions within them. This method, thus, dislodges ordinarily understood meanings and demonstrates the perpetually elusive nature of the essence of meaning, since intelligence is frustrated or distorted by the mediation of concepts-in-words between pure meaning and the subject.

CLS applies this deconstructionist technique to legal doctrine. This enables it to point to the value-bearing character of legal language and to conclude that an interpretation of a text or a social action is a function of power, not proof. The CLS deconstructionism exposes the indeterminacy of the text and delegitimizes liberal legalism's claim about the existence of a knowable, objective, and value-neutral law.

6. *Hermeneutics.* The idealized notion of judicial activity perceives the judge as a neutral facilitator interpreting objectively the intent of the law or the intention of the parties in dispute. CLS maintains that since objective meaning is an impossibility, law cannot be value-free. Interpretation is not a neutral or apolitical task. The interpreter's value judgments, his or her thought process, and his or her social context are inextricably woven into the interpretation.

7. *Ideological Unmasking.* To CLS, what appears as natural forms of human association are

nothing but unexamined social conventions or constructs. Law reinforces these constructs. CLS debunks legal reasoning as a subterfuge for ideologies. The ideological unmasking of law is executed by showing that a system of legal rules and practices is applied differentially by favoring some interests over others. Much of the CLS work in labor law has concentrated on this unmasking.

8. *Exposing Indeterminacy.* The essential claim of CLS is not so much that the systems are biased as that they are indeterminate. They are erected upon contradictory assumptions. Therefore, their failure to produce a necessary outcome results not from the insincerity of the decision maker but from the indeterminacy produced by the contradictory nature of the system's assumptions. The appearance of law's ability to provide that outcome derives from the privileged position given unconsciously to one element of the contradiction over the other.

9. *Rejection of Formalism.* CLS understands legal formalism as the notion that law is a self-contained deductive system, so that decisions result from applying principles, precedents, and procedures without reference to the political, economic, and social context, social goals, and values. CLS rejects the notion that society can resolve disputes through a value-neutral system of rules and doctrine. It maintains that all decision making is contingent on the beliefs of the decision maker. It argues for the rejection of formalism for the pur-

pose of enabling individuals to recognize injustices and inequalities perpetuated by liberal legalism. According to it, there can be no plausible legal theory without a social theory.

10. Rejection of Positivism. CLS adopts the anti-positivist approach of the Frankfurt School and rejects the notion that empirical or scientific knowledge is possible in law.

11. Rejection of Reification within Law. The notion of reification of concepts is borrowed from Marxist theory. Under it, the concept is endowed with qualities additional to the qualities of the particular human beings who either created it or use it. The concept thus acquires an independence from its social context. CLS finds in this reification of legal concepts the fallacy of confusing human nature with historically contingent social experience.

12. Rejection of Rationality in Law. Liberalism claims that it is rationality that distinguishes legal discourse from other kinds of social force, that in law there is a rational foundation for doctrine and development. CLS rejects this notion as a myth. Passion or will, it claims, is not expunged from law.

13. Exposing of Contextuality of Law. CLS claims that the individual's institutional or imaginative assumptions are shaped by his context, which is determined by his political, social, and economic surroundings. It debunks liberalism for ignoring this type of contextuality. The significance of understanding this contextuality in law and society lies in the realization that any context can be broken or changed. One context-breaking creates another context, so that there is no ultimate context-breaking. However, individuals achieve self-assertion by experimenting with new relationships through context-breaking.

14. *Establishing Unity of Law and Politics.* For CLS, law is nothing but an expression of politics. The Marxists viewed law as an instrument of the ruling class for coercion. However, the neo-Marxists, which the CLS scholars tend to be, see it as an instrument of political propaganda that legitimates the class structure by masking exploitation with apparent fairness, with the consequence that the exploited are co-opted into supporting the system that exploits them. Thus, for example, theft is viewed as departure from a normatively justified system of property rights rather than as a part of the struggle for control over resources, or limiting victim's consent at the time of the criminal act is viewed as the vindication of an economy characterized by unrestrained market and contractual deals.

15. *Rejection of Reform and Call for Transformation.* The CLS program is not interested in reforming the existing legal system. Instead, it aims at transforming social, political, and legal institutions.

16. *On the Possibility of a General Theory.* The CLS scholars are divided on the issue whether it is either possible or desirable for them to construct a

general theory. While some argue for elaborating
an alternative general theory, others, influenced
by modern pragmatist philosophy, deconstruction,
and post-structuralism, argue that constructing a
general theory is senseless.

   17. On the Epistemological Explanation. The
above assertions of the CLS are generally not subject to proof or refutation in empirical terms. CLS,
therefore, claims that the validity of their propositions is a matter not of empirical proof but of
evaluating the appropriateness of their questions
about the legal rules. It argues that since the
purpose of explanation of a legal rule is to assist in
making a normative judgment about it, it follows
that the explanation must be in terms that reveal
the normative structures of the rule.

CRITICISMS

1. As to Realist Ancestry

   The claimed connection of CLS with American
Legal Realism, especially the claim that CLS is a
matured version of Realism, is not well taken.
Even though there are common points of methodology between the two, namely, the debunking of
formalism, the demystifying of the law, and the
exposing of the indeterminacy and non-objectivity
of law, the essential difference lies in the fact that
while Realism's objective was to aim its critique
toward making law an effective instrument of
sound public policy, the aim of CLS critique is to
delegitimize law.

The difference is fundamental, both methodologically and substantively.

Methodologically, the Realist approach derives from the scientific rationalism of the Enlightenment and finds its roots in an empirical search for common principles in law, as pioneered by Blackstone's systematizing of categories of precedents and developed by Langdell's case method of tracing the growth of doctrines through a series of cases. The CLS methodology, on the contrary, is grounded in the critical theory of the Frankfurt School and is directed against the rationalist position.

Substantively, Realism proceeded from the fundamentally positivist position that law and morals are separable, and it believed that just decisions would result if the decision makers used scientific procedures of inquiry. Therefore, it proposed behavioral research in the judicial process. Realism's attack was not so much on the formalist tradition's claim to neutrality of legal reasoning as on its choice of the first principles that constituted the premises for arriving at the legal conclusions, which choice was made by formalists on the basis of their personal ethical choice. That is why it became fundamental to the Realists that fact (is) be consciously distinguished from value (ought). The Realists' pursuit was to prevent formalism from distorting law at its abstract level by insisting on moral neutrality during legal investigation. On the contrary, CLS rejects the very proposition of the Realists that an objective decision is possible at all. For CLS, there is a basic indeterminacy of legal doctrine that makes a value-free jurisprudence impossible.

2. As to Repudiation of Liberalism

The CLS' repudiation of liberalism is worrisome.

There are various schools of liberal thought in Europe, where it originated, and in the United States. Thus, while some liberals think that freedom means being able to do what one wants to do, others think it means being able to do what one ought to do. Or, while some see freedom as something that belongs to the individual and to be protected from the encroachment of the state, others see it as belonging to the society and the state can be made to enlarge and improve it. In modern jurisprudential thought, there are several traditions of liberalism. For example, one tradition considers political autonomy of law as essential to democratic pluralism (Otto Kirchheimer and Franz Neumann). Another maintains the primacy of freedom of citizens and their freely-formed associations against the state (F.W. Maitland and J.N. Figgis). Another propounds a legal order that its citizens accept as legitimate (H.L.A. Hart). Yet another emphasizes the need to recognize friend-enemy relations and the state of exception in the formulation of the rule of law (Carl Schmitt). CLS slurs over these various thoughts.

Liberal pluralism believes that the freedom of citizens and their associations is of primary value, that public power itself must be rule-governed, and that freedom exists because of the conflict of interests when regulated by law. It maintains that a legal order depends upon the existence of the state. It maintains that a pluralistic civil society has law and a political system in which distinct political forces compete to influence the public power, in which their competition is based on a broad associational pluralism, in which no body of citizens is excluded from participation in this competition, and in which no body is subordinated to another. It does not tolerate informal justice. It regards law not merely as a constraint but as a guide to action. It assigns to the public power a limited set of functions for regulating the interaction of agents and associations. It implies acceptance of ethical pluralism.

This sort of thought is rejected by CLS. However, in order to persuade people to throw away these propositions of liberal pluralism, CLS must provide not only an alternative but a better one. It has been lacking in that. The CLS critique of liberalism lacks persuasiveness when it concentrates on ideology and ignores social experience. Thereby it fails to show how the ideological content is incorporated into institutions.

It indulges in an excessive reductionism when it uses its dualisms of contradictions, mentioned above.

Further, its occupation with deligitimation, deconstruction, and so on has deflected its attention away from proving that liberalism has been inadequate in meeting people's needs, fulfilling their desires, and providing an evaluation of law in terms of justice.

Finally, the CLS critique entertains the assumption that there is a necessary relationship between liberalism and capitalism and that liberalism must bear the responsibility for the ills of capitalism. However, it is difficult to accept that liberalism considers market relationships natural or necessary. In fact, some liberals are quite critical of capitalism. Hume, for example, denies that property rights are natural. He considers them a social convention, instead. The liberal support for capitalism had been contingent, granted only as long as it served the security and welfare interests of ordinary people.

3. As to Fundamental Contradiction

The CLS assertion of fundamental contradiction that all normative concepts contain unresolvable conflicts is too dogmatically made and not proven or argued. It simply is claimed, in the manner of a moral axiom. Moreover, although the term contradiction is used not in the ordinary sense of propositions negating each other but in the dialectic sense of conflicting social forces, any possibility of compromise or adjustment between them is nevertheless denied totally. This is incomprehensible, since the dialectic sense makes synthesis possible, not impossible.

4. As to Deconstruction

The use of Derridean deconstruction by CLS ignores the fact that while the technique might be quite suitable for literary or philosophical texts, it may not be appropriate for legal texts. Derrida used his technique on texts of great thinkers that contained elaborate metaphorical structures. These structures provided opportunities for deconstruction. However, judicial opinions are not of this nature.

Moreover, a deconstructionist analysis turns out to be less than satisfying, since it is more in the nature of an indulgence of the analyst's imagination than a logical argument.

Finally, since the technique erodes an integrated view of society, it lacks the ability for providing a foundation for an alternative social theory.

5. As to Indeterminacy

The indeterminacy thesis of CLS argues that law is not independent of the social order and that historical meaning is subjective. It maintains that if there is no clear meaning of the text, i.e., the Constitution, then the rule of law is nothing but a rule of those in power.

However, there are problems with this thesis. In the first place, the ideal of the rule of law is just that, an ideal, rather than a specific content. Therefore, the arbitrary or illegitimate nature of decisions might challenge the political and legal order of the society but not the ideal of the rule or law. Secondly, the concept of the rule of law has many aspects, including the laying down of procedural rules for safeguarding against the abuse of power. However, the CLS critique has not explored the various aspects of the concept it criticizes. Thirdly, constitutionalism provides checks on the power of the sovereign. CLS rejects constitutionalism but it has failed to provide an alternative means for checking this power.

6. As to Unity of Law and Politics

In this respect CLS betrays an inability to distinguish political reasoning from legal reasoning. While political reasoning is characterized by teleological justification, legal reasoning is characterized by deontological justification. These are two different methods of justification, not, as CLS claims, one and the same.

7. As to Supplying an Alternative

CLS has thus far been short in providing an alternative of its own to institute in place of that which it has set out to destroy.

B. FEMINIST JURISPRUDENCE

Feminism as a public issue in the United States goes back to the proposals made during the American Revolution (1775) for giving women full citizenship, although those proposals never succeeded. In 1824, Frances Wright came to America from England, where she had been friendly with the English jurist and reformer Jeremy Bentham. In America she campaigned for women's rights and for abolition of Negro slavery. The American movement for female suffrage, organized in 1848 at a convention in Seneca Fall, New York, issued a bill of rights for women. The nineteenth amendment to the U.S. Constitution came into effect in 1920, giving women their voting rights.

Feminist legal activity found its first prominent manifestation in the mid-nineteenth century in efforts surrounding the passage in various states of the Married Women's Separate Property Acts. In more recent times, a major feminist legal activity is seen in the abortion litigation that culminated in the U.S. Supreme Court's decision of 1973 in Roe v. Wade. However, the theoretical work of feminist jurisprudence did not appear until the late 1970's when, as a result of the women's liberation movement of the 1960's, feminist legal scholars began presenting critiques of law from the viewpoint of the experiences of women.

We now have a considerable literature and a number of writers in this field, analyzing women's subordination and seeking ways of changing the situation. There is diversity in their work. We shall take note, below, of the common feminist themes, the various schools of feminist jurisprudence, and the feminist methodology.

1. Common Themes

a. *Critique of History*

According to the feminists, traditional historians wrote history from the male point of view that excluded the female point of view. These historians did not inquire into women's role in making history, structuring society, and living their own lives. Inclusion of women in writing history (his-story v. her-story) began in the 1970's. These writings endeavor to show, firstly, the falsity of history that excludes a consideration of women. They challenge the traditional periodization of history. For example, the period of Renaissance is traditionally considered a period of rebirth of western civilization even when women were being burned as witches, domesticated as bourgeois wives, and excluded from liberty-equality-fraternity formulation of the Revolution. Secondly, they show that the male-written history has created an androcentric bias in our conceptions of human nature, gender potential, and social arrangements. It has thereby perpetuated patriarchy.

b. *Critique of Patriarchal Jurisprudence*

The feminist scholars regard mainstream jurisprudence as patriarchal, from which they distance themselves. They show that legal doctrine defines men and protects them, not women, and they argue that by discounting gender differences, the prevailing conceptions of law perpetuate patriarchal power.

This male-dominated system of law subordinates women. Men have had the bulk of social, economic, and political power, which they have used to subordinate women in the public spheres of politics and economy as well as in the private spheres of family and sex. The feminists point to the legal doctrine, legal practice, and legal language to show sexism in these. They argue that patriarchy has had the power of naming and since naming creates categories of things to be valued or not, counted or not, or noted or not, the male-created language reinforces male values. Sexual intercourse, for example, is male experience of penetration and not female experience of enclosure, or the woman is described through the visual imagery of the male and not touch and other senses of the female, or even the gender "woman" is constructed by man to describe what man is not, she the object he the subject. They point out that since name and language are created by men, the male is used as the norm even without being explicit about it. The result is that the implicit or unstated male norms have distorted our understanding, so much so that if we expunged male biases from the concepts of our political and social systems, there would be nothing left of these concepts. These concepts are passed off as neutral or objective, whereas objective reality is a myth, only a projection of the male psyche. Moreover, they point out, not seeing this solipsism of the male norm results in our lawyerly tendency to seek comprehensive rules in accordance with that norm. They claim that the male ontology defines the world in false oppositions, such as the self-other opposition. They question the dualisms of male ontology and espouse a feminist ontology which relies not on opposition but on relation, such as the self-other relation.

c. Critique of Biological Determinacy

They challenge biological determinacy, for this determinacy has the consequence of curtailing women's power and their options. They maintain that gender is created socially, not biologically. Sex determines such matters as genitalia or reproductive capacity but not the psychological, moral, or social traits assigned to each gender.

d. Adoption of Sex/Gender Dialectic

They challenge the patriarchal-style dualist separation of sex from gender. They point to a dialectical relationship between the two. They see an interaction between them. The two are not completely independent of each other but they argue that the patriarchal dichotomy prevents us from seeing other components of this interrelationship.

e. Certain Common Commitments

The research agenda of the feminist scholars is varied. However, it does reflect certain common commitments. First, politically, they seek equality between men and women. Second, analytically, they make gender as a category of analysis for the purposes of reconstituting legal practices that have excluded women's interests. Third, methodologically, they use women's experiences to describe the world and to point out the needed transformations. They primarily rely upon an experiential discourse for analyzing such matters of their concern as gender hierarchy, sexual objectification, and social structures. They use this method to discover the authentic sexuality and the reality of women's condition. However, their writings do sometimes reflect the worry whether this method isn't too individualistic.

2. Various Schools

The diversity of feminist jurisprudence may be demonstrated by identifying various schools of thoughts within it. These include (1) the liberal, or equal-opportunity, or formal equality, or symmetricist feminism, (2) the assimilationist feminism, (3) the bivalent, or difference, or special treatment feminism, (4) the incorporationist feminism, (5) the different-voice, or cultural, or relational feminism, (6) the dominance, or radical feminism, and (7) the post-modern feminism.

a. The Liberal, or Equal–Opportunity, or Formal Equality, or Symmetricist Feminism

Under this approach, the central goal is formal equality of women. The claim is made that women must be treated same way as men. Women and men are argued to be rights-bearing, autonomous human beings. This approach anchors its thoughts in the core concepts of liberal political theory (rationality, rights, equal opportunity), and argues that women are just as rational as men. Therefore, they should have equal opportunity to make their own choices. It challenges the assumptions of female inferiority and it seeks to eliminate gender-based distinctions recognized in law, thereby enabling women to compete equally in the marketplace.

The critics of this approach point out its fallacy in that it takes maleness to be the norm. Women's success is measured by their performance in the male institutions, in building of which institutions women have been excluded. They argue that this approach accepts the reasoning of the patriarchal jurisprudence and thereby it cannot achieve a real change in women's status. The claimed similarity of men and women only perpetuates patriarchal values, since the concept of woman continues to be male-constructed.

The defenders of this approach maintain that it expands possibilities for female life experience, instead of reducing women to men. The approach works, it is argued, since it speaks the language that the legal system understands. It has the further advantage of attracting non-feminist people to the movement. They do not deny sex differences but they argue that non-sex-specific legal solutions are preferable to sex-specific laws. They maintain that sex-based legislation perpetuates discontinuous categories of men and women, whereas they insist on their right, not the state's right, to say who they are. Formal equality requires that the state deliver in a symmetrical form whatever measures it delivers concerning women's equal participation and economic viability.

b. *The Assimilationist Feminism*

This is a more extreme version of the liberal approach. It argues for a non-sexist society in which no distinctions would be made on the basis of sex, whether on the legal, or institutional, or personal level. Physical dissimilarities are argued to have no relevance to social arrangements that distribute political, institutional, or interpersonal concerns. As to the distinguishing factor of pregnancy, it makes two arguments to eliminate pregnancy from the social experience. Firstly, it argues that artificial reproduction and extra-uterine gestation can free women from the tyranny of their reproductive biology. Secondly, even if the physiological capability remains unchanged, the effects of pregnancy can be nullified by developing appropriate social institutions, such as creating the category of disability for pregnancy or abolition of the heterosexual nuclear family and creation of social institutions for raising children.

The critics of this approach point out that it trivializes sex. By committing society to creating similarity between male and female, it precludes our enjoyment of sex differentiation. Moreover, this approach, like the liberal approach, accepts maleness as the norm. They argue that treating either of the sex roles as a paradigm would yield invidious sex-role differentiation.

c. The Bivalent, or Difference, or Special–Treatment Feminism

This approach maintains that the ideal of equality forces women to conform to the male norm. It, therefore, emphasizes sex difference. It argues for a dual system of rights, namely equal and differential. Equal rights disregard a person's individual qualities. Differential or special rights, on the contrary, are based on human differences. This approach believes that differences between men and women are not cultural but psychological, which are connected to physiological differences. Law, it argues, must take an account of these differential qualities. Political, institutional, and social arrangements would, thus, depend to some extent upon sex differences. Women deserve special treatment or special benefits because they are different from men. The sameness (equality) argument hides from vision the underlying structural conditions that are detrimental or disadvantageous to women.

The critics point to three main defects of this approach. Firstly, it is extremely difficult to determine what these differential qualities are. Problems relate to identifying the differences, deciding which differences are legally relevant, and distinguishing between real and stereotyped differences. The defenders might propose a definitive list of differences and consequent special rights for women. However, the critics insist that this process only promotes the objectification of women and eliminates the gender issue, rather than affirming it. Secondly, it reinforces stereotypical assumptions about female dependency, instead of accounting for the historical exclusion of women on the basis of difference in reproductive capabilities. Thirdly, by taking the disadvantages of women as given, this approach, too, like the equality approach, deflects from tackling the underlying structural conditions.

d. The Incorporationist Feminism

This approach proposes a strictly limited way for law to account for sex differences, limited only to the two aspects unique to women, namely, pregnancy and breastfeeding. It, thus, neither nullifies the sex differences nor extends it to all areas of legal, political, and institutional matters.

The difficulty with this approach is that it obscures the fact of domination by regarding the sexist injustice as mere irrationality that can be fixed, instead of exposing male supremacy as a complete social system.

e. The Different–Voice, or Cultural, or Relational Feminism

This approach focuses upon the difference between men and women and celebrates that difference. Women have different life experiences which make them speak in a different voice from that of men. While men emphasize competition, aggressiveness, and selfishness, women's voices emphasize caring, nurturing, and empathy. While men seek autonomous individualism, women seek connection and relationship. While men view human beings as distinct and unconnected, the reality of women's lives shows their essential connectedness. While men focus on a hierarchy of abstract rights, women value relationships and make contextualized adjustments issuing from relationships. While maturity for men consists in separation, for women it consists in connection. While men view intimacy as threatening, women see in separation the failure of the ethic of care. This woman's difference, it is claimed, is good. What is sought, then, is a recognition of such values as child-raising and care-giving, which are women's special contribution to society. The objective is to give equal recognition to women's moral voice. Changes are sought in the existing conditions so as to recognize woman-valued relationships, such as, for example, the special relationships between mother and child. The complaint under this approach is not that the category of woman has been misdefined but that it has been ignored. The male perspective in law must, according to this approach, be reconstructed to take account of the above-mentioned feminine values. In expressing this different voice of caring and communal values, this approach criticizes possessive individualism which is so integral to domesticity. It promises that women's survival in a predominantly male professions does not require for women to surrender their female values of compassion, relationships, and nurturing.

The critics point out several disturbing aspects of this approach. One, they point to its essentialism and show that such essentialism is misleading in that, under it, gender alone determines the attitude of men and women about a broad range of issues. Two, it tends to marginalize women, since it excludes from women's personality the values of competition and self-interest and, consequently, excludes them from economic enterprises where the mainstream values are competition and self-interest. Three, under this approach the category of woman seems to possess a discoverable essence, whether natural or socially constructed. If natural, this voice invites the question of how do we know this is woman's voice, especially since, as some critics maintain, it is not possible for women to speak for themselves so long as they continue to be victimized by male subordination. If socially constructed, this different voice is merely another voice of patriarchy, since it has been constructed in response to patriarchy. Finally, cultural feminism affirms traits which only promote women's collaboration with their oppressors. Thus, women who do

not recognize that voluntary heterosexual intercourse is nothing but a type of intrusion by men
perpetuate, the critics argue, this pattern of wom-
en's subordination.

f. The Dominance, or Radical Feminism

This approach views women as a class, not individual human beings as in the liberal feminism,
and it claims that this class has been dominated by
another class, namely, men. Gender inequality of
women is viewed as the consequence of a systematic subordination, not a result of irrational discrimination. Traditional gender roles have accepted sexually dominated gender hierarchy as natural
or intrinsic to those roles. Men have produced the
social construction of sexuality in order to establish this gender hierarchy. Thus, the social construction of heterosexuality, which protects male
domination, has been produced by the social relations of dominance and submission in gender roles.
The truth, it is pointed out, is that if a woman
finds pleasure in heterosexuality, she finds pleasure in her own subordination. That which is experienced as true intimacy is only a false consciousness.

Gender, for this approach, is a question of power.
Therefore, it is not satisfied with creating legal
categories to accommodate present reality. It criticizes that very reality. Both the gender-neutrality
principle   and   the   special-protection-for-women
principles take maleness as their referent. What

is needed, it is argued, is a reconstruction of sexual
equality on the basis of woman's difference from
man, not a mere accommodation of that difference.
Her identity of difference thus becomes central to
normative debates about re-structuring the world.
Had, for example, women had their share in designing the workplace, the pregnancy issue would
be not of accommodations to be made by employers
for pregnancy but of structuring of the workplace
in which pregnant workers would not be at vari-
ance from the norm.

Since this approach believes that the socially
constructed class of women is different from men,
it rejects liberal equality arguments. The issue for
it becomes that of power. Approaching it not from
the viewpoint of equality but of domination and
sexual subordination, this approach demands
changes in law that would end the inequality in
power. Such changes would include (i) protection
of women from sexual harassment, rape, battering
by men, and so on, (ii) prohibition of pornography,
since pornography contributes to women's sexual
subordination, and (iii) provision for reproductive
freedom and voluntary sexual intercourse.

The critics of this approach make four major
points. One, they maintain that the emphasis on
women as a class is mistaken. It merely highlights
differences between men and women but ignores
differences among women. Secondly, by viewing
women in this singular way this approach defines
women in some essential way. It seems to say that

there exists a female essence. The protagonists of this approach deny that such essentialism exists in their viewpoint, since they maintain that women are socially constructed. Their deconstruction of woman has as its objective not a discovery of the true essence of woman but a challenge to the male construction of her. The resultant category may well be a woman-defined social construct of woman, but that, being woman defined, would be an improvement. Thirdly, the critics claim that special protections for women tend to lead to inequality. For example, by asking the state to ban pornography this approach gives the state the power to define acceptable sex but, state being a creature of male power, that definition cannot be of female persuasion. Moreover, pornography is not always pernicious. One needs to distinguish, the critics say, between pornography that does violence from erotica that celebrates women's release from repressive mores of the Victorian era. A further danger in banning pornography lies, the critics argue, in suppressing speech, which would eventually suppress women's speech as well. Finally, not all women agree that the experience of the genuine intimacy of sexual intercourse is merely a false consciousness. The critics deny the alleged self-deception of sexual experience which this approach ascribes to women.

g. The Postmodernist Feminist

The postmodern thought is anchored in the epistemology of W.V.O. Quine. The most influential theory of scientific knowledge from the seven-teenth to the twentieth century has been positiv-ism, with all its emphasis on the empirical basis. In the 1950's, Quine disputed the positivistic idea that knowledge is a correspondence between con-cept and world and that its process is that of building from the simple to the complex. He of-fered his own holistic epistemology, wherein truth of a proposition is not a function of its relationship to the world but, instead, of how it hangs together with everything else taken to be true. The totality of our knowledge or beliefs is a field of force whose boundary conditions are experience, so that a con-flict with experience at the periphery causes read-justments in the interior of the field. Therefore, re-evaluating one statement must require re-evalu-ation of some others. Consequently, it is mislead-ing to speak of the empirical content of an individ-ual statement or proposition. Knowledge is not a matter of building up from foundations but a func-tion of one's ability to move within a holistic com-plex.

Consistently with this epistemology, postmodern feminism is neither detained by the issue of objec-tive reality or unitary truth nor does it have any difficulty in accepting the proposition that gender categories are social constructs of patriarchy in need of feminist reconstruction. Its claim is that there is no such thing as the essential woman, the woman's point of view, a single theory of equality good for all women, a single goal best for all women. Woman has multifarious manifestations.

Femininity and masculinity relate to broader net-work of discourses on gender, instead of being circumscribed in one master discourse. The cate-gory of woman is an identity that is not possible to determine. Instead of focusing upon a category called woman, this approach focuses upon the situ-ated realities of women. It believes that defining woman, even by feminists, constricts the identity of an individual to her identity as a woman.

What is emphasized in this approach is practical solutions to concrete situations. Sometimes an ethical feminism is proposed which denounces the process of deriving what woman ought to be from the reality of what is and calls for a collective imagining, informed but not limited by women's realities, in which all women can find themselves.

This approach claims the advantages of avoiding essentialism because of its rejection that any cate-gory, including that of race or gender, is always determinative. It points to the context and main-tains that only in some particular context may such a category be determinative. It, therefore, does not accept any such thing like woman's voice as determinative of behavior in all situations. A person is situated in a complex of social and psy-chological factors that interact in multiple and different contexts. The self is continually refigur-ing itself, rather than being determined by belong-ing to a particular social category.

3. Methodology

The aspects of feminist methodology include experiential discourse, consciousness-raising, asking the woman question, and feminist practical reasoning.

a. *Experiential discourse*

To a large extent, the feminist critique utilizes experiential discourse as a basis for knowledge for analyzing social structures, gender hierarchy, and sexual objectification. This experiential analysis takes concrete experiences at its starting point, instead of working deductively from abstract principles and conceptual schemes. It then integrates these experiences into theory in order to attain a deeper understanding of the experiences. Personal consequences of institutionalized injustice are narrated. The focus is put upon the experience of being dominated, as distinguished from just thinking about it.

This method has several problems. For example, in its zeal to speak from women's experience, the method tends to gloss over diversities that arise from such factors as period of history, culture, class, race, age, sexual orientation, ethnicity, and so on. Moreover, it does not take into account the experiences of those women whose experiences are not in keeping with the feminist premises. The problem becomes even more serious if we consider the research claims made by some investigators that for a great majority of women the terms of experiencing the world are not the same as those adopted by the feminists. There is also the dispute even among the feminists as to which experiential account among several should be controlling. Furthermore, the question arises as to wherein lies the authority for an experiential account. More specifically, why should gender experience be a more privileged account of subordination than, say, class, race, ethnicity, or sexual orientation.

b. Consciousness–Raising

Essentially, consciousness-raising consists in women listening to each other's personal stories, stories which have been lost in the din of the dominant discourse. Knowledge is gained of women's experiences through consciousness-raising, promoting reflection upon the range of women's experiences, and destabilizing the apparent consensus concerning the meaning of social life. Personal hurts are transformed into a collective experience of oppression. The subordinate experience is shared, which leads to exposing the class-based nature of these experiences, which, thereby liberates women from self-blame.

The consciousness-raising method operates at two levels, namely, personal growth group level and institutional level. In personal growth groups, it takes the experience and integrates it into theory, which theory is, in turn, validated or modified by the experiences. The individual and social dimensions of experience are thus made to connect. At the institutional level, the method publicly shares the experiences of oppression in order to change public perceptions thereof and challenge the patriarchy. The insights gained from this consciousness-raising are then proffered as normative propositions of the legal process, such as, for example, the proposition that a growth in women lawyers would improve legal process or a growth in women judges would promote collaborative decision-making among judges.

Consciousness-raising among women has also had the consequence of bringing forth disagreements among them on such issues as heterosexuality, motherhood, pornography, surrogate motherhood, military draft, and so on. The method is sometimes criticized as intimidating women into politically correct positions.

c. *Asking the Woman Question*

Asking the woman question consists in identifying gender components and gender implications of a rule or practice that is claimed to be neutral. Sometimes the woman question is refined as the question of the excluded, the refinement being the taking into account of the broad range of oppression experienced by different women and even men. Gender analysis is, thus, put within the context of multiple identities.

The woman question explores the gender implications by inquiring how the existing law prefers
male values over female values and how it could be
corrected to remove the female disadvantage. The
method is not designed to reveal any inherent
attributes of women but to expose the institutional
arrangements, such as family, workplace, child-
bearing patterns, and so on, that subordinate wom-
en.   In the courtroom, it challenges the prece-
dential value of a case. The method is intended to
make a difference, or, in other words, shape substance. It does so by enlarging the decision-mak-
er's substantive preferences, since it makes precedents increasingly indeterminate.   It provides a
method of interpretation that does not accept the
status quo and reveals the hidden bias in law.

d.   Feminist Practical Reasoning

This method immodestly ascribes to women
alone the attributes of sensitivity to context, open-
ness to evolving insights, and care for the practical-
ities of everyday life. However, substantively, it
minimizes the givens of any situation and treats as
open questions the issues of what, why, and how
something should be done in a specific context. It
has little use for abstract reasoning, since it believes that problems are not dichotomous conflicts
to be resolved by choosing one principle over another but, rather, they are dilemmas characterized
by a multiplicity of perspectives which need be
reconciled in a particular context. It does not

reject rules. However, it points to the necessity of reconciling rules to the contingencies of new facts, as opposed to the method of reducing contingencies to rules. In this procedure it brings in the woman question, discussed above, to challenge the rules that pretend to speak normatively for the entire community but which, indeed, conceal gender exclusion. Reasoning from context is used to expose the otherwise unnoticed injustice.

Thus, feminist jurisprudence has certain common themes, various schools of approach, and a particular methodology.

C. CRITICAL RACE THEORY

Critical Race Theory aims at maximizing the human status of blacks in American society. To that end it analyzes the relationship of law and racial subordination in the United States. Its first Workshop was held at the Institute of Legal Studies, University of Wisconsin, in July 1989. Its particular focus is upon the contemporary civil rights phase in the evolution of this status.

The previous phases of this evolution have been (1) the early seventeenth century bondage in colonial America without a clear definition of the status of a slave, (2) the late seventeenth century legislative activity in colonial legislatures and the early eighteenth century slave codes that made slavery not only a lifetime condition but hereditary as well, (3) the continued denial of legal personality to the blacks in the American Revolution and in the new Republic that followed and the enactment of post-Revolutionary slave codes, (4) the detailed regulation in the nineteenth century slave codes of black-white relationship whereunder a black person had no right to family, freedom of movement, choice, and legal capacity to sue or testify in a case involving a white person, supported by complementary penal statutes for the blacks, (5) the Free States phase in pre-Civil War era when the northern Free States put restrictions on the employment of blacks, their education, franchise, accommodation, and legal personality, a situation that was dramatically sustained by the United States Supreme Court in Dred Scott v. Sanford (1857), (6) the post-Civil War Black Codes which were passed after the abolition of slavery to govern the marriage, work relations, movement, and other aspects of life of the freedman, supplemented by the share-cropping statutes and the vagabond- and convict-leasing statutes, (7) the systematic codification of racial segregation of the society, upheld in the separate-but-equal doctrine of the Supreme Court in Plessy v. Ferguson (1896), aided by the legal devices of poll tax, literacy test, and the Grandfather Clause in the constitutions of southern states limiting right to vote, all designed to keep political power away from the blacks, and (8) the phase of change that began with the Supreme Court decision in support of desegregation in Brown v. Board of Education (1954) and the subsequent advent of civil rights legislation. Critical Race Theory focuses upon the contemporary civil rights phase and it makes a break with the dominant civil rights discourse by resorting to a refined race-consciousness.

It argues that the perception and experience of the world are differentiated by one's position in the race structure of the society, that race makes a difference in how legal topics are approached, that everyday institutional practices are embodiment of white norms despite their pretense to neutrality, and that legal categories are the product of dominant cultural assumptions that extort cultural conformity from the members of the minority races in exchange for their legal recognition.

Its major themes include (1) critique of integration, (2) critique of anti-discrimination doctrine, (3) critique of analogy with sexism, and (4) search for multiple consciousness.

1. Critique of Integration

Critical Race Theory makes an argument for race consciousness as a liberating, not repressive, element. Race consciousness took on a repressive meaning as a result of the invention of integration and black nationalism as the two contrasting views of racial justice in the 1960s and 1970s. Racial integration in this particular development has not materialized into a comprehensive critique of the social structure but, instead, has become merely a part of the dominant cultural rhetoric. That dominant rhetoric speaks the language of liberal American ideas of enlightenment and points to the universal characteristics shared by whites and blacks, so that white supremacy becomes false and black nationalism as an alternative becomes an equivalent of white supremacy. Progress lies in ensuring that race does not make a difference.

Integration and black nationalism, thus, emerge as opposed ideologies, the latter being marginalized as an extreme ideology. Race consciousness becomes arbitrary and unenlightened, integration reasonable and enlightened.

This approach, it is pointed by the proponents of Critical Race Theory, is mistaken. By reducing the white-black disparities to nonracial concepts of poverty and class, it merely ignores race and fails to present a satisfactory definition of racial justice in terms of relations of distinct communities.

2. Critique of Anti–Discrimination Doctrine

Critical Race Theory criticizes what is sometimes called the single-axis framework of the present anti-discrimination law in which there is either gender discrimination or race discrimination but not the compounding of the two.

This framework has resulted in the denial to the black woman of the right to claim discrimination as a member of a subgroup that is distinct from both black men and white women. It has resulted in the denial to her in a sex discrimination suit of the right to represent a class that includes white women. It has resulted in the denial to her in a race discrimination suit of the right to represent a class that includes black men. This narrows the scope of what is considered discrimination and marginalizes those whose experiences cannot be comprised within these narrow limits. The approach of treating race and sex claims only in the alternative suffers from the fallacious assumption that racism and sexism always operate independently. The assumption is fallacious since the plaintiff can belong both to a subordinated race and a subordinated gender, e.g., a black female.

This approach is seen as having been designed from the perspective of white males. As a result, its doctrine regards gender discrimination as an ill against white women and race discrimination as an ill against black men. The black woman is granted protection only to the extent her experiences fit into either of these categories. In the same vein, the black plaintiff is denied certification in discrimination suits as class representative of white females and black men.

Moreover, it is pointed out through cases applying the Civil Rights Act of 1964 (Title VII) that while the black woman is not allowed by courts to make a compound claim, the white man's reverse-discrimination claim has not been disallowed on the ground of compounding the race and sex claims. This law is, thus, criticized as marginalizing the black woman and privileging the white man.

3. Critique of Analogy With Sexism

The practice of analogizing racism to sexism is criticized as contributing to the perpetuation of racial discrimination by obscuring the very particular role of race as a tool of oppression in society. This is seen to occur in several ways. For example, it is pointed out that the practice of lumping together of socially-subordinated groups tends to represent the problem of oppression as a uniform problem, thereby obscuring the particular complexities of racism. Or, it tends to divert attention from black people back to white issues. Or, it promotes an essentialism that assigns exclusive categories to women and blacks that marginalizes black women. Or, it promotes among whites a false sense that since they understand the oppression of women they understand the oppression of race as well. This results in over-emphasizing similarities between the two and under-estimating the differences.

4. Espousal of Multiple Consciousness

Critical Race Theory seems to be leaning toward multiple consciousness of the postmodern thought that denies the grounding of values in foundationalist absolutes like humanity, nature, or reason and insists upon their locally contingent nature. It seems to be moving in the direction of searching for a way to correcting racial injustice in society without having to be trapped into a single universalizing norm or a single vision of the good.

CHAPTER 14

LEGAL POLYCENTRICITY

Legal polycentricity is the name given to a movement in legal thought inaugurated in 1990 at the Institute of Legal Science, University of Copenhagen. Its first workshop was held in Copenhagen in April 1992.

It accepts the non-universality of law, as shown in Chapter 2, and the non-universality of values within a legal system. Proceeding from these facts, it aims at making the legal system responsive to the pluralism of values.

It rejects the single-value approach to matters of morals and law as well as the radical relativism of values, and it accepts moral pluralism.

The single-value approach contends that all true values are compatible. Therefore, there is one ultimate right answer to moral questions. The task, then, becomes of developing a single set of moral principles to resolve conflicts. Legal polycentricity considers this unitary, absolute, monistic system both misleading as well as dangerous. It is misleading in two ways. One, it obscures the fact that values are many and they are not all harmonious. Its insistence that conflicting values are reconcilable under one truth is an inaccurate rep-

347

resentation of common life experience. It is dangerous in that, firstly, its inherently deterministic picture of the moral field as a unified totality that is possessed of its own single truth breeds pessimism, secondly, it distorts reality by giving us a false notion of comprehensiveness that contains all solutions within it, and, finally, by insisting upon one right answer it provides a convenient justification for tyranny.

Legal polycentricity also rejects the radical relativism of values that precludes moral standards for criticism and maintains that anything goes. Anthropology, psychology, and sociology help us develop those standards, as indicated in Chapter 4.

It accepts the pluralism of moral values. Accordingly, it conceives of the problem of legal relationships in terms of relations among various normative orders. It seeks their recognition within the legal system. Its program is not merely to describe the normative interrelationships among various normative orders and provide a cognitive postulate for legal reality that comprehends this pluralism but also to reform state law so as to give an adequate recognition of this pluralism within the legal system.

This approach opens the way for maximizing the legitimacy of legal order, promoting tolerance, promoting a non-coercive methodology by expanding the freedom to choose one's own preferred value, promotes stability by providing individuals and associations their own morally preferred space, provides a framework for understanding the inter-action between dominant groups and subordinate groups, avoids the Marxist contradiction of crushing class enemies to attain a freer society, and avoids the necessity of having a privileged unitary perspective.

The possible dangers against which it must guard are the neglect of struggles within a particular social field and the dominance of interest groups.

Its goals may be realized through a variety of modes, including use of pluralism-compatible doctrines of law, use of facilitative law empowering persons to realize their particular objectives, developing categories of individuals on the basis of value sectors, and designing institutional structures of administration of law which would respond to the demands of the pluralistic values.

Its challenge, therefore, is dual: (a) identification of pluralistic values, and (b) devising modes of their realization.

CHAPTER 15

CONCLUSION: ON DEFINING LAW

Returning to the central investigation of this book, namely, definitions of law, we have seen in previous chapters that it has not been possible to define law satisfactorily. Three reasons combine to explain the failure of these theories in providing the desired universal definition of law, namely, the non-universality of law as a principle of social organization, the multiplicity of irreconcilable epistemologies underlying these theories, and the pluralism or non-universality of legal values. We have discussed these factors in previous chapters, especially in Chapter 2.

These theories have responded to the challenge of these factors in four ways, all very unsatisfying.

One, some theories have simply assumed that law exists everywhere. For example, Aristotle maintains that law (true law, natural law) is the same everywhere, just as the same fire burns in Greece as well as in Persia. This assumption, as we have seen, is erroneous.

Two, some theories have ascribed a civilizationally superior status to the Western societies for the fact of being possessed of law, so that law becomes the highest achievement of human societies. For example, Sir Henry Sumner Maine of the historical school argues along these lines. This claim of cultural superiority of the Western societies is not only pernicious for being chauvinistic, it is also unsustainable either in history or in contemporary scene of these societies. Evidence is lacking to show that in moral matters, to which law belongs, Western societies are superior to non-Western societies. I am, of course, not asserting the moral superiority of the latter, either.

Three, some theories have made an ideological statement incipiently and set up that preferred value as philosophy conveying the universal truth. We have pointed out this incipience through the course of our examination of these theories, as, for example, in natural law, Kant, Hegel, Stammler, Savigny, Duguit, American realism, and the phenomenological theories.

Four, the positivist theories have responded to the challenge of non-universality of legal values by expunging values altogether from their definition of law, as in Bentham, Austin, Kelsen, and Hart. The result is that their definitions are so skeletal for excluding law's crucial value element that they fail to provide a complete grasp of the phenomenon of law.

The clarifications attempted in this book have two important consequences of practical significance. One, the non-universality of law must make us question any professed inevitability for it.

It must make us reconsider our crusade for law in such movements as, for example, human rights in the world. Two, a society contains conflicting values and a choice among them is made in law and morals. This choice does not result from philosophy, whose concern is objective truth, but ideology. We must be alert to watch how and by whom that choice is made, so that its maker does not fool us with a philosophical disguise for an ideological choice.

INDEX

353

COMTE, AUGUSTE—Cont'd
Metaphysical phase of human history, 230
Scientific phase of human history, 230
Theological phase of human history, 230

CONFUCIANISM
Interpretation of old texts, 28

CONFUCIUS
Analects, 33

CONSTANTINE
Emperor of Byzantium, 13

COSSIO, CARLOS
Egological theory of law, 292

CRITICAL LEGAL STUDIES
Contextuality of law, 312
Critical Legal Conference (Great Britain), 295
Criticism of Critical Legal Studies theory of law, 314–320
Critique du Droit, 296
Derrida, 309–310
Formalism, 311
Hermeneutics, 310
History, 296–297
Ideological unmasking of law, 310–311
Liberalism, delegitimation, 309
Reification within law, 312
Relativist epistemology, 300–306
Unity of law and politics, 312

CRITICAL RACE THEORY
Cases under Civil Rights Act of 1964
Compounding of gender and race discrimination, 344–345
Critique of analogy with sexism, 346
Critique of anti-discrimination doctrine, 344–345
Critique of integration, 343–344
Multiple consciousness, 346
Relationship of law and racial subordination, 341–343

CRITICAL THEORY OF THE FRANKFURT SCHOOL
Cognition and liberation, 298
Origins of Critical Legal Theory movement, 297
Reinterpretation of Marx and Engels, 297–298
Role of self-reflection, 299

†